DEVELOPMENTS IN E-GOVERNMENT

Innovation and the Public Sector

The functioning of the public sector gives rise to considerable debate. Not only the efficiency and efficacy of the sector are at stake, but also its legitimacy. At the same time we see that in the public sector all kinds of innovations are taking place. These innovations are not only technological, which enable the redesign of all kinds of processes, like service delivery. The emphasis can also be put on more organizational and conceptual innovations. In this series we will try to understand the nature of a wide variety of innovations taking place in the public sector of the 21st century and try to evaluate their outcomes. How do they take place? What are relevant triggers? And, how are their outcomes being shaped by all kinds of actors and influences? And, do public innovations differ from innovations in the private sector? Moreover we try to assess the actual effects of these innovations, not only from an instrumental point of view, but also from a more institutional point of view. Do these innovations not only contribute to a better functioning of the public sector, but do they also challenge grown practices and vested interests? And what does this imply for the management of public sector innovations?

Series Editors:

Prof. Dr. Victor J.J.M. Bekkers
Erasmus University, Rotterdam, The Netherlands

Prof. Jean Hartley
The University of Warwick, Coventry, United Kingdom

Prof. Sharon S. Dawes
University at Albany/SUNY, Albany, NY, USA

Volume 13

Recently published in this series

This series is a continuation of "Informatization Developments and the Public Sector" (vols. 1–9, ISSN 0928-9038)

ISSN 1871-1073

Developments in e-Government

A Critical Analysis

Edited by

David Griffin

Philippa Trevorrow

and

Edward Halpin

Leeds Metropolitan University, Leeds, United Kingdom

Press

Amsterdam • Berlin • Oxford • Tokyo • Washington, DC

ISBN 978-1-58603-725-3
Library of Congress Control Number: 2007923237

Publisher
IOS Press
Nieuwe Hemweg 6B
1013 BG Amsterdam
Netherlands
fax: +31 20 687 0019
e-mail: order@iospress.nl

Distributor in the UK and Ireland
Gazelle Books Services Ltd.
White Cross Mills
Hightown
Lancaster LA1 4XS
United Kingdom
fax: +44 1524 63232
e-mail: sales@gazellebooks.co.uk

Distributor in the USA and Canada
IOS Press, Inc.
4502 Rachael Manor Drive
Fairfax, VA 22032
USA
fax: +1 703 323 3668
e-mail: iosbooks@iospress.com

Cover Design
Joost van Grinsven

LEGAL NOTICE
The publisher is not responsible for the use which might be made of the following information.

PRINTED IN THE NETHERLANDS

Contents

Part 4. Evaluation of e-Government

Developments in e-Government
D. Griffin et al. (Eds.)
IOS Press, 2007

Preface

The Irish Government hosted a very successful conference on e-government in Dublin Castle in June 2004. The theme of the conference was "Towards Innovative Transformation in the Public Sector". As my predecessor as Minister for the Information Society, Ms. Mary Hanafin, T.D., remarked at the time, this conference provided "an exciting opportunity for a wide range of international e-government stakeholders to assess the evolution, economics and expectations of e-government".

The inspiration for this book came from the formal presentations as well as the informal discussions which took place at the conference. It is appropriate, therefore, that half of the chapters in this book have been contributed by academics and practitioners who presented papers at the conference.

The purpose of this book is to continue the evaluation of e-government progress and practice from a wide range of expert perspectives, with authors drawn from across the European Union and beyond.

I am delighted that this book is part of the legacy of the conference hosted by my Government and am sure that the perspectives on e-government contained within it will be useful to stakeholders who wish to remain apprised of the ongoing debate in this extremely important aspect of the Information Society.

Mr. Tom Kitt T.D.
Government Chief Whip and Minister of State to the Taoiseach
Irish Government

Contributors

Pierre Balestrini
Pierre Balestrini is a Marketing lecturer at the School of Management, University of Surrey. In industry, Pierre has worked as a Sales and Marketing executive for companies mainly in the packaging industry both in France and Britain, managing inter alia foreign accounts.

Frank Bannister
Dr. Frank Bannister is a senior lecturer in Information Systems and Head of the Department of Statistics at Trinity College. Dublin. His research interests include e-government, e-democracy, IT value and evaluation and questions of privacy and trust. He has written extensively on IS related topics and has published a book on the Financial Management of IT. He is editor of the Electronic Journal of e-Government as well as being on the editorial boards of several other academic journals. He is a member of the Institute of Management Consultants in Ireland, a Fellow of the Irish Computer Society and a Chartered Engineer.

Rob Brookes
Rob Brookes is IT Systems Manager at Conwy County Borough Council in North Wales and has a background in systems development. His interest in e-government issues stems largely from the experience of producing Conwy's first Implementing Electronic Government statement. Rob has an MSc with distinction in Managing IT from the University of Salford and is a member of the conference committee for the European Conference on e-Government and the SOCITM (Society of IT Managers) Wales benchmarking sub-group.

Anthony Bryant
Dr. Antony Bryant is Professor of Informatics at Leeds Metropolitan University. His current research interests include Public Sector Innovation, Self-Organizing Communities, and Ethical Issues in the realm of ICT. He has recently published *Thinking Informatically; A New Understanding of Information, Communication & Technology* (Edwin Mellen Press), including a preface by Zygmunt Bauman, and an introduction by Frank Land. He is Senior Editor for the forthcoming *Handbook of Grounded Theory* (SAGE). His teaching includes Information Systems Modelling, Public Sector Innovation, and Research Methods.

Luca Buccoliero
Dr. Luca Buccoliero is an assistant professor of Public Management, e-Government and e-Health at Bocconi University, Italy. He has a degree in Business Management, (Bocconi University, Milan, Italy) and a Ph.D. in Public Administration Management (Università degli Studi of Parma, Italy). He is the education initiatives coordinator at the Center for Research on Health and Social Care Management of Bocconi University. His research interests include information and communication technologies in the public sector; financial accounting information systems in the healthcare sector and in local government (e-government, e-health).

Stefano Calciolari

Dr. Stefano Calciolari is an adjunct professor of Public Administration at Aosta Valley University, Italy. He is also a research fellow of Public Management at Bocconi University, Italy and an assistant professor at the Division of Public Management of the School of Management of Bocconi University, Italy. He has a degree in Business Management, with a major in Public Administration and International Institutions from Bocconi University, Milan, Italy, a Master of Public Administration, Maxwell School of Syracuse University, USA and a Ph.D. in Public Administration Management, Università degli Studi of Parma, Italy. His research interests include the strategic management of public sector organizations, with particular emphasis on information technology management in the healthcare sector (e-health) and in local governments (e-government), financial accounting and change management in the public sector.

J. Ignacio Criado

J. Ignacio Criado is a lecturer in Politics and Public Administration, Department of Political Science and International Relations, Autonomous University of Madrid. He has published several chapters and peer-reviewed articles on e-government issues, specially about the local and regional tiers in comparative perspective. His book *Building the Local e-Administration* (published in Spanish, *Construyendo la e-Administración Local*. Madrid, EuroGestión Pública, 2004) was awarded in the III Fermin Abella y Blave Prize (Spanish Ministry of Public Administration). His research interests cover also public sector reform and modernization, quality and knowledge management in public organizations, and information society policies. He is editorial board member of the International Journal of Public Sector Management. He may be contacted at ignacio.criado@uam.es.

David Gilbert

Dr. David Gilbert is Professor of Marketing at the School of Management, Surrey University. He has 21 years' academic experience in higher education and over 8 years' operational marketing experience for the private sector, having worked as a Product Manager and as a Marketing Manager for Rank leisure. He specialises in the teaching of marketing related to: Relationship Marketing, Consumer Behaviour, Market Research, Research Methods and the functions of Marketing Management and was the founder of the MSc in Tourism Marketing at Surrey. Alongside his academic duties, he has worked with several government and private organisations and consultancies on tourism project work. He was the research director of the Thomas Cook Research Centre at the University of Surrey and has in-depth knowledge of marketing in relation to the service industry.

David Griffin

David Griffin is a senior lecturer in Information Systems at Leeds Metropolitan University. His research interests include e-government, social innovation and youth participation. Before becoming an academic he spent 20 years working in local government IT as a project manager and a chief business analyst. He is a member of editorial board of the Electronic Journal of e-Government. He is a member of the British Computer Society and a Chartered IT Practitioner. He may be contacted at: d.griffin@ leedsmet.ac.uk.

Edward Halpin
Dr. Edward F. Halpin MA, MCLIP, is Associate Dean in the Leslie Silver International Faculty, at Leeds Metropolitan University. He has a background in politics, community development and social informatics. He has a number of publications on e-government and has researched the use of information and ICTs for human and child rights; including work as an expert for the European Parliament Scientific and Technical Options (STOA) Unit. This work has involved him in working alongside organizations such as Save the Children, the Child Rights Information Network (CRIN) and Amnesty International. He has published widely on these subjects including the book *Human Rights and the Internet* (Palgrave, 2000) and co-edited the recently published book *Cyberwar, Netwar, and the Revolution in Military Affairs* (Palgrave, 2006).

Alisa Kolsaker
Alisa Kolsaker is a lecturer in e-Business and Marketing in the post-graduate Management School of the University of Surrey. Before becoming an academic she worked for some years in the telecommunications industry in Norway and as a manager in the education sector in the UK. Her research interests centre around the role of technology in modern society, specifically; e-government, e-business applications and technology-driven marketing.

Davy Janssen
Davy Janssen has an M.A. in Germanic Philology (Katholieke Universiteit Leuven), and has additional degrees in International Relations and Business Economics. He is a research assistant at the Universiteit Antwerpen, Belgium. His research interests lie in the area of e-democracy and the use of ICT in state-citizen relations. Since 2001, he has been involved in research projects concerning e-government strategies, e-government benchmarking, e-government prioritization and the influence of ICT on state-citizen relations. He may be contacted at: davy.janssen@ua.be.

Jungwoo Lee
Dr. Jungwoo Lee is currently an associate professor of Information Systems in Graduate School of Information at Yonsei University in Korea. He received his Ph.D. in computer information systems from Georgia State University. Before coming to Yonsei, he worked for University of Nevada, Las Vegas. His research interest focuses on systems analysis and design but spans over towards the competence of firms in using information technology, impact and management of conflicts during IS/IT utilization process, and developmental issues related to e-government initiatives. He has published articles in Information & Management, Information Systems Journal, Government Information Quarterly, Journal of Computer Information Systems, and numerous conference proceedings. He may be contacted at: jlee@yonsei.ac.kr.

Albert Jacob Meijer
Dr. Albert Jacob Meijer works as an assistant professor at the Utrecht School of Governance in the Netherlands. He teaches various courses on public administration and policy sciences at the bachelor and master level. He does research on public accountability, on informatization in public administration and on the use e-mail by government organizations. He has published in journals such as Information Polity, The Information Society and Government Information Quarterly. In addition, he is one of the chairs of the permanent study group on informatization in public administration of the European Group for Public Administration.

M. Carmen Ramilo

M. Carmen Ramilo is a research fellow and PhD candidate in the Department of Political and Administration Sciences, Basque Country University. Master in Public Management, Complutense University, Madrid. Her research interests are Information Society and policy networks in the regional and local level. She participates in different research projects for the analysis of e-government in the Basque Country and has collaborated with Mr. Criado since 2000 in research and publications. She has been a visiting researcher in the Department of Organisation Studies at Tilburg University, Department of Politics and Management at Konstanz University; and the Department of Statistics at Trinity College in Dublin. She may be contacted at: mentxu@gmail.com.

Dan Remenyi

Dr. Dan Remenyi is a visiting professor at Trinity College Dublin and a visiting academic fellow at Henley Management College in the United Kingdom. His original academic interests are in the field of Political Science and Economics. Later he worked with information systems management with special emphasis on the evaluation of information and communications technology investment. In this regard he has worked with various applications including knowledge management and e-government. He holds a B Soc Sc, MBA and PhD.

Sabine Rotthier

Sabine Rotthier has an M.A. in Political Sciences (Universiteit Gent). She is a research assistant at the Hogeschool Gent, Belgium. Her research interests lie in the area of local e-government. Since 2002, she has been involved in research projects concerning e-government strategies, e-government benchmarking, e-government prioritization and the adoption of e-government at the local level. She may be contacted at: sabine.rotthier@hogent.be.

Kris Snijkers

Kris Snijkers has an M.A. in Political Sciences (Katholieke Universiteit Leuven) and a Postgraduate in Business Economics (Vlekho Business School, Brussels). He is a research assistant at the Public Management Institute, Katholieke Universiteit Leuven, Belgium. His research interests lie in the area of e-government and the use of ICT in the public sector; especially issues concerning intergovernmental ICT projects and process innovation. Since 2001, he has been involved in research projects concerning intergovernmental task allocation, e-government strategies, e-government benchmarking, e-government prioritization and intergovernmental e-government projects. He is the co-ordinator of an e-government training program for civil servants. He may be contacted at: kris.snijkers@soc.kuleuven.be.

Philippa Trevorrow

Dr. Philippa Trevorrow is a research officer and lecturer at Leeds Metropolitan University. She has a BSc B(Ed) Hons in Mathematics and Education, and a PhD from the University of Exeter. Her current research interests include youth participation and the use of new technology by young people specifically mobile phones and WIKIs. She has recently co-edited *Cyberwar, Netwar and the Revolution in Military Affairs* (Palgrave, 2006).

C. William R. Webster
Dr. William Webster is a lecturer in Public Management at the University of Stirling. He is Director of the BA (Hons) Public Management and Administration and Public Sector Management MBA programmes. He has a long standing research interest in the policy processes and governance structures surrounding the emergence of CCTV systems in public places across the UK, and has published numerous times in this area. His other research interests include developments in the delivery of electronic public services, information age governance, electronic democracy, and the relevance of telecommunications policy and its regulation to these innovations. William is a member of the European Group of Public Administration's (EGPA) permanent study group on 'Information and Communications Technologies in Public Administration', the International Research Society for Public Management (IRSPM), and of the Information Resources Management Association (IRMA). He may be contacted at: c.w.r.webster@ stir.ac.uk.

Diana Wilson
Diana Wilson is a lecturer in Information Systems at Trinity College, Dublin, Ireland. Her research is particularly concerned with the social relations of technology and the labour process. Her background in the metal and chemical industries has also informed her work on the historicism and philosophy of technology and its interrelationship with organisations and society. As a result, Diana has published work on technology and teams, computers and gender, and socio-economic factors affecting technology uptake and diffusion.

List of Abbreviations

ANOVA	Analysis of Variance
CBA	Cost Benefit Analysis
CCTV	Closed Circuit Television
CRM	Customer Relationship Management
CSF	Critical Success Factor
DAF	Department of Agriculture and food
DOI	Diffusion of Innovation (Theory)
EU	European Union
FBI	Federal Bureau of Investigation
FAC	Fight Against Crime
GDP	Gross Domestic Product
HTML	Hyper Text Mark-up Language
ICT	Information and Communications Technology
IEG	Implementing Electronic Government
IS	Information Systems
IT	Information Technology
NPV	Net Present Value
TAM	Technology Acceptance Model
UK	United Kingdom
UN	United Nations
UNPAN	United Nations Online Network in Public Administration
US	United States of America
VOIP	Voice over Internet Protocol
WWW	World Wide web

Introduction
e-Government: A Welcome Guest or Uninvited Stranger?

David GRIFFIN, Philippa TREVORROW and Edward HALPIN

Leeds Metropolitan University

"Twenty-first Century Government is enabled by technology – policy is inspired by it, business change is delivered by it, customer and corporate services are dependent upon it and democratic engagement is exploring it. Moreover, modern governments with serious transformational intent see technology as a strategic asset and not just a tactical tool [1]."

This claim was made by the UK Government in 2005, towards the end of a five-year modernization programme that moved government services onto the Internet. There is an underlying assumption of technological determinism in this statement. It suggests that the application of technology to organizations and to society will lead to an improvement for all. This volume of essays sets out to provide a more critical evaluation of developments in e-government. The analytical tools, frameworks and theoretical perspectives employed by the contributors should enable students and practioners to analyze and critique local, national and global progress in undertaking technology-enabled change in the processes of government.

The scope of the book includes the area traditionally associated with e-government, i.e. service delivery by various levels of government. In addition, it examines the emerging area of e-democracy, in which technology is being utilized to provide a digital presence for the democratic processes of government. The book is a synthesis of theoretical contributions and empirical investigations. The contributors have been assembled from across the European Union and beyond to present empirical evidence from studies undertaken in a number of different countries. The knowledge gained from the implementation of e-government on an international scale, at the national and local level, should provide a useful reference point for policy makers and academics that are steering and evaluating future developments in e-government.

1. Is e-Government a Welcome Guest?

Most public administrations involved in the design, development and implementation of e-government programmes have adopted structured techniques which emphasize planning and control by the host organization based on the organic metaphor. Ciborra [2] offers an alternative metaphor for thinking critically about the relationship between the host organization, the technology and the people who are intended to interact with it. This is the hospitality metaphor.

According to Ciborra, hospitality is a 'time-economizing' institution. Its rituals and practices serve to reduce the time taken for a temporary relationship to be formed between people of different cultures and beliefs. The linguistic root of hospitality provides an insight into the challenges involved in the receiving of strangers into the home. In Latin, the word *hostis* can mean both guest and enemy. Ciborra uses the term 'ambiguous stranger' to encapsulate these potential alternative outcomes of the interaction. A successful host will temporarily relinquish their power and control within the hosting environment and will become the servant to the incoming stranger. The encounter requires both parties to enter this temporary relationship with a degree of trust in each other and a desire not to control the other.

How might this metaphor help us to analyze the e-government programme? We can explore the use of the metaphor in at least two ways. Firstly, we can envisage the public administration as the host and the e-government system as the guest. The technology may be received by some staff in the organization as a welcome guest and by others as a threat to their current practices and, in some instances, a threat to their livelihood. Secondly, we can consider how welcoming the e-government system itself is to those citizens and businesses which come into contact with it. In this situation, these 'strangers' are crossing the public administration boundary and being received within the virtual e-government sphere.

There are a number of questions that immediately come to mind when employing the hospitality metaphor in this manner:

- How should the host public administration change so that the encounter with the technology will be more like a meeting of relatives than a chance meeting between strangers?
- Should this technological stranger be treated as merely an artifact that will impact upon the host or is the encounter shaped by the culture, skills and experiences of the host as well as the characteristics of the technology?
- If the encounter is socially-situated, will the technology be welcomed in different ways by other host public administrations and will the encounter shape-up and develop in different ways?
- Is the public administration, as host, accountable to wider community stakeholders for the success of e-government systems?
- How welcoming is the e-government system to the citizens and businesses that will come into contact with it?
- What are their attitudes and feelings about this encounter?

These issues are all raised, debated and answered at various points in the chapters of this book.

2. The Shape of the Book

There are four parts to this volume. In Part A, *policy and theoretical perspectives* are introduced, through which e-government developments may be viewed. In Chapter 1, Bryant opens the debate by challenging policy-makers and government officials to ask fundamental questions about the approach they are taking to modernize services. Following Beer, he asks 'given the existence of ICT, what is the nature of government?'

He asserts that the e-government programme needs to be more radical than merely placing existing government services on the Web. He argues, along with Bauman, that society is in a state of liquid modernity and, as such, e-government plans and policies need to take account of this. In Chapter 2, Webster presents a theoretical framework for examining the workings of public sector policy processes. He examines a policy associated with a single technology employed by local authorities and other public bodies, CCTV. This chapter provides a thought-provoking deliberation about the working of the public policy process. Webster builds a new theoretical framework for analyzing policy processes. This framework explores existing theory by considering a series of different perspectives from which the development and diffusion of this innovation may be examined.

Part B investigates *issues connected to the ICT-enabled transformation of government service delivery*. In the first of three chapters in this section, Lee analyses recent e-government stages of growth models in order to further clarify and develop the model he previously produced with Layne [3]. His examples are taken from government services in the United States. He argues that the four stages presented in this chapter are not the complete journey. Further stages may be added as technological innovation develops. Furthermore, he argues that it is not implied that all should begin at the first of the four stages. Developing countries just embarking on e-government may learn from the experiences of others and start at a subsequent stage. In Chapter 5, Criado and Ramilo provide a comparative analysis of local public administration on the Web in two municipalities in Spain. They argue that there is a more complex relationship between organizations and technology than is implied by existing diffusion of innovation theory. The implementation of website technology, for example, is affected by the political, economic, social and cultural factors. Their empirical study explores this complex relationship. During the e-government programme, administrations, at all levels, have benchmarked their own performance in service delivery with that of others. In Chapter 6, Snijkers, Rotthier and Jannsen critique 18 international e-government benchmarks in order to inform the development of future benchmarks. They identify that, to date, most benchmarks concern themselves with the products of e-government policy, typically the front-office website presence. They argue that attention also needs to be given to back-office benchmarking, to help administrations decide how to innovate to improve the services that lie behind the customer-facing systems and processes.

Part C explores *the impact that the modernization of the information systems and processes of government is having on democracy and accountability*. In chapter 6, Remenyi and Wilson start by clarifying the definition of e-democracy as being the use of ICT to facilitate democratic processes. They identify four democratic processes – debating, campaigning and canvassing, lobbying and voting – and analyze the potential contribution of ICT to each. They conclude that is too early to say whether technology will energize democratic engagement or sap its strength. The next two chapters examine accountability. In the first of these, Meijer suggests that discussion of e-government has mainly concentrated on service delivery. There has been much less debate about how ICT may be employed to facilitate public accountability. He argues that a new conceptualization of accountability is required, one in which the government is only one of a number of societal actors considered to be responsible for public affairs. In the following chapter, Griffin continues this exploration of the potential effect of ICT on accountability. The emphasis here is to analyze whether the innovative use of ICT has affected government accountability for the e-government programme. He presents the results of an empirical study of the scrutiny processes of UK local authorities. He argues that ICT has had little effect on accountability. It has opened up scrutiny to a small, new community of interest, but there has been little change in the overall scrutiny processes. A significant finding of this study is the gap in accountability for partnership working. As most UK councils are now members of 100+ partnerships, this is an area of concern. In Chapter 9, Trevorrow discusses how a specific technology, the mobile phone, may be used to raise participation in democracy by young people. She presents the findings of her empirical research conducted with UK local councils and young people. She concludes that, whilst young people have the required skills and access to the technology being used to raise youth participation by councils, the real issue is whether they want to engage with public administrations.

The complete book is a critique and evaluation of developments in e-government. However, Part D contains a selection of essays which specifically *evaluate the progress towards fully e-enabled service delivery*. In Chapter 10, Bannister examines the economics of e-government at the macro, micro and 'pica' levels. For context, he draws on examples of the Irish e-government services at the national level. His discussion, and examples of the layers of the typical public sector, provide an informative context for considering competing definitions of e-government. He argues that an economic consideration of e-government is required for three reasons: to understand the full contribution of government IT spending to the economy; to provide a guide for future investment; and to improve the allocation of scarce resources. In Chapter 11 Buccoliero and Calciolari make an economic appraisal of two Italian healthcare projects. Although these are examples of ICT-enabled change within the wider public sector, we feel that this chapter is worthy of inclusion here as it provides a detailed consideration of the costs and benefits associated with ICT change projects. They argue that the range of impacts of public sector investments need evaluation approaches that include multiple measures to fully capture the variety of costs and benefits. In particular, measures should be available to account for intangible benefits and the secondary benefits to projects following on from the one being appraised. In Chapter 12 Gilbert, Balestrini, Kolsaker and Littleboy provide a timely examination of citizen perceptions of electronic service delivery and their attitudes and intentions towards using it. They present the findings from an empirical study undertaken in Guildford, UK, which identifies nine factors that determine citizens' attitude to using web-based public services. They argue that government could improve resource utilization by paying attention to these factors when taking decisions about new online services. In Chapter 13 Brookes continues the evaluation of e-government from the citizen perspective in a study of digital exclusion. He examines the UK public policy towards citizen access to ICT using empirical evidence obtained from his study in North Wales. He identifies that government policy has concentrated on providing access to ICT as a means of reducing digital exclusion from the information society. He argues that ICT exclusion does not simply equate to lack of access to the technology. There are a number of other significant factors at play.

Acknowledgements

The production of an edited book is a lengthy process which depends for its successful completion on the co-operation and effort by numerous parties. We wish to thank all the individual chapter authors for their patience and prompt responses throughout the development of this book. We are also very grateful for the assistance of Elaine Exon and Gillian Wood, both of whom cheerfully helped us to navigate through the intricacies of the copy-editing within a short timescale whilst, at the same time, ensuring the quality of the final product. However, of course, any errors or omissions that still remain in the text are our sole responsibility.

References

[1]   Cabinet Office, *Transformational Government Enabled by Technology*, The Stationery Office, London, 2005.
[2]   C. Ciborra, The Labyrinths of Information: Challenging the Wisdom of Systems, Oxford University Press, Oxford, 2002.
[3]   K. Layne and J. Lee, "Developing Fully Functional E-Government", *Government Information Quarterly*, Summer 2001.

Part 1

Policy and Theoretical Perspectives

Developments in e-Government
D. Griffin et al. (Eds.)
IOS Press, 2007

Government, e-Government
and Modernity

'The times they are a-changin';
and even the changes are *a-changin*

Anthony BRYANT
Innovation North: Faculty of Information and Technology,
Leeds Metropolitan University, UK

1. Introduction

Ideas about e-government sometimes amount to not a great deal more than 'Government-as-usual + ICT'[1]. This can be seen as the 21st century version of the old Leninist slogan 'Communism = Soviet power + Electrification'. Slogans may serve a progressive purpose if they rally support and provoke action; but they can also obscure and impede. *E-government* is, for now, a fashionable catch-all label that can be pasted on to a variety of activities, initiatives, programmes, and platforms emanating from government, inter-government and intra-government sources. In many cases these are simply attempts to re-badge what are in effect *business-as-usual* administrative activities; except that for many the close association or near-complete merging of government and business is not at all usual.

The more incisive commentators and researchers on e-government understand that harnessing the power and potential of ICT is far more complex. In fact the very metaphor of *harnessing* – i.e. adding the horse-power of ICT to extant activities – is itself simplistic and misleading. To paraphrase the words of Stafford Beer, the question which asks *how to use ICT in government?* – or anywhere else – is the wrong question; a better formulation is to ask *how government should be run given the existence of ICT?* The best version of all is the question; *given the existence of ICT, what is the nature of government?*[2]

A similar process of interrogation was induced, if not welcomed, when the commercial world discovered the internet in the 1990s. At first there was enormous excitement and enthusiasm often based on the mistaken belief that e-commerce was the equivalent of *Business-more-or-less-as-usual + ICT*, and the result would be more customers, bigger margins, faster turn-around: essentially something-for-nothing. Some of the initial *successes* of the internet-as-market-place seemed to indicate precisely this, and there was a great deal of talk – and many learned papers and presentations – about 'new business models', 'disintermediation', and 'the friction-less market'. Economic reality soon re-asserted itself with the various 'market adjustments' of the late 1990s. Current ideas about e-commerce – a term that now sounds almost quaint and bizarre – are far removed from any early excess exhilaration. Taking the boom and bust of the internet economy as a chastening lesson, we should all heed J. K. Galbraith's admonition in a lecture at the London School of Economics in 1999 [1], '[W]hen you hear it being said that we've entered a new era of permanent prosperity … you should take cover'.

The experiences of the 1990s should not have come as a surprise. Those involved with ICT should all too easily have recognized that *we have been here before* – several times. Indeed there is a whole literature devoted to the ways in which the processes of adapting to, and accommodation of, technological innovation have to be seen as learning processes or stages of maturation.

2. Models of growth and maturity

The most notable, and one of the earliest efforts at explaining these phenomena in the context of ICT can be found in the work of Nolan and Gibson [2] dating from the early 1970s. They presented a model based on a relatively cursory piece of research prompted by nothing much more than a series of hunches on Nolan's part that organizations went through a small number of stages or phases in applying computer technology; and that the stage which an organization reached was dependent on or at least indicated by the organization's computing budget. Their research resulted in a classic 'S-curve' – or learning curve – of expenditure against time, and so evoked the concept that organizations went through a learning process in utilizing computer technology. Nolan later extended the original four stage model to six stages, the final stage being termed 'technological maturity'. Ever since the appearance of Nolan's later paper, in 1979, the ICT literature has been replete with commentaries and critiques of the model. Is the model historically specific to the uptake of (main-frame) computer technology in North America in the 1960s and 1970s; or does it have wider application? How useful is 'expenditure' as an indicator? And so on. Whatever its specific shortcomings[3], the fact that it continues to attract a wealth of attention testifies to its explanatory profundities. The model has recently been used as a focus of discussions about e-commerce, internet banking and knowledge management – and e-government as will be seen later.

The model is elegant and simple, yet simultaneously compelling and provocative. Work by McFarlan *et al* in the early 1980s extended the central concepts of the model to encompass technology in general, focusing on the ways in which organizations 'assimilated technology' [3]. Whether they realized it or not, McFarlan *et al* were using Piaget's concepts, taking them from the context of cognitive psychology and applying them to organizations. For Piaget [4] individuals learn through *adaptation* which itself consists of two, complementary processes; *assimilation* and *accommodation*. When a child has novel or unexpected encounters or experiences its cognitive equilibrium is disturbed, and it can only achieve a new equilibrium through a combination of *assimilation* – i.e. incorporation of novelty into existing cognitive structures or schema – and *accommodation* – i.e. modification to existing structures as a result of the experience. McFarlan *et al* were implying that organizations could be seen to be responding in a similar fashion. Overall they will tend to move from experimentation and piloting of innovative technology to a final stage of technology transfer, and effective and managed utilization. In the process of moving through these phases the organization and the technology will undergo mutual adaptation. The organization will seek to find balance between *assimilating* the technology – adapting the technology itself by incorporating it into existing structures, routines and practices – and *accommodating* to the technology – changing practices and processes in the light of the technology. The new equilibrium will involve both the organization and the technology undergoing modification.

It is no coincidence that Nolan, and McFarlan *et al* used the concept of *maturity*. When technological developments are heralded as unmitigated panaceas there is usually an initial phase of excitement, optimism and anticipation as the technology is introduced and used as a basis for experiment and innovation. One result of this is that well-entrenched routines and procedures are brought into question; perhaps having previously been completely unstated and unstatable, and hence assumed to be natural and inevitable. Gibson and Nolan argued that the introduction of computer technology in the late 1960s and early 1970s 'shocked the organization': Again this echoes Piaget's approach whereby learning involves disturbance of one's equilibrium. —

Uncertainty increases and there can be ramifications for people, groups and organizations with regard to their own profile and self-image. Have the innovations undermined people's autonomy and depth of control? Do organizations need to reconsider their place in the market or their relationships with suppliers, competitors, and customers? Given this undermining of certainty and the concomitant increase in doubt and insecurity, it is not surprising that any initial zeal is replaced by a more tempered orientation or even shadings of despair and despondency. The innovations and accompanying changes are themselves often personalized so that various individuals become seen as heroes or villains: Sometimes the same person can fulfil both roles – the prime example for our age would be Bill Gates. Far from *maturity*, this combination of traits – technological excitement, experiment and innovation, uncertain profile and self-image, heroes and villains, retreat from routine or procedure, high optimism coupled with deep despair – is a fairly accurate summary of *adolescence*.

So perhaps the metaphor of maturity has some useful extensibility; organizations will need guidance and insight – perhaps wisdom – in order to move beyond juvenile phases of coping with and reacting to technology and novelty. In a context of inherent novelty, however, this may be some Sisyphean task; and Nolan's model implies that perhaps maturity is a stage that can never be attained, but on the other hand has continually to be striven for.

As a swift aside it needs to be pointed out that use of the concept of *maturity* in the context of ICT can also be found in work emanating from Watts Humphrey's application of Crosby's [5] Quality framework to IS/ICT; in particular with respect to software and systems development. This has given rise to an entire industry of quality inspection and assessment now encompassed by the Capability Maturity Model[4]. Humphrey's model [6] is derived from Crosby's work which distinguished between five levels of quality management maturity. The five levels, from least to most mature being *uncertainty, awakening, enlightenment, wisdom, certainty*. The general trend is from confusion to understanding or insight; and Crosby's work has been highly influential in many spheres of activity. The choice of terminology is, however, flawed; as will be argued later, with wisdom there ought to come an understanding that the quest for certainty is an erroneous and misguided objective.

3. e-Government growth models

Within the context of e-government there have been several attempts to apply Nolan's model in recent years. A recent report from the Australian Government includes a contribution from Pearce [7] in which he discusses two such attempts by Layne and

Lee [8][5], and by Moon [9]. Layne and Lee's model seeks to explain 'government's use of technology, particularly web-based Internet applications, to enhance the access to and delivery of government information and services to citizens, business partners, employees, other agencies and government entities' ([8, p. 123] – quoted in [7]). As such they offer a four stage model starting with *Cataloguing*, going on to a *Transaction* stage, followed by *Vertical integration*, and eventually *Horizontal integration*. The cataloguing stage is not much more than establishing a presence on the internet with some inactive web-pages, but not allowing any interaction from users. This only occurs in the next stage where such things as applications can be submitted and various payments made. The latter two stages focus on the internal workings and structures of government, drawing on parallel ideas from the commercial world, where different aspects of the existing organization have to be brought together (vertical integration), and then where the internal – departmental and potentially diverting and divisive – structure has to be overcome to allow faster and more effective processing (Pearce likens this to Business Process Re-engineering).

Pearce is quick to point out the shortcomings of this somewhat mechanistic interpretation and application of a stages-of-growth model. Layne and Lee fail to account even for the complexities of the organizationally-oriented model itself, let alone seek to incorporate such critically distinctive aspects of governmental organizations as citizenship, and the general political processes and pressures. Layne and Lee's model in their 2001 paper exemplifies the equation given at the start of this chapter: e-government = government-as-usual + ICT. In Lee's revised or amplified account of the model in this volume (chapter 4), he is far more circumspect. Lee tempers any simple-minded interpretation of a four-stage model by noting that it is a 'general metaphor based on organic growth'; also that governments need not have to start at stage one and continue progressing through the other stages. He also distance their model from the 'classic' maturity models of, for example, Gibson and Nolan; their model 'does not assume saturation or maturity as suggested in other growth models', governments may develop 'beyond the four stages'.

Lee concludes his chapter with various caveats and a discussion pointing out that '[p]ractical realization of e-government requires reconceptualization of government'. This is a useful clarification, since Layne and Lee's earlier paper was far more obviously anchored to Beer's first level of questioning – how to use ICT in government: But, if we revise Beer's words, 'the question which asks how to use *ICT* in *government* is, in short, the wrong question'. We have to move to Beer's third question, but perhaps we can only reach this as the result of a process of conceptual growth which moves through Beer's three questions.

The strength of Layne and Lee's work is that they clearly set out the argument that e-government is not simply a case of plug-and-play or *plug-and-preside*; some processes of learning and development are called for, and presumably some managing of progression through the stages is demanded.

The second model described by Pearce is from the work of Moon. Moon uses a definition of e-government taken from a report published by the United Nations *and* American Society for Public Administration in 2001. Although Pearce gives a slightly condensed version of this definition, it is worth giving at some greater length; 'e-government includes the use of all information and communication technologies, from fax machines to wireless palm pilots, to facilitate the daily administration of government.' In addition, e-government should improve 'citizen access to government information, services, and expertise to ensure citizen participation in, and satisfaction with the government process'[6].

So this at least places the citizen at the heart of the phenomenon and specifically addresses participation and satisfaction. Moon contends that there are four aspects of e-government; establishment of reliable, high performance and secure government computer systems; web-based service delivery; application of e-commerce for transaction handling; and e-democracy. These aspects are developed during a five stage model starting with *Information Dissemination and Cataloguing*, moving to *Two-way Communication*, then *Service and Financial Transactions,* and *Vertical and Horizontal Integration*, ending with *Political Participation*. Pearce argues that combining vertical and horizontal integration is a weakness in comparison with Layne and Lee's model, but the overall effort is redeemed by inclusion of political participation. Interestingly Pearce makes no comment about the inclusion of issues of performance and security.

Pearce builds upon both models, adding a sixth stage. This results in a sequence originating with *Informational*, proceeding to *Transactional*, then on to *Process Redesign, Full Integration, E-Democracy*, and *Maturity*. So Nolan's model is adhered to more strictly, both in terms of having six stages, and with an end point of maturity.

> *"The six stages can actually be considered as a series of three consecutive pairs ... stages 1 and 2 can be considered as e-government/commerce, dealing ... with provision of information and enabling of transactions to external entities. ... 3 and 4 are focused on internal effectiveness of horizontal and vertical integration ... considered to be e-government/administration ... 5 and 6 have a socio-political focus and may be considered to be e-government /civic."* [7, p142]

Pearce justifies locating e-democracy only in the penultimate stage because it is only at that point that the complex socio-political issues – such as consideration of direct versus representative democracy – come into consideration.

One of the common features of all these models is that they mix management of the technology with management of governmental and administrative structures; and in the case of Moon and Pearce's models they also incorporate issues of political participation. Pearce recognizes this characteristic of his own model, but seems confused about its ramifications.

> *"The fact that beyond stage 2 the emphasis of the model is no longer on technology, but on organisational processes, structures, culture and the socio-political environment weakens the model's utility for wholesale change efforts."*

Gibson and Nolan's original model stressed that progression through the stages of growth was in effect a move from managing the technology to managing the 'data' or 'data resource'; which we might now term moving from IT-management to information management. This seems a useful way of thinking about organizational maturity. So why is Pearce not content with a model that moves from a focus on technology to a focus on organizational, cultural and socio-political aspects? The answer seems to be that his initial focus was too oriented towards the technology; something he readily admits. But he then contends that 'inspection of the model showed that the effort, if directed to effective change management, rather than focusing on the technology, would work'. His solution is to place the model against a change management framework, specifically Lewin's [10] three-phase approach of unfreezing, implementing change, re-freezing.

Although Pearce displaces Lewin's model to an extent, as will be seen below, essentially Pearce's argument seems to be that the stages-of-growth-model is appropriate and useful, provided it is supplemented by and located against a framework of change management and organizational development. He concludes that this then provides a 'suitable, comprehensive, holistic management model' for e-government. Moreover it provides an effective response to the 'challenge to apply management *more stringently* to e-government' (stress added). Having moved far ahead of Beer's first question – the wrong or inadequate one – we now seem to be back where we started. Yet Pearce himself has provided the objective that ought to have left him dissatisfied with his own conclusions. In the introduction and synopsis to his own paper he noted that:

> "e-Government is not simply a public good that provides another channel of communication between governments and their constituents; it is an opportunity to employ new technologies in order to enable transformation of government to a model more appropriate to the 21st century "(stress added).

Unfortunately he has not heeded his own words – although it might be contended that a phrase such as '*transformation of government to a model more appropriate to the 21st century*' conceals more than it reveals: Yet Pearce implies that the only transformations will be centered on vertical and horizontal integration.

The work of Heeks and his co-authors [11] is a useful corrective to Pearce's modest and constrained objectives. In his introductory essay Heeks stresses that although any application of ICT could also be accomplished by other, non-technological means; in practice ICT allows the accomplishment of tasks that otherwise 'could not be contemplated'. This does not quite engage with Beer's third question, but it comes fairly close.

The stages-of-growth model, however, has at least one distinct strength: It immediately focuses attention on issues such as progress and development, and learning and experimentation. If those using the approach have sufficient grasp of the literature, it should also lead to consideration of the extent to which *growth* will necessitate or result in fundamental re-thinking of the context within which the evolution is charted. If the final stage is associated with *maturity*, then there should also be an intimation that such a stage is usually tantalizingly beyond reach, but constantly present as an ambition. When applied to any context within which technology plays an initiating role, stages-of-growth models should also move from a focus on the technology itself to more broadly-based considerations of the ways in which the context itself changes – as a result of both assimilation and accommodation. This will then preclude falling into the trap of technological determinism: Recognition of the applicability of Piaget's dual-natured concept of adaptation prevents allocation of primacy to either the technology or the surrounding context.

Furthermore, establishing stages affords a basis for benchmarking which can be helpful to practitioners and policy-makers and other stakeholders. Moreover this implies that the model should be couched in terms to which these constituencies can relate, so that the model can be revised and modified accordingly. In the context of e-government it is crucial to understand that the learning process is undergone by component institutions and bodies within governmental structures, as well as by *government* itself: And this includes those *being governed*. Ideas about e-government should prompt stakeholders to ask Beer's second and third questions:

- How should government be run given the existence of ICT?
- Given the existence of ICT, what is the nature of government?

One of Beer's fundamental assumptions – at least in his early work – is that organizations develop as systems, but are themselves immersed in a systemic – even systematic – environment. The metaphorical basis of this, one which permeates his work, is that organizations are in some sense *organic*; hence two of his key books are entitled *The Brain of the Firm* and *The Heart of the Enterprise*[7]. Correspondingly the concepts of learning and maturation assume that organizations can be considered to be organic – they grow, evolve, mature and perish. This organic metaphor has great power and is part of the – implicit – basis of applying a stages-of-growth model to e-government. But the metaphor has its limitations, and one of them is that it usually encompasses the assumption that the environment within which the organism grows is relatively constant – certainly far more so than the individual organism itself. So in the context of e-government it is often assumed that governance takes place in a relatively stable environment. This compounds the failure to pursue the third of Beer's questions or challenges.

What has to be grasped is that the very nature of government and governance are altering as a result of massive socio-political changes and ruptures. The current socio-political context has been variously labelled – *the information age, the knowledge society, the digital economy*, and the *informational form of capitalism*; depending on which author you read. Yet these all fail to encapsulate one of the key aspects of contemporary society: Constant and continuously unpredictable change on a global scale but with local and specific impacts. The recent work of Bauman [12] [13] [14] [15] [16], and also that of Beck [17], Giddens [18] and Sennett [19] amongst others, offers a valuable resource against which issues such as e-government can be understood in this light. In what follows I will focus specifically on what Zygmunt Bauman has termed *liquid modernity*, and the ways in which strategies for e-government need to take account of this fluid socio-political formation.

4. Liquid modernity – flux and turbulence

In a landmark paper in the 1960s, Emery *and* Trist [20] distinguished between four types of 'causal texture'; thereby focusing on different environments within which organizational activities and developments take place. The four types ranged from the placid to the turbulent. Each causal texture or environment was characterized by the distribution of what they termed 'goals and noxiants': or in the words of Sellar and Yeatman [21], 'good things and bad things'.

In the *placid-randomized* case these goals and noxiants are 'relatively unchanging in themselves and randomly distributed'. This corresponds to 'the economist's classical market' which takes little or no account of discontinuities. In such causal textures, there is no distinction between tactics and strategy. Tactics can be learned by simple trial and error, and then generalized across the entire environment. The placid-randomized environment sounds more like an idealized context than anything that might actually exist; but in ecological terms Emery *and* Trysts likened it to large areas of grassland such as the Steppes, where vast barren expanses are punctuated by small concentrations of food.

The *placid-clustered* environment differs slightly from the randomized one, since 'goals and noxiants are not randomly distributed but hang together in certain ways'. Strategy and tactics are now distinct since it becomes important to be able to decipher the non-uniform environment, gaining an understanding of which parts to avoid and which to approach. The ecological exemplification given by Emery *and* Trist is an area of scrub land with clearings and forested areas; the latter being both sources of danger from attack as well as food and shelter. In organizational terms, in such contexts there is a need to develop long-term plans and devise resource management strategies accordingly. This also necessitates the development and encouragement of (vertical and horizontal) division of labour, or what Emery *and* Trist term 'distinctive competences', accompanied by centralization and hierarchy aimed at optimizing co-ordination and control.

The third type of causal texture they termed *disturbed-reactive*. The key difference between this texture and the previous one is that as well as the environmental aspects, account has to be taken of competitors. As a consequence strategies have to incorporate ways of anticipating the actions of others and also anticipating their responses to such expectations, and so on. As well as tactics and strategy, the concept of *operations* is required. This brings together 'a planned series of tactical initiatives, calculated reasons by others, and counter-actions'. One key ramification of this additional facet is that some de-centralization is required since there is a 'premium on quality and speed of decision at various peripheral points'. Emery *and* Trist base this observation on the derivation of *operations* from the military context, where the lack of any – or any reliable – real-time communications necessitates decentralization of precisely this sort. Organizations have to decide on the extent to which they are prepared to decentralize, allowing operational decisions to be taken rather than waiting for authorization from command-and-control centres[8].

Organizations have to choose between strategies that range from the fiercely competitive to the openly co-operative; and will have to judge when to move across this range. Ecologically this can be likened to an environment with several groups of chimpanzees, in close proximity to baboons, leopards, and the like; in other words where there is co-location of competitors and predators. This is a context that will encourage the appearance of an oligopoly with non-zero sum competition, and so necessitates that actors foster alliances and out-think competitors. 'One has to know when not to fight to the death'.

The fourth type of causal texture is the *turbulent* field. Emery *and* Trist argued that in this context the dynamic processes themselves lead to the triggering of other dynamic processes, some of them emerging from the turbulent field itself: 'The *ground* is in motion'. This is akin to the phenomenon of 'soldiers marching in step over a bridge'; the Millennium Bridge over the Thames in London provides a recent example[9]. Furthermore they also argued that in such contexts there is an 'increasing reliance on research and development … [leading] to a situation in which a change gradient is continuously present'. In other words the only thing that remains unchanging is change itself.

In ecological terms turbulence is exemplified by disrupted eco-systems such as rain-forests in the 20th century, and even more so now in the 21st century. It also applies to the current global economic system; 'the dynamic properties arise not simply from the interaction of the component organizations, but also from the field itself. The *ground* is in motion'.

> "*These trends mean a gross increase in ... relevant uncertainty. The consequences which flow from ... actions lead off in ways that become increasingly unpredictable: they do not necessarily fall off with distance, but may at any point be amplified beyond all expectation; similarly, lines of action that are strongly pursued may find themselves attenuated by emergent field forces.*" [20]

In other words, large changes can have negligible effects, and small ones can have significant ones: What is now sometimes referred to as 'the butterfly effect'.

Writing in the 1960s Emery *and* Trist were clear that the response to turbulent fields cannot be simply a larger, more bureaucratic and over-arching hierarchy. On the contrary, their tentative solution called not for stronger, more powerful or extensive structures; but rather relied on 'the emergence of *values that have overriding significance for all members of the field*' (stress in original). They justified this by arguing that in conditions of persistent 'relevant uncertainty', attempting to select a course of action on the basis of its consequences is self-defeating and largely pointless; there is no way of having or developing any insight or understanding of future effects. They suggested that people will need to have recourse to 'rules ... to provide them with a guide'. These days we might use the term *heuristics* and contrast them with *algorithms*; the former implying more flexibility as opposed to the rigidity of the latter.

Emery *and* Trist did not, however, specify how such rules or values - 'such as the ten commandments' – will emerge and be sustained. They simply offered the imperative statement that strategic objectives can no longer be formulated in terms of location (which was deemed appropriate for clustered fields) or capabilities (appropriate for disturbed fields); but 'must now be formulated in terms of *institutionalization*': Which they defined as the state an organization reaches 'through the embodiment of organizational values which relate them to the wider society'.

There is a striking resonance between Emery *and* Trist's ideas, and the recent work of Zygmunt Bauman [14][10] on *Liquid Modernity*. This second phase modernity is a result of modernity's melting powers, initially applied to 'traditional' or 'pre-modern' social entities, now acting upon modernity itself: So that earlier reference points and concepts, presumed to be fixed and immutable, have been emptied of meaning and content. This phase of social development

> "*sets itself no objective and draws no finishing line; ... it assigns the quality of permanence solely to the state of transience. Time flows – it no longer marches on.*" Bauman [14]

The disruption initiated by modernity now acts upon modernity itself in a fashion that has no end point: Like the sorcerer's apprentice, social forces have been unleashed and continue to develop out of control – and there is no sorcerer who on his return will break the spell.

According to this analysis, Emery *and* Trist's turbulent field is no longer restricted to particular organizational contexts or sectors, but has now become the axial principle of society. Consequently there is little or no chance that organizations can break out of turbulence by seeking to embrace, or orient themselves towards more stable and solid values from society in general. The core values of society are themselves those of flux, innovation, change, transformation and competition.

So these are further obstacles to add to the more common problem of reconciling commercial interests with those of society as a whole. Society in the 21st century has been described by Ulrich Beck [17] as undergoing a process of *second modernity*. One result of this is that previously fixed points, rich with meaning and significance for social actors – and for organizational and institutional orientations – have lost their fixity and significance. Beck terms them *zombie categories* and *zombie institutions*, and examples include *family, class, and neighborhood*. Bauman develops this insight by noting that we have a 'redistribution and reallocation of modernity's *melting powers*'. Initially aimed at 'extant institutions' these melting powers have now moved on to undermine 'configurations, constellations, patterns of dependency and interactions'. 'The liquidizing powers have moved from the *system* to *society*, from *politics* to *life-policies*'. In such an environment concepts of citizenship, participation, government and governance are stripped of their meaning. Reinvention of government and governance is not a choice; it is ineluctable and essential; mandated by the context.

So the turbulent field of Emery *and* Trist is no longer an organizational or local context, it is now ubiquitous; and any hope that society and well-founded institutions could provide stability to counter this turbulence is unfounded. Society and social institutions are not the solution, on the contrary they are at the heart of the problem; and so this has severe repercussions for consideration of government and governance – with or without the e-prefix. Any prospect that e-government could simply be some 21st century *Cyber-Leninism* has to be ruled out of hand. The *business of government* has changed, and will continue to do so; there is no end-point to which it can be directed.

5. e-Rational government – player piano and cloud minders

In his earlier work on globalization, Bauman [12] made the point that the state has been dismantled. In particular its foundational tripod of military, economic and cultural sovereignty has been destroyed; all three legs have been broken, the economic most of all. To a large extent governments have responded to this catastrophic loss of sovereignty by re-inventing themselves as employment agencies, touting their workforce as skilled, flexible (i.e. easy to get rid of), and cheap. A quick tour of the websites of governments and governmental agencies bears this out. As such there is a basis for the argument that citizenship in the 21st century is dependent on being able to register as an adaptable and employable person, and to sustain that employability. Much of the language about e-government uses concepts such as *inclusion*, and *participation*; but a glance at the EU websites on E-Inclusion[11] (sic!) indicates that for all the talk of *inclusion*, E-Citizenship is for the most part targeted primarily, and perhaps even exclusively, at those able to prepare themselves to be employable – i.e. perpetually-flexible – knowledge workers for the globalized information society.

In his more recent writings, Bauman has looked at *waste* [14]; both in terms of consumerism and people. Thus he stresses that liquid modernity demands that people throw out yesterday's innovative consumer products in order to make way for today's. It is not only yesterday's newspapers that are used to wrap fish and chips; everything that is 'old news' is due for disposal in one way or another. Similarly, people themselves can be consigned to the scrap heap; the term *redundancy*, now often replaced by some management-speak euphemism, such as *flexibility, down-sizing, right-sizing, market-factoring*, testifies to this. A stark evocation of this was actually provided in Kurt Vonnegut's novel *Player Piano* [22] written in the 1950s, where the few 'fortunate' enough to employed in the corporate world – where they are at the beck-and-call of the truly fortunate, extremely powerful and wealthy elite – are separated from those for whom there is no longer any employment, other than occasional menial tasks. An episode of *Star Trek, 'The Cloud Minders'*, runs along similar lines (clearly derived from Lang's cinematic masterpiece *Metropolis*), with a depiction of life on the fictional planet of Ardana. Here the floating city of Stratos appears to offer the most cultured and cerebral civilization in existence – however far one may have boldly gone. But the apparent idyll has a less pleasant aspect; the Troglytes who dwell on the surface perform all the menial tasks and drudgery for those floating above them. Also the gas on the surface of the planet causes the Troglytes to suffer from retarded mental development, and leads to psychological disturbances such as anger and aggression. Thus the city dwellers can separate themselves from the surface dwellers, justifying this in terms of the Troglytes' coarse and vulgar behavior. As the ever-perceptive and unpretentious Mr Spock observes: 'This troubled planet is a place of the most violent contrasts. Those who receive the rewards are totally separated from those who shoulder the burdens. It is not a wise leadership.'

Developing the *Star Trek* motif we might say of the realities and potentials of e-government: *It's government Jim, but not as we know it.* Or we might restate Beer's third question: *What, given liquid modernity, should e-government actually be?* Those working on e-government, or government in a technological age, really ought to contend with the insights and admonitions of those such as Vonnegut and the Star Trek writers; but few actually do so. Far too much writing on the subject takes off from an un-examined rationalism that assumes that e-government is the desirable and desired end result of some rarefied, ultra-rational, well-planned process that will inevitably lead to *better* government; because it will incorporate and be partially based upon technology. In this sense e-government is irrational, rather than *e-rational*: It is certainly not 'wise leadership'.

Those suffering under such misapprehensions may well be doing so for the best of motives; surely this is the basis for a wise and enlightened society? But if this is what they really think then they need to consider the work of, for instance, Stephen Toulmin [23], who has argued that if we wish to take our lead from the Enlightenment, we should aim at a humanism derived from Montaigne as opposed to a rationalism derived from Descartes.

An overly rationalistic and mechanistic view of government, all too readily convertible to the 'e' form, is one based on certainty; a certainty beyond wisdom along the lines of Crosby's model. But as Voltaire noted; 'doubt is an uncomfortable position, but certainty is a ridiculous one'. If we are not careful our concepts of e-government will simply be prescriptions for automating a residual and out-moded form of government; an on-line employment agency, boasting the lowest costs, easiest redundancies and termination, lowest overheads, simplest extrication and disengagement: Perhaps with additional, value-added services for waste disposal and security. We need to pay regard to Beer's third question and to the nature of the liquid modern context; and then re-evaluate the nature of government, citizenship and public participation.

There is a danger that the current faddish concern with e-government will turn out to be mere persiflage; failing to engage with the real complexities of the liquid modern age, and by way of conclusion I can offer nothing more pithy and succinct than the words of that great liquid modernist – Bob Dylan [25]...

Then you better start swimmin'
Or you'll sink like a stone
For the times they are a-changin'

Endnotes

1. Information and Communications Technology – a more inclusive and expansive term than simply IT
2. 'the question which asks how to use the computer in the enterprise, is, in short, the wrong question. A better formulation is to ask how the enterprise should be run given that computers exist. The best version of all is the question asking, what, given computers, the enterprise now is ([26[27], stress in original)
3. In particular some commentators criticize the model because its final stage – maturity – can never be fully attained, if at all. For others this horizon-like objective is part of its appeal.
4. See for instance the website for CMM at the Software Engineering Institute http://www.sei.cmu.edu/cmm/
5. Pearce refers to Layne and Lee's article of 2001; the current volume includes Lee's more recent paper, and I have benefited from having had access to a draft version of their chapter – hence some references are made to this later version.
6. This version is taken from [28].
7. His later work was devoted to explication of 'the viable systems model'; which extended the organic metaphor, and which links directly to work on complexity and chaos.
8. Any idea that in the context of an information society it is now largely possible to overcome this dilemma with the introduction of reliable real-time communications and monitoring is almost certainly mistaken!
9. When this new footbridge over the Thames opened late in 2001, everyone flocked to walk across. In so doing they set up vibrations that caused the bridge to sway and so forced its closure and re-engineering.
10. These ideas are also developed in his other recent work such as Wasted Lives, Society Under Siege, and In Search of Politics.
11. See for instance www.einclusion-eu.org/

References

[1]   J.K.Galbraith, *The Unfinished Business of the Century*; lecture given at LSE June, 1999.
[2]   R. Nolan and C. Gibson, Managing the Four Stages of EDP Growth. *Harvard Business Review* **52** (1974), (1), 76-78.
[3]   F.W. McFarlan, J.L. McKenney and P. Pyburn, P, The information archipelago: maps and bridges. *Harvard Business Review* 60 (1982),109-119.
[4]   J. Piaget, *The Child's Conception of the World*, Rowman *and* Littlefield, London, 1975.
[5]   P. Crosby, *Quality is Free*, Signet, London, 1992.
[6]   W. Humphrey, *Managing the Software Process*, Addison Wesley, Reading MA, 1989.
[7]   L. Pearce, New Government, Digital Government: Managing the Transformation, *Future Challenges for E-government, Discussion paper 20*, 2004, available at http://www.agimo.gov.au/publications/2004/05/egovt_challenges
[8]   K. Layne and J. Lee, Developing Fully Functional E-Government: A 4 Stage Model. *Government Information Quarterly*, **18** (2001), 122-36.
[9]   M.J. Moon, The Evolution of E-Government among Municipalities. *Public Administration Review* **62** (2002),(4), 424-33.
[10] K. Lewin, *Field Theory in Social Science*, Harper and Row, New York, 1951.
[11] R. Heeks, ed, *Reinventing Government in the Information Age*, Routledge, London, 1999.
[12] Z. Bauman, *Globalization*, Polity, Cambridge, 1998.
[13] Z. Bauman, *In Search of Politics*, Polity, Cambridge, 1999.

[14] Z. Bauman, *Liquid Modernity*, Polity, Cambridge, 2000.

[15] Z. Bauman, *Society Under Seige*, Polity, Cambridge, 2002.

[16] Z. Bauman, *Wasted Lives*, Polity, Cambridge, 2004

[17] U. Beck, *Risk Society*, Sage, London, 1992

[18] A. Giddens, *The Consequences of* Modernity, Polity, Cambridge, 1991.

[19] R. Sennett, *The Corrosion of Character*, WW Norton, New York NY, 2000.

[20] F.E. Emery and E.L. Trist, 'The causal texture of organizational environments', *Human Relations,* 18, 21-32, 1965.

[21] W. C. Sellar and R.J.Yeatman, *1066 and all that*, Methuen, London, 1998.

[22] K. Vonnegut, *Player Piano*, Bantam, New York NY, 1952.

[23] S. Toulmin, *Cosmopolis*, Macmillan, London, 1990.

[24] Star Trek, Cloud Minders, available at http://www.startrek.com/startrek/view/series/TOS/episode/68808.html

[25] B. Dylan, *The Times They Are A-changing*, Columbia Records,1964.

[26] S. Beer, *The Heart of the Enterprise*, Wiley, New York NY, 1994

[27] S. BEER, *The Brain of the Firm: Managerial Cybernetics of Organization*, Allen Lane, London, 1981.

[28] E.M. Bernick, B. Bunch and P. Byrnes (2004) *The Illinois E-Government Factbook*, University of Illinois – available at http://cspl.uis.edu/NR/rdonlyres/8112B523-0973-4D95-B213-E05FFC9CFD90/0/ILEGovtFactBook.doc

Developments in e-Government
D. Griffin et al. (Eds.)
IOS Press, 2007

Myths, Rhetoric and Policy in the Information Age: The Case of Closed Circuit Television

C. William R. WEBSTER

Department of Management and Organization, University of Stirling

1. Introduction

> *"In Britain it is now virtually impossible to move through public (and increasingly private) space without being photographed and recorded...in almost every area to which the public have access we are under surveillance from CCTV"[1:3].*

This chapter explores the policy processes surrounding the rapid emergence of new Closed Circuit Television (CCTV) surveillance systems in public places across the UK. In particular, it highlights the importance to technological diffusion of the myths, discourse and political rhetoric embedded in the public policy-making process. The enhanced surveillance capabilities offered by new ICTs make CCTV systems inherently powerful. Yet despite this and despite limited knowledge about whether the cameras work or not, their introduction has been relatively uncontroversial. One explanation for the popularity of these systems is an unnerving faith in the technology, a general belief that the cameras 'work' and that they are a 'good thing'. This perception has been encouraged by political rhetoric and shaped by key institutional forces in the policy process. Ultimately, the case of CCTV shows, that discourse and myths about a technology are as important to its diffusion as the technological artifact itself. Consequently, creating myths, influencing discourse and shaping perceptions are core aspects of policy-making in the information age.

The underlying theme of this chapter is a desire to explain the rapid diffusion of CCTV systems in the UK. The chapter begins by setting out the UK CCTV policy environment and establishing the extent of CCTV diffusion. It then goes on to consider the dominant academic approaches that seek to explain technological diffusion, namely, diffusion theory and social shaping theory. Although both of these approaches offer useful and differing insights into the reasons for the diffusion of CCTV, neither give adequate importance to the role and significance of state institutions and the public policy-making process. To address this limitation, the chapter brings forward a theoretical framework of understanding based on different perspectives of the policy process. Four policy perspectives are brought forward, they are, the institutional, systems, individual choice and power perspectives. Each offers a different way of conceptualizing the policy process, and consequently a different way of explaining the development of policy and the diffusion of technology. Developing a framework around these different policy perspectives is important, because it highlights the importance of seeing the diffusion of CCTV as a policy phenomenon as well as a technological one, and because it shows that policy and diffusion processes are closely intertwined. Ultimately, it is argued, that where powerful technologies like CCTV are concerned, it is not possible to explain their introduction, and subsequent diffusion, without a full account of the role of the public policy-making process.

2. The diffusion of closed circuit television: A surveillance revolution

'CCTV' is a widely used generic term to denote the use of video surveillance cameras and systems in public places, where camera technology is linked in 'real-time' to a control room in which monitoring and surveillance takes place, usually by human operatives. A typical system consists of a number of cameras linked through a dedicated information and communication network, or 'closed circuit', to a centre containing the technical capability for displaying, storing, retrieving and reviewing the images captured by the cameras. The CCTV systems of interest here are those located in 'public places', where the public have free and unhindered access, and where the systems are financed and operated by public agencies. Theses systems are of particular interest because they are being introduced for the 'benefit of society' and because their use must be publicly accountable. Such systems are distinct from the myriad of privately operated systems found in shops, banks, petrol stations and other 'private' locations.

Since the mid 1990s the UK has undergone a surveillance revolution, a revolution that has swept the nation with limited resistance. The rapid deployment of CCTV in this period has been noted by a number of authors, and in particular, Bulos and Sarno [2], Fyfe and Bannister [3], Goodwin *et al* [4], Graham [5], Graham *et al* [6], Norris and Armstrong [1], Norris *et al* [7] and Webster [8, 9, 10, 11, 12]. CCTV systems have been introduced into a wide range of public places, including, town and city centers, schools, hospitals, libraries, car parks, and in residential and rural areas [8, 9, 10, 11, 12]. Norris *et al* argue that there are now over 4 million CCTV cameras in public places across the UK [13], and go so far as to state that Britain is the most heavily surveyed country in the world [1]. In general, these systems have been installed because there is a widespread belief that they can help 'prevent and detect crime, and offer the public reassurance against the rising fear of crime' [14:3]. Moreover, the apparent success of CCTV in reducing crime and the fear of crime, has led to remarkable levels of support for CCTV amongst politicians, public agencies, the general public and the media. The extent of this support has paved the way for an unprecedented speed of uptake; CCTV is without doubt a phenomenon of the late 20th and early 21st centuries.

2.1. The law and order context of the revolution

The law and order context for the introduction of CCTV in the 1990s was dominated by the rapid rise in crime levels and the subsequent political importance of the 'fight against crime' (FOC). Although the basic components of CCTV had been around since the 1970s, the political law and order climate in the 1970s and 1980s retarded its development as a mass surveillance tool. However, the rapid rise in crime levels in the late 1980s and early 1990s, the growth of 'proactive intelligence led policing', and the search for technological solutions to crime problems, combined to create a climate in which politicians were willing to consider new initiatives, which demonstrated to a concerned public, that they were tackling crime, disorder and the FOC.   Early evaluations of trial systems showed a massive fall in crime rates and a massive increase in detection rates, suggesting CCTV could represent a vital breakthrough in the fight against crime [15].

In 1993, the tragic death of Jamie Bulger dramatically launched CCTV into public consciousness.   Although CCTV had not saved the toddler, it was clear that the fuzzy images contributed to the identification of the killers and the process of abduction. Furthermore, the initial success of CCTV as a crime reduction tool was presented as enhancing citizens' rights to personal protection, safety and freedom of movement. The populist rhetoric, 'if you've got nothing to hide, you've got nothing to fear', dominated to such an extent that even civil liberties groups did not oppose CCTV, but merely argued for its statutory regulation [16, 17].   By the mid 1990's CCTV had become a central part of the government's law and order policy.

2.2. The emergence of a formal closed circuit television policy

In 1994, CCTV emerged as a formal policy when the then Home Secretary, Michael Howard, announced the availability of £2 million to fund new CCTV surveillance systems [18].   The Home Office's Crime Prevention Agency Unit and the Scottish Office's Crime Prevention Unit funded the provision of CCTV through annual 'CCTV Challenge Competitions'.   These 'competitions' contributed up to 50% of the capital costs of new schemes, but only where it could be demonstrated that there was a need for CCTV, where 'community partners' included the local authority and police force, and where the majority of capital costs were paid for by private businesses.   The competitions also required bids for funding to demonstrate how the future running costs would be met, that a code of practice concerning the use of cameras existed, and that appropriate evaluation procedures were in place.   Home and Scottish Office statistics (summarized in [11]) show that the challenge competitions distributed approximately £40 million to nearly 700 new schemes across the UK.   The significance of this funding is noted by Goodwin *et al*, 'the extent of Home Office backing for and reliance on CCTV is indicated by the fact that…78% of the Home Office budget for crime prevention was being used to fund schemes to put CCTV in public places' [4:3].

After the election of New Labour the CCTV Challenge Competition was replaced by the 'CCTV Initiative' [19].   This initiative formed part of the Crime Reduction Programme announced in 1998 and was managed jointly by the Home Office, The Department of Environment, Transport and the Regions and the National Assembly for Wales.   Under the CCTV Initiative, £153 million was made available for CCTV in England and Wales.   A separate 'Make Our Communities Safer' Challenge Competition operated in Scotland.   The initiative differed from the earlier challenge competitions in three key respects.   Firstly, funding was available on a rolling 'first come first served basis', secondly, the initiative funded up to 100% of capital costs, and thirdly, the initiative was explicit in targeting new system in residential and community areas [19].

The Home Office and Scottish Office backed up financial assistance with policy and operational guidance.   Both have published detailed policy guidance documents providing advice on the location, design and operation of CCTV [14, 20].   These documents were intended to give potential operators access to basic knowledge about the technology and a plan of how best to proceed in installing the most appropriate system. Also, the 'Application Prospectus' for the CCTV Initiative sets out the types of bid and system that were likely to be awarded funding [19], whilst the Home Office's Police Scientific Development Branch (PSDB) published a range of materials covering the technical issues of CCTV operation [21]. Interestingly, the proliferation of cameras has not been accompanied by specific legislation restricting and controlling their use [12]. Instead CCTV falls under generic legislation such as the Data Protection Act 1998, the Human Rights Act 1998 and the Crime and Disorder Act 1998. The CCTV policy arena is largely self-regulated through voluntary codes of best practice, including the Data Protection Commissioners 'CCTV Code of Practice' [22]. Although these codes are designed to safeguard civil liberties and govern the use of systems they are not legally enforceable and differ considerably in content [23].

2.3. Creating the myth: CCTV works

One notable feature of the CCTV revolution is the extent to which the introduction of CCTV appears to have widespread public support [6, 8, 9, 10]. Part of the explanation for this, is a general belief that the cameras work in preventing, detecting and deterring crime. CCTV has been promoted against this belief and marketed to the general public as a 'state-of-the-art' technological tool to combat crime. Norris and Armstrong argue, 'there is a common assumption: CCTV actually produces the effects claimed for it…an unquestioning belief in the power of the technology' [1:9]. Public perception surveys, such as those conducted for the Home Office [24, 25], by independent academics [26] and for prospective operators [4, 27], show clearly that the public believes CCTV to be a highly effective tool and that civil liberties are not a major concern. For example, the earliest independent public attitude survey, conducted for the Home Office by Honess and Charman [24], found that between 85% and 92% of respondents welcomed the installation of CCTV in their area. The view that CCTV actually reduces crime has been widely and successfully disseminated across society, and accordingly there is widespread support for CCTV amongst politicians, policy-makers and the general public. This has been central to the government's claim that the roll out of CCTV has been a legitimate policy.

The overwhelming support for CCTV is unquestionable and it is noticeable how little debate there has been across society, on the use and impacts of these sophisticated surveillance systems [9, 10]. The belief that CCTV 'works' and that society needs these systems, especially since the events of 9/11, have overridden any dissenting voices who question their effectiveness and impacts. Debates about CCTV have been led and shaped by political rhetoric which has wholeheartedly supported the technology. Consequently, public discourse has focused on the success and benefits of the cameras and not on the more complex issues associated with extending the states surveillance capabilities. Absent from any debate is any discussion about the appropriate use of CCTV, the implications of using such technology in the community, the impact on civil liberties of the surveyed, and the changing relations between citizens and the state arising from the use of CCTV [28]. Questions about whether CCTV actually reduces crime, whether displacement occurs, whether CCTV is a threat to civil liberties, and whether there should be specific legislation governing the use of CCTV are often not even asked.

2.4. Some concerns about the revolution

The absence of public debate about the implications of using CCTV technology so widely in society is intriguing, since it is in the public who become subject to increasing levels of surveillance. Academics on the other hand, typically raise two main concerns about the proliferation of CCTV systems. Firstly, that their use signals the emergence of a 'surveillance society' where citizens are the subject of greater levels of surveillance and control, and secondly, that CCTV systems are not as effective in reducing crime as initially thought.

The emergence of a surveillance society [29, 30, 31, 32, 33] based on the enhanced capabilities offered by new information and communication technologies points to CCTV being essentially about power and control [34, 35], and in particular, the extent of power and control over citizens exercised by agencies of the state. In this approach CCTV represents both a threat to civil liberties and a tool of social control, perhaps even similar to 'big brother' in Orwell's classic distopian novel 'Nineteen Eighty-Four' [36]. This is because CCTV is part of the 'architecture of conformity', which ensures that individual citizens assume that they are constantly being surveyed and therefore internalize power and conform to socially acceptable behavior [37]. In this way the proliferation of CCTV is likened to a modern day electronic version of Bentham's panoptic prison [1, 3, 32, 38, 39]. At the crux of this argument is that surveillance is a form of power, and this form of power has been dramatically enhanced by the development of sophisticated CCTV technology.

Alongside sociological critiques of the panoptic potential of CCTV criminologists have attempted to discover the 'effectiveness' of CCTV and its ability to deliver reductions in crime and disorder. Although political discourse is based on the belief that the cameras work, there is actually very little reliable evidence to support this proposition. Moreover, whilst CCTV has proliferated there have been very few systematic evaluations measuring its effectiveness [40, 41]. Here 'effectiveness' is usually gauged in terms of measurable reductions in levels of crime and the FOC, and improvements in detection and 'clear-up rates' For Short and Ditton, the early evaluations, which claimed such huge successes for CCTV, were actually inconclusive and 'fairly contradictory regarding the effectiveness of CCTV as a crime prevention method' [42:11].

The most recent research into the effectiveness of CCTV [43, 40, 44] suggests that it is most effective in reducing property crime and deterring offences like vehicle crime and burglary, perhaps on the basis that potential offenders perceive the risk of apprehension to outweigh the benefits. However, in crimes involving alcohol, such as public disorder, where 'rationality' is often lost, then the deterrent effect of CCTV is weakened. In an attempt to ascertain a clear picture of the crime reduction effects of CCTV, the Home Office commissioned a review of all CCTV evaluations considered to be methodologically sound [44]. The initial findings of this study are that CCTV has a very small, but statistically significant, reduction in crime of about 3%. More specifically, the review also suggests that CCTV appears to have no effect on violent crimes, a significant effect on vehicle crime and is most effective when used in car parks. They also suggest that CCTV is most beneficial when used in conjunction with other crime reduction measures and when its use is tailored to its local setting. So, despite the proliferation of CCTV systems in the last decade, research to date suggests that CCTV is not always as successful at reducing crime as it is claimed to be and the extent to which CCTV can act as an effective crime prevention measure is very much dependent upon the context in which it is applied.

Concerns over the emergence of a surveillance society and about the cameras' ability to reduce crime raise questions about the extent of rationality in the policy process, about power relationships in the CCTV policy arena, and about the dominant discourse through which policy agendas are constructed and resolved. Why then is CCTV so popular and what is the logic of installing so many systems, if there is limited evidence that it works and if its use has largely unknown consequences for human behavior and citizen-state relations? The focus on whether CCTV works or whether it leads to a surveillance society detracts from a detailed understanding of the reasons how and why CCTV has diffused so widely across society. CCTV needs to be understood in a much wider context – if surveillance is a form of power, then CCTV surveillance systems are uniquely powerful new technologies that can contribute to social order and control. Moreover, because they are inherently associated with power and control, they are inherently 'political' technologies, and as such explaining the reasons for their introduction is vitally important.

3. Technological perspectives of diffusion: The diffusion and social shaping approaches

The two dominant approaches to understanding technological diffusion and development are 'diffusion theory' and 'social shaping theory'. Both approaches offer useful insights into the reasons for technological uptake.

Diffusion Theory focuses on a technology that diffuses [45, 46, 47]. According to diffusion theory the process of diffusion involves an innovation that diffuses a population of individuals or organizations that decide when to adopt the technology, and a flow of ideas about the technology which influences adopter's views about the technology. This approach predicts that the characteristics of certain technologies make them inherently useful and that once a 'superior' technology has been invented, technological uptake is inevitable. Not only is uptake inevitable but it also follows a predictable 'natural trajectory' where the pattern of diffusion follows an s-shaped diffusion curve, with the rate of diffusion speeding up and slowing down during the lifecycle of the technology in question [48]. Diffusion theory argues that the diffusion of a new technology is determined by its technological capabilities and impacts, and consequently its usefulness. This suggests that to understand the diffusion of a new technology we have to identify and recognize its impacts and how it is useful. In the case of CCTV, the technology is recognized as being very effective in reducing and deterring crime, the FOC, anti-social and undesirable behavior. The ability of CCTV to deliver these impacts therefore explains its diffusion.

Social Shaping Theory [49, 50, 51, 52, 53, 54] is at odds with the deterministic nature of diffusion theory and offers a different set of explanatory factors for technological diffusion. At its simplest social shaping theorists point to technologies as social creations, that is, they are constructed by humans to meet certain purposes. As such they do not contain inherent capabilities that result in inevitable impacts and use, but instead follow a trajectory that is shaped and influenced by choices made by actors at the various stages of technological design and implementation [53]. In this perspective human agency and not technological capability determines whether or not diffusion occurs. Therefore to better understand why a new technology diffuses the social dynamic in which the technological artifact is embedded has to be accounted for. This includes identifying the different forces and actors that influence and shape the artifact [49].

Social shaping theories point to the creation and diffusion of technologies as a 'means to an end', in that their design and use is intended to meet purposes defined by society. In the case of CCTV, the technological components of systems are relatively old technologies, but their configuration into CCTV surveillance systems is fairly new. This suggests that it was not the inherent capabilities of the technology that secured its diffusion but a realization that if certain technologies were configured in a certain way then they could be used to address certain problems in society, primarily problems associated with crime and disorder. In this account the diffusion of CCTV is explained as a tool created to assist in the 'fight against crime'. To meet this 'purpose' CCTV is embedded in the social structures and arrangements of those agencies that are responsible for addressing these issues. If we take this perspective then it is possible to see that CCTV is shaped by social forces and is closely integrated with those agencies using the technology.

Diffusion and social shaping approaches represent the two dominant academic accounts of technological diffusion and both offer important insights to comprehending the diffusion of CCTV. Both perspectives seek to explain technological diffusion, but in doing so, they both offer deterministic accounts of the diffusion process. For diffusion theorists the characteristics of a technology determine diffusion, whereas for social shapers, society and social forces determine which technologies diffuse. A combined position would point to CCTV being a 'socio-techno phenomena', which should be understood as a technology that has influences on society, but which is also influenced and shaped by society. In other words, to understand why and how a technology diffuses it is important to recognize the complex inter-relations between technology and society.

The main drawback of both these approaches is that they downplay the influence of the political and policy-making processes. In diffusion theory the inevitability of diffusion renders the policy process irrelevant, whereas from a social shaping perspective, policy influences are just one of many influences shaping diffusion. The problem here is that certain technologies, because of the way they are used and the way in which they impact on society, are inherently political and powerful, and therefore their diffusion can only really be understood through their political and policy settings. This suggests that for certain technologies, like CCTV, not all shaping forces are equal and that certain forces in society are more influential than others, namely, the state, its institutions and processes. For this reason technologies like CCTV are not just socially shaped but are more specifically 'politically' and 'policy' shaped. By downplaying or ignoring the significance of policy-making in the diffusion process both the perspectives negate the most important influences in society. The point here is that certain technologies can only be legitimately operated by the state and therefore we can only fully understand their diffusion by taking account of the processes that have led to their diffusion, these processes ultimately being about policy and politics.

4. Explaining diffusion: Perspectives of the policy process

To consider the importance of policy and political processes for the diffusion of a new technology like CCTV it is important to have a clear understanding of the 'workings' of the policy process, and how these processes shape and influence technological diffusion. Although 'the policy process' is usually understood to mean the methods, strategies, techniques and decisions taken by actors to develop a policy there are actually many ways of conceptualizing the process. This is achieved here by constructing a theoretical framework that identifies established ways of thinking about the policy process. This framework locates existing theory within a series of overarching 'perspectives', each of which identifies a core idea or concept and its development over time [11]. The four key policy perspectives brought forward here are, the institutional, systems, individual choice and power perspectives. Constructing a framework of understanding in this way allows for different features of the policy process to emerge as significant in the shaping and making of new policy, and consequently different ways of 'seeing' and explaining the diffusion of CCTV. This is significant as it shows that CCTV must be understood as a policy and a technological phenomenon, and that the processes that explain policy development and technological diffusion are closely intertwined.

4.1. Institutional perspectives of the policy process

Traditional institutional perspectives of the policy process explain the development of policy in terms of formal legal arrangements and activities [55, 56]. At its crudest the focus is on the existence of formal rules, procedures and organizations involved in the forming and execution of policy. The key to this approach lies with formal constitutional power and those organizations that have the legitimate legal authority to make and execute decisions in a particular policy area. New institutional perspectives are more sophisticated because they go beyond the formal institutions of government by explaining policy in terms of the norms, values and beliefs embedded in institutional activity [57, 58]. Here the profound and subtle influence of institutions is because they comprise of the belief systems and conventions of behavior, as well as being the formal apparatus of government. In this perspective institutions matter because they shape the policy process by influencing and constraining the choices of actors, and because institutions embody past decisions which in turn structure the formation and implementation of new policies. Institutions therefore become durable because they adapt and change slowly over time as new policies and activities are integrated into existing structures, procedures and norms [59, 60, 61]. In this sense new policies and the policy process are 'framed' by their institutional settings.

In this perspective, state institutions, however they are defined, are the dominant influence shaping policy and diffusion [62, 63]. This suggests that one way of comprehending the CCTV revolution is to explore the institutional setting of the technology. In the case of CCTV, Parliament has enacted legislation that applies to CCTV, central government departments have formed national CCTV policy and established funding programmes, while local authorities and police forces have been the main agencies responsible for implementing CCTV. At its simplest, the strength of this approach is that it identifies the various organizations within the architecture of complexity that is the policy process. The fundamental difference between this approach and social shaping accounts is that institutions are placed at the heart of the diffusion process and their involvement determines why one technology diffuses and another does not. 'Institutions matter' [64] because they can be identified as responsible for forming CCTV policy and for implementing CCTV as a service.

4.2. Systems perspectives of the policy process

Systems perspectives of the policy process explain the development of new policies by placing the relevant actors, institutions and activities in their broader 'political' setting or system. In this perspective new policies and new technologies do not exist in isolation but are part of a larger system where the policy process converts political demands into policy outcomes [65]. Within 'the system' the policy process is typically conceptualized as either consisting of a series of functional stages through which policy emerges, or through the existence and influence of complex networks of actors involved in each stage of the policy cycle.

The policy cycles approach breaks down the policy process into a series of sequential stages from policy conception, to policy formation, implementation and evaluation [66, 67, 68, 69]. This is useful as it allows the researcher to track policy through the different stages of the policy cycle, thereby identifying the different actors and organizations involved in the policy process. Policy network approaches challenge the idea that the policy derives from formal institutions and processes, arguing instead that policy emerges as a result of informal, as well as formal, patterns of association [70, 71, 72, 73]. In this account, stable networks of actors with shared interests are able to transcend formal institutions to promote policies that are in the network's interests [74]. This approach is useful because it tells the researcher to look beyond the formal institutions involved in a policy and to consider which groups in the broader system have a shared interest in securing a particular policy.

This perspective suggests that one way of comprehending the diffusion of CCTV is to see it as a rational policy response to demands in the broader political system. If this is the case, then the introduction of CCTV is a direct response to environmental demands for a safer better society, with less crime, less disorder, less undesirable behavior and less FOC. Here the policy process is simply converting these demands into policy outcomes, which in this instance happens to be the provision of CCTV. This perspective suggests that within the political system the policy process is a rational process traveling through a series of 'stages' to ensure that policy implementation addresses policy concerns. This suggests that the best way of comprehending diffusion is to see it as a rational process, which through the policy cycle, ensures that identified goals and objectives are delivered.

4.3. Individual choice perspectives of the policy process

At its simplest, individual choice perspectives of the policy process explain the development of new policies as arising from the myriad of choices made by rational self-interested actors. Here, the assumption is that individuals are rational agents who continuously seek to maximize their own personal utility [75]. Therefore, to understand the policy process we must first seek to understand the individual choices and motivations of the different actors involved in the process. The idea that individuals are self-interested agents also extends to organizational settings and suggests that organizations pursue polices and strategies to enhance their standing and ensure their continued existence. For example, public choice [76, 77, 78, 79] and bureau-shaping [80] approaches are based on a set of assumptions which explain the behavior of individuals and firms. These approaches suggest that one notable feature of the modern state is the way in which large state bureaucracies have grown by serving themselves rather than the public interest.

This perspective suggests that one way of comprehending the diffusion of CCTV is to identify those groups and actors in the policy process that have their self-interest served by the provision of CCTV. A number of groups and individuals can be seen to benefit from the provision of CCTV, with each having a different rationale for supporting and promoting its diffusion. Arguably police forces are the main beneficiaries of the introduction of CCTV, mainly because it is typically used as a tool to aid general policing. In practice, these systems are used to alert the police to incidents as they occur, thereby allowing the police to manage their resources more efficiently. They are used to generate information to be used as evidence in prosecutions, thereby allowing the police to meet their goal of catching criminals, and they are used to monitor and control well known offenders, thereby allowing the police to maintain order and control. Unsurprisingly then, the police have been vocal advocates of CCTV, even though in most cases they are not solely responsible for its installation or operation. Within local authorities political representatives have benefited from the introduction of CCTV because they have been able to demonstrate that they were doing something to address local crime concerns. Their self-interest was served because they believed supporting CCTV would make them more electable.

4.4. Power perspectives of the policy process

The core idea underpinning power perspectives of the policy process is that the development of policy reflects the underlying power structures in society. In this perspective those who exercise and structure power in society shape and control the policy process and consequently determine diffusion. Power is not just the legitimate authority to act or a reflection of individual or organizational choice, but it is reflected in the overarching societal structures that pervade and determine policy activity. In this perspective diffusion and policy either consciously or subconsciously reflect wider societal forces, either through the process of governing, the shaping of discourse, the delivery of service, or the existence of powerful relationships between elites and those who govern.

In the structural account technological diffusion is not an autonomous phenomenon, but inextricably linked to processes structured into the existing political, social and economic system [81, 82]. Consequently, the introduction of a new policy is driven and shaped by powerful forces that ensure the interests of the current – capitalist - system are protected and enhanced. This account is critical of the other perspectives for giving undue weight to the autonomy of institutions, networks and individual choices, while neglecting to appreciate the significance of wider more powerful forces. If this account is accurate then the diffusion of technology reflects existing socio-economic structures in society and simply reinforces the established hegemony and social order. This suggests there is an alternative explanation for the diffusion of CCTV, namely that its diffusion is intended to protect the capitalist system and maintain social order. Significantly, CCTV can be perceived to be a direct 'tool of social control' because it is used by the police to help maintain order and control, and thereby protect the capitalist system. In this respect CCTV is a tool to help the police perform their core function whilst at the same time discouraging behavior that is deemed undesirable by society. In this way CCTV ensures that the current hegemony is maintained. If this account is accurate then it *does not* matter if CCTV works as a crime reduction tool, because its success and purpose lie in its ability to control and shape behavior and in maintaining general order.

Ideas or discourse approaches of the power perspective stress the importance of language, knowledge and communication in the policy process as key explanatory factors in the development of a new policy. In this account, ideas about policy problems and potential solutions have a 'life of their own' and gain influence independently of the policy process, yet are significant in determining policy activity [83, 84, 85]. This is because the process of policy-making is permeated by discourse, discussion, debate and dispute about different ideas and beliefs, and ultimately it is these beliefs that shape policy activity. Therefore, it is the process by which ideas become important and beliefs become established that explains policy activity [86]. This approach suggests that one way of comprehending the diffusion of CCTV is to recognize the significance of how the technology is perceived and presented, and how it is packaged [87]. Discourse about CCTV has been instrumental in establishing a general belief about what the technology can achieve. CCTV has been presented as a very effective tool for reducing crime and disorder. The positive perception of the technology has been promoted and reinforced by political rhetoric. Politicians have espoused the virtues of the technology presenting it as the latest high-tech tool in the 'fight against crime', whilst the media by broadcasting programmes like 'Police Camera Action' have portrayed CCTV as a highly effective tool. These discourses have created a situation where there is overwhelming support for CCTV and a policy environment receptive to its diffusion. The dominant discourse is that 'CCTV works' and this view has filtered down into the general consciousness of the population. The extent to which this view dominates is highlighted by the lack of debate about CCTV and the rare occurrence of negative views about CCTV. This is partly due to the overwhelming positive message about CCTV and partly because those with opposing views have been marginalized in the policy process.

The key insight offered by this approach is that CCTV diffusion can be explained by society's overwhelming belief in the technology, despite there being limited evidence that it actually works. This suggests that powerful forces in society have shaped the policy process by influencing how the technology is perceived and understood. The point here is that it *does not* really matter if the technology *does not* work, because the general belief is that it does, and so long as this belief is maintained and reinforced then the policy will continue to be popular. If this is the case, then ideas and the beliefs they generate become the defining feature of diffusion.

5. Reconsidering the CCTV revolution: A policy-diffusion process

Each of the policy perspectives discussed in this chapter offer a unique and valid way of comprehending the complexity of contemporary policy processes. Each is based on the significance of a core idea or concept and therefore offers different insights into the diffusion of CCTV. Institutional perspectives tell us that the diffusion of CCTV is shaped and regulated by existing institutions in society. Systems perspectives offer insights into how CCTV diffusion has been processed and how networks of interested actors influence diffusion. Individual choice perspectives explain the diffusion of CCTV as meeting the interests of certain individuals and organizations in the process.

And finally, power perspectives tell us that the diffusion of CCTV can be explained because it supports the existing societal system and because the belief structure surrounding the technology influences how it is perceived and consequently how it is diffused. Each of these perspectives point to different factors as being influential in shaping diffusion. Taken together they offer a comprehensive account of the policy-diffusion process.

Constructing a theoretical framework in this way is significant because it highlights that the diffusion of CCTV is not just shaped by policy, but by different aspects of the policy process. This represents a significant advance over traditional social shaping accounts which downplay the importance of policy shaping in the shaping process. In the case of CCTV, these perspectives have shown that the processes of governance are central to shaping and determining the development of policy and the diffusion of the technology. Here it is evident that the process has been shaped by powerful interests, be they institutions, networks, choices, structures or ideas, to encourage and manipulate the diffusion of CCTV. The significance of the state, public agencies and of policy to the diffusion of CCTV suggests that the diffusion process should be seen as a policy-diffusion process.

It is evident that the institutions of governance have played a crucial role in developing a policy environment malleable to the development of a technology with powerful surveillance capabilities. For example, the role played by the Home Office in making funds available for new systems, demonstrating its effectiveness in offering policy advice and guidance, and providing political rhetoric has been critical. This suggests information age policy processes are managed by key institutions of the state, possessing the ability to control and disperse information and knowledge. It is therefore apparent that for information age technologies, like CCTV, who determines and controls information about the technology invariably controls its diffusion and use. This suggests that the policy processes surrounding new technologies might be different to other more traditional policy areas. This is because a new technology is 'new' and its impacts and effects are not known, and consequently perceptions of, and beliefs about the technology become all-important. In this respect the diffusion of ideas and beliefs about information age technologies are paramount to their successful diffusion and use.

6. Conclusion

This chapter has sought to account for and explain the rapid diffusion of CCTV surveillance systems in public places across the UK. It is argued that where the diffusion of an inherently political technology is being considered a policy focus must be taken. Theories of technological diffusion, such as diffusion theory and social shaping theory underestimate the significance of the institutions of governance, and therefore are unable to offer a valid account of the diffusion process. By taking a policy perspective the different policy forces influencing the diffusion of CCTV can be considered and it can be demonstrated that its diffusion is closely allied to the policy process. Therefore, we should interpret its introduction and uptake as a 'policy-diffusion process'. The recognition that the processes of policy development and technological diffusion are inherently intertwined signifies an important development in our understanding of how policy emerges in the information age.

Although each of the policy perspectives brought forward here have descriptive and explanatory power there are certain features of the process that appear to be especially significant for information age technologies. Firstly, is the significance of the state and the institutions of governance in creating a policy environment malleable to the implementation of a new policy. Secondly, and underpinning the first point, is the extent to which ideas and discourse about the technology are crucial to securing its diffusion. In the case of CCTV, it is apparent that the institutions of governance have shaped the policy process by manipulating knowledge about the new technology. This has created a situation where CCTV is believed to be very effective and consequently there is considerable pressure to install new systems. This suggests that to understand the diffusion of a new information age technology like CCTV its belief structure and institutional setting must be accounted for and explained.

References

[1]   C. Norris and G. Armstrong, *The Maximum Surveillance Society: The Rise of CCTV*, Berg, Oxford, 1999.

[2]   M. Bulos and C. Sarno, *Closed Circuit Television and Local Authority Initiatives: The First Survey*, School of Land Management and Urban Policy, London, South Bank University, 1994.

[3]   N.R. Fyfe and J. Bannister, City watching: closed circuit television in public spaces, *Area*, **28**, 1 (1996), 37-46.

[4]   M. Goodwin, C. Johnstone and K. Williams, *New Spaces of Law Enforcement: Closed Circuit Television, Public Behaviour and the Policing of Public Space*, Paper presented to the Association of American Geographers Annual Conference, Boston, MA, March (1998)

[5]   S. Graham, CCTV - big brother or friendly eye in the sky?, *Town and Country Planning*, **65**, 2 (1996), 57-60.

[6]   S. Graham, J. Brooks and D. Heery, Towns on television: closed circuit television surveillance in British towns and cities, *Local Government Studies*, **22**, 3 (1996), 1-27.

[7]   C. Norris, J. Moran and G. Armstrong, (Eds*)*, *Surveillance, Closed Circuit Television and Social Control*, Ashgate, Aldershot, 1998.

[8]   C. W. R. Webster, Closed circuit television and governance: the eve of a surveillance age, *Information Infrastructure and Policy*, **5**, 4 (1996), 253-63.

[9]   C. W. R. Webster, Closed circuit television and information age policy processes, In B.N. Hague and B.D. Loader, (Eds), *Digital Democracy: Discourse and Decision Making in the Information Age*, Routledge, London, 1999.

[10] C.W.R. Webster, Relegitimating the democratic polity: the closed circuit television revolution in the UK, In I. Horrocks, J. Hoff and P. Tops, (Eds), *Democratic Governance and New Technology: Technologically Mediated Innovations in Political Practice in Western Europe*, Routledge, London, 1999.

[11] C.W.R Webster, The diffusion, regulation and governance of closed-circuit television in the UK, *Surveillance and Society*, **2**, 2/3 (2004), 230-50.

[12] C.W.R Webster, Evolving standards and regulation: exploring the development and provision of closed circuit television in the UK, *Knowledge Technology and Policy*, **17**, 2 (2004), 82-103.

[13] C. Norris, M. McCahill and D. Wood, Editorial. The growth of CCTV: A global perspective on the international diffusion of video surveillance in public accessible space, *Surveillance and Society*, **2**, 2/3 (2004), 110-35.

[14] Home Office, *Closed Circuit Television: Looking Out For You*, Home Office, London, 1994.

[15] Audit Commission, *Helping With Enquires: Tackling Crime Effectively*, HMSO, London,1993.

[16] Liberty (National Council for Civil Liberties*)*, *Who's Watching You? Video Surveillance in Public Places*, Briefing No.16, October, Liberty, London ,1989.

[17] Scottish Council for Civil Liberties (SCCL), *Civil Liberties and Video Cameras*, Briefing No.2, SCCL, Glasgow, 1994.

[18] Home Office, *Preventing Crime into the Next Century*, Michael Howard, News Release, 22 November, Home Office, London, 1995.

[19] Home Office, *Crime Reduction Programme: CCTV Initiative, Application Prospectus: Crime Reduction - CCTV*, March, Home Office, London, 2000.

[20] Scottish Office, *CCTV in Scotland: A Framework for Action*, J4499 4/96, HMSO, Scotland, 1996.

[21] Police Scientific Development Branch (PSDB), *CCTV Operational Requirements Manual*, PSDB, Home Office, London, 1994.

[22] Data Protection Commissioner, *CCTV Code of Practice*, The Office of the Data Protection Commissioner, London, 2004.

[23] M. Bulos and C. Sarno, *Codes of Practice and Public Closed Circuit Television Systems*, Local Government Information Unit, London, 1996.

[24] T. Honess and E. Charman, *Closed Circuit Television in Public Places: Its Acceptability and Perceived Effectiveness*, Home Office Police Research Group, Crime Prevention Unit Series, Paper 35, Home Office, London, 1992.

[25] B. Brown, *CCTV in Town Centres: Three Case Studies, Crime Detention and Prevention Series*, Paper No.68, Home Office Police Department, Home Office, London, 1995.

[26] J. Ditton, Public support for town centre CCTV schemes: Myth or reality?, In C. Norris, J. Moran and G. Armstrong, (Eds), *Surveillance, Closed Circuit Television and Social Control*, Ashgate, Aldershot, 1998.

[27] D. Ross and J. Hood, Closed Circuit Television (CCTV) - The Easterhouse Case Study, In L. Montanheiro, B. Haigh, D. Morris and N. Hrovatin, (Eds), *Public and Private Sector Partnerships: Fostering Enterprise*, Sheffield Hallam University Press, Sheffield, 1998.

[28] C.W.R. Webster, Changing relationships between citizens and the state: the case of closed circuit television surveillance cameras, In I.Th.M. Snellen and W.B.H.J. van de Donk, *Public Administration in an Information Age, A Handbook*, Informatization Developments and the Public Sector Series, No.6., IOS Press, Amsterdam, 1998.

[29] D. Flaherty, The emergence of surveillance societies in the western world: toward the year 2000, *Government Information Quarterly*, **5**, 4 (1988), 377-87.

[30] S. Davies, *Big Brother: Britain's Web of Surveillance and the New Technological Order*, Pan Books, London, 1996.

[31] O.H. Gandy, The surveillance society: information technology and bureaucratic social control, *The Journal of Communication*, **39**, 3 (1989), 61-76.

[32] D. Lyon, *The Electronic Eye: The Rise of the Surveillance Society*, Polity Press, Cambridge, 1994.

[33] G. Marx, The surveillance society: the threat of 1984-style techniques, *The Futurist*, June, 21-6, 1985.

[34] J.R. Beniger, *The Control Revolution*, Harvard University Press, Cambridge, MA, 1986.

[35] S. Cohen, *Visions of Social Control*, Polity Press, Cambridge, 1985.

[36] G. Orwell, Nineteen Eighty-Four, Martinr, Secker and Warburg, London, 1949.

[37] M. Foucault, *Discipline and Punish: The Birth of the Prison*, Vintage, New York, 1977.

[38] A. Reeve, The panopticisation of shopping: CCTV and leisure consumption, In, C. Norris, J. Moran and G. Armstrong, (Eds), *Surveillance, Closed Circuit Television and Social Control*, Ashgate, Aldershot, 1988.

[39] M. Crang, Watching the city: video surveillance and resistance, *Environment and Planning*, **28**, 12 (1996), 2099-104.

[40] J. Ditton, E. Short, S. Phillips, C. Norris and G. Armstrong, *The Effects of Closed Circuit Television on Recorded Crime Rates and Public Concern About Crime in Glasgow*, The Scottish Office Central Research Unit, Scottish Office, Edinburgh, 1999.

[41] N. Tilley, Whys and wherefores in evaluating the effectiveness of CCTV, *International Journal of Risk, Security and Crime Prevention*, **2**, 3 (1997), 175-85.

[42] E. Short, E. and Ditton, J. (1995) Does CCTV affect crime? CCTV Today, 2(2), 10-2.

[43] R. Armitage, *To CCTV or not to CCTV? A Review of Current Research into the Effectiveness of CCTV Systems in Reducing Crime*, NACRO Community Safety Practice Briefing, NACRO, London, 2002.

[44] B.C. Welsh and D.P. Farrington, *Crime Prevention effects of Closed Circuit Television: A Systematic Review*, Home Office, London, 2003.

[45] S. Davies, *The Diffusion of Process Innovations*, Cambridge University Press, Cambridge, 1979.

[46] E.M. Rogers, *Diffusion of Innovations*, Free Press, New York, 1962.

[47] E.M. Rogers, *Diffusion of Innovations*, Third ed. Free Press, New York, 1983.

[48] R.R. Nelson and S.G. Winter, *An Evolutionary Theory of Economic Change*, Harvard University Press, Massachusetts, 1982.

[49] W.E. Bijker, *Of Bicycles, Bakelites and Bulbs: Towards a Theory of Socio-Technical Change*, MIT Press, Cambridge, MA, 1995.

[50] W.E. Bijker, T.P. Hughes and T. Pinch, (Eds), *The Social Constructions of Technology Systems*, MIT Press, Cambridge, MA, 1987.

[51] W.E. Bijker and J. Law, (Eds), *Shaping Technology/Building Society: Studies in Socio-technical Change*, MIT Press, Cambridge, MA, 1992.

[52] D. Edge, The social shaping of technology, In N. Heap, R. Thomas, G. Einon, R. Mason and H. Mackay, (Eds), *Information Technology and Society*, Sage, London, 1994.

[53] D. MacKenzie, *Knowing Machines: Essays on Technical Change*, MIT Press, London, 1996.

[54] D. MacKenzie and J. Wajcman, (Eds), *The Social Shaping of Technology: How the Refrigerator Got its Hum*, Open University Press, Milton Keynes, 1985.

[55] P. Self, *Administrative Theories and Politics: An Introduction to the Structure and Process of Modern Government*, Allen and Unwin, London, 1972.

[56] D. Judge, *The Parliamentary State*, Sage, London, 1993.

[57] V. Lowndes, Varieties of new institutionalism: a critical appraisal, *Public Administration*, **74** (1996), 181-97.

[58] P.A. Hall and R.C.R. Taylor, Political science and the three new institutionalisms, *Political Studies*, **XLIV** (1996), 936-57.

[59] J.G. March and J.P. Olsen, The new institutionalism: organizational factors in political life, American *Political Science Review*, **78** (1984), 734-49.

[60] J.G. March and J.P. Olsen, *Rediscovering Institutions: The Organizational Basis of Politics*, Free Press, New York, 1989.

[61] D. North, Institutions, *Institutional Change and Economic Performance*, Cambridge University Press, Cambridge, 1990.

[62] E. Ostrum, *Governing the Commons: The Evolution of Institutions for Collective Action*, Cambridge University Press, Cambridge, 1990.

[63] T. Skocpol, Bringing the state back in: stages of analysis in current research, In: P.B. Evans, D. Reuschemeyer and T. Skocpol, (Eds), *Bringing the State Back In*, Cambridge University Press, Cambridge, 1985.

[64] R.K. Weaver and B.A. Rockman, *Do Institutions Matter?*, Brookings Institution, Washington D.C., 1993.

[65] D. Easton, *A Systems Analysis of Political Life*, John Wiley, New York, 1965.

[66] B.W. Hogwood, *Trends in British Public Policy*, Open University Press, Buckingham, 1992.

[67] B. Hogwood and L. Gunn, *Policy Analysis for the Real World*, Oxford University Press, Oxford, 1984.

[68] H.D. Lasswell, *The Decision Process: Seven Categories of Functional Analysis*, University of Maryland, College Park, 1956.

[69] W. Parsons, *Public Policy: An Introduction to the Theory and Practice of Policy Analysis*, Edward Elgar, Aldershot, 1995.

[70] D. Marsh and R. Rhodes, (Eds), *Policy Networks in British Government*, Clarendon, Oxford, 1992.

[71] R.A.W. Rhodes, Power dependence, policy communities and intergovernmental networks, *Public Administration Bulletin*, **49** (1985), 4-31.

[72] R.A.W. Rhodes, *Beyond Westminster and Whitehall*, Unwin Hyman, London, 1988.

[73] M. Smith, *Pressure Power and Policy*, Harvester Wheatsheaf, Hemel Hempstead, 1993.

[74] P. Sabatier and H.C. Jenkins-Smith, (Eds), *Policy Change and Learning*, Westview, Boulder CO, 1993.

[75] H. Ward, Rational choice theory, In D. Marsh and G. Stoker, (Eds), *Theory and Methods in Political Science*, Macmillan, Basingstoke, 1995.

[76] A. Downs, *An Economic Theory of Democracy*, Harper Collins, New York, 1957.

[77] A. Downs, *Inside Bureaucracy*, Little Brown, Boston, 1967.

[78] W. Niskanen, *Bureaucracy and Representative Government*, Aidine, Chicago, 1971.

[79] G. Tullock, *The Politics of Bureaucracy*, Washington D.C., Affairs Press, 1965.

[80] P. Dunleavy, *Democracy, Bureaucracy and Public Choice*, Harvester Wheatsheaf, Brighton, 1991.

[81] C. Ham and M. Hill, *The Policy Process in the Modern Capitalist State*, Harvester Wheatsheaf, Brighton, 1993.

[82] M. Marinetto, *Studies of the Policy Process: A Case Analysis*, Prentice Hall, Hemel Hempstead, 1999.

[83] M. Edelman, *The Symbolic Use of Politics*, Illinois University Press, Urbana, 1964.

[84] M. Edelman, *Political Language Words That Succeed and Policies That Fail*. Academic Press, New York, 1977.

[85] G. Majone, *Evidence, Argument and Persuasion in the Policy Process*, Yale University Press, New Haven, 1989.

[86] T. Kaplan, Reading policy narratives: beginnings middles and ends, In F. Fischer and J. Forrester, (Eds), *The Argumentative Turn in Policy Analysis*, UCL Press, London, 1993.

[87] B. Franklin, *Packaging Politics: Political Communications in Britain's Media Democracy*, Edward Arnold, London, 1994.

Part 2

Transforming Service Delivery

Developments in e-Government
D. Griffin et al. (Eds.)
IOS Press, 2007

Search for Stage Theory in
e-Government Development

Jungwoo LEE
Yonsei University, Korea

1. Introduction

The literature reports that experiences with e-government initiatives are unmanageable [1, 2, 3] and the development of on-line services is only in an infant stage despite the recent surge of investment in e-government initiatives. Recent studies revealed that e-government initiatives present a number of challenges[1]. While there are many emerging programs and initiatives on e-government throughout the world, it seems that the actual development and implementation may take another decade or so, as infrastructures must be built, policy issues resolved, and interoperability established. It took more than a century for accompanying social changes and relevant organizational structures to be stabilized after the initiating invention of energy-matter transfer technology during the Industrial Revolution. Assuming the information revolution would take a similar path, the technological changes of today may take longer to stabilize with the appropriate social and organizational changes, than might be anticipated by technology optimists today.

E-government is a technological initiative but without appropriate social and organizational changes, it would not be fully functional. E-government is not a one-step process or implemented as a single project. It is evolutionary, involving multiple stages or phases of development. This chapter explores models developed and contested about stages of e-government by comparing and contrasting previous work. These stages outline the structural transformations of governments as they progress toward electronically-enabled government including how Internet-based government models become amalgamated with traditional public administration, implying fundamental changes in government functions.

2. Stage models of e-government

'Stage model' is a general metaphor based on organic growth, applicable to and used in many areas. In management literature, product life cycle seems to be a specified version of the stages of growth model. In e-government literature, other growth models begin to appear during the same period as the Layne and Lee model from which this chapter has developed [4]. In this section, these models are reviewed and compared against the Layne and Lee model. With this analytical comparison, Layne and Lee model will be refined and presented with revised details.

Hiller and Belanger identified four stages of electronic government: (1) **information**, (2) **two way communication**, (3) **transaction, and (4) integration** [5]. Here the 'information' phase is similar to the 'cataloguing' phase of this model and their third phase of 'transaction' is similar to the second stage of the model under discussion. The fourth stage of 'integration' would encompass both the third and fourth stages of the stages of growth model. However, Hiller and Belanger add a fifth stage to their proposed model called 'participation', in which online registration and voting along with posting comments online are provided. These services would not be separated from other transaction based services in the fully functional e-government model discussed here.

United Nations Online Network in Public Administration (UNPAN) presents five stages of e-government as (1) **emerging web presence**, (2) **enhanced web presence**, (3) **interactive web presence**, (4) **transactional web presence**, and (5) **fully integrated web presence** [6]. The 'emerging' stage includes a formal but limited web presence through a few independent government websites with static organizational or political information. The 'enhanced presence' refers to the expansion of websites with content of dynamic and specialized information and links to other official pages including government publications, legislation newsletters. The 'interactive presence' includes a sophisticated level of formal interactions between citizens and service providers such as e-mail and post comments areas. The capacity to search specialized databases and download forms and applications or submit them is also available. The 'transactional presence' offers secure transactions like obtaining visas, passports, birth and death records, licenses, and permits. The 'fully integrated or seamless presence' refers to the stage where lines of demarcation are removed in cyberspace.

In the handbook developed to help e-government efforts in developing countries, World Bank also presented a stage model consisting of three phases: **publish, interact**, and **transact** [7]. This model is a simpler version than that offered by UNPAN and has been created for less developed e-government initiatives in developing countries.

Gartner Research also developed and present four phases of e-government [8]: (1) **presence stage** in which the primary goal is to post information such as the agency mission, addresses, opening hours and possibly some official documents of relevance to the public, (2) **interaction stage** in which basic search capabilities are provided, downloadable forms are hosted, links with other relevant sites and e-mail addresses of offices or officials, (3) **transaction** stage where the focus is to build self-service applications for the public to access online, but also to use e-government complementary to other channels, and (4) **transformation stage** where the delivery of government services is redefined by offering a single transparent point of access to citizens.

These five models of e-government are compared in table 1 below. As can be seen from the comparison, these models are very similar in terms of their classification of stages. Three of these models designate 'integration' as the last stage of e-government and simple web presence as the beginning stage while Gartner named the last stage as transformation and World Bank closes their model with transaction as the final stage. 'Integration' is defined in most cases with broad terms such as "one stop shopping for services" or the removal of "line of demarcation" in government services. What is less clear is how this integration would happen across different levels of government except the Layne and Lee model in which vertical integration is proposed before horizontal integration considering current organizational structures of government. It seems clear that vertical integration would precede horizontal integration as the gap between functional areas is much larger than the one between different levels of government.

It should be noted here that integration or transformation is not the end. These models present stages of growth without specific reference to life cycle metaphor in which the saturation point leads to decline and demise. The point is that the growth models compared here are expected to evolve as technology progresses, and new stages may be added leading on to another curve towards evolution. It is more of a process towards more advanced stages of e-government which may not be visible now.

Also, these models are somewhat similar because these are frameworks developed from a technological perspective in which Internet and connectivity related technologies are assumed to be the basis of growth or development of e-government. These models were built on a 'data or information' centric view where information posting is a starting point leading towards the integration of information and databases and the mature stages. The service-centric view which is becoming more popular in other areas of public administration is not considered at all, although 'transformation' stage implies a little bit of service-orientated changes in e-government.

Reflecting these shortcomings identified from a comparative analysis of different stage models, Layne and Lee model is revised and presented here in Figure 1. The major revisions are: (1) further stages are implied in the figure, (2) an arrow is added to represent the changing role of technology which suggests further stages to be identified, and (3) a standing arrow is included, representing recent trends of ubiquitous and service-centric transformation of public administration.

Discussions and anecdotes in this chapter are based on a United States (US) model with its multi-layers of governments among federal, state and local agencies. Discussion begins from state government because it is in the middle of this structure, but emphases are added to the connections and linkages to federal and local level. These underlying theories of growth and related cases are also applicable to governments outside the US because it is a general theory for administrative structure striving towards seamless coordination using information technology.

Table 1. Summary of Stages in e-Government

Layne & Lee	Hiller & Belanger	UN/ASPA	World Bank	Gartner
Cataloguing	Information	Emerging web presence	Publish	Presence
		Enhanced web presence		
Transaction	Two-way communication	Interactive web presence	Interact	Interaction
	Transaction	Transactional web presence	Transact	Transaction
Vertical Integration	Integration	Fully Integrated Seamless web presence		Transformation
Horizontal Integration				

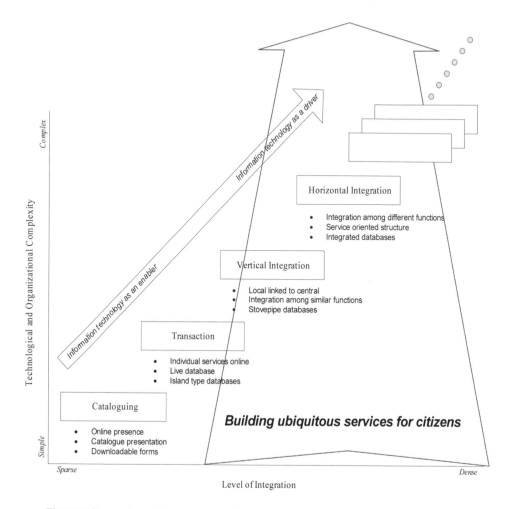

Figure 1. Stages of growth in e-government

The next section explains each of the four stages in detail. Each stage is described from three different but related aspects: (1) definition, (2) types of functionality involved, and (3) technological and organizational challenges. Key issues involved in e-government initiatives based on this model are presented afterwards, followed by a conclusion.

2.1. Stage I: Cataloguing

At the beginning, governments create a 'state website' mostly due to a great deal of pressure from the media, technology-literate employees, demanding citizens, and other stakeholders to get on the "net". At this stage, governments do not have much Internet expertise, and they prefer to minimize the risk by doing a small project. Mostly non-transactional information is presented on the website. There are several reasons why any government would want to move to this 'electronic cataloguing' stage, but mostly, many citizens and businesses have access to the web. As they are able to access information on services from the private sector on the web, they expect the same access to information on government services[2].

Accordingly, more and more citizens will look for government information on the web instead of flipping through the yellow pages and going through touch-tone voice processing systems, and they will be disappointed if they cannot find information about their government. From the government side, as much government staff time is consumed in answering basic questions about government services and procedures, the web presence will increase citizens' convenience and reduce the workload on frontline employees. More importantly, such information is available 24 hours a day seven days a week. With government web presence, citizens use this information to learn the specifics of policies and procedures, find out where to go for government services and post-service support. Citizens could still use existing service processes such as a phone call, personally standing in line, etc, but to a lesser extent. The idea of government services being available to all people - universal access - requires that some off-line capabilities continue to exist for citizens not on-line [1].

2.1.1. Types of functionality

For "citizen as customer", this stage offers the least amount of functionality for the customer. As this stage progresses, the quantity of posted information increases, and governments will begin to see the need for an index or portal site that provides links to other sites. Usually at first the index site is organized on the basis of functions or departments as opposed to service access points. Consequently, if the citizen is unsure for which department he or she is searching, a search for the necessary agency will be required before being able to obtain the information about the process. The typical government department home pages at this stage have a description of the department, notices, news, employees and their tasks, and some links to other pages. It establishes a departmental "presence" as opposed to providing service access points to the customer.

The next step of progression is re-organization of information by services, by different actions or by different events. An example at the federal level in US is the Firstgov.gov site (http://www.firstgov.gov) and at a state level, an example would be a portal project by the State of Nevada (http://silversource.state.nv.us). This offers a 'clearinghouse' providing a central site that presents a comprehensive list of forms to be downloaded by the user, organized by services. No transactions take place electronically, but the form can be downloaded and filled out before arriving at a state facility [10].

2.1.2. Challenges

Although the technology at this stage is relatively simple, there are several challenges on managing these sites. Different departments require different amounts of on-line presence and demand that resources be allocated to them. Resource allocation in a political organization is always a problematic issue. Another important issue is the maintenance of the information. Along with procedural and policy changes, web pages need to be updated as data presented on government websites may be temporal. Date and time stamping may be essential at this stage, along with issues of consistency in format and user-interface from one agency to the next.

Privacy will also surface as an issue at this stage, as it is possible for the government to track on-line activities like frequently accessed products, the length of time spent on each page, and the length of time spent searching. Whilst this tracking information can be used to improve the website and its offerings, the temptation to sell this information to external parties may also exist. Thus, several policy issues must be decided by the agency in establishing the site[3].

Due to the scope of the website under this stage, organizational challenges are limited. The first challenge is assigning responsibility for the overall coordination and planning of services on the state website as well as having each agency assign responsibility for the maintenance of a website. One central agency may assume responsibility for the coordination and planning efforts, such as a department of information technology, or an ad hoc group may be convened for this purpose. In Nevada, the Governor's Executive Order decreeing a website presence also created the Silver Source Steering Committee which was assigned the task of developing a plan for "utilizing electronic technology to improve the delivery of governmental services and to expand the opportunity for economic development [10:1]." The Governor's Chief of Staff chairs the committee, and the State Department of Information Technology coordinates the e-government program and establishes the electronic infrastructure, and develops policies and procedures related to e-government initiatives [9].

Individual agency's assignment of website development and maintenance is more problematic. Outsourcing to a private vendor or state information technology agency is one solution. Outsourcing at this level may present problems in terms of the allocation of maintenance responsibility once the site is developed. In many cases, at this stage, an internal champion emerges among internal employees who have non-technical job classifications. Many department directors in the state of Nevada indicated that an internal person was assigned the maintenance responsibility for the site. Often these people's jobs are related to information technology, e.g., the staff person working for the Commission on Educational Technology handles the Department of Education website[4]. Over a period of time, this part-time responsibility may create problems of inappropriate use of resources as the person may come to spend more time on site development and maintenance. Having an internal person whose skill at developing websites is secondary to other skills may limit the ability of the site to meet customer needs, especially in terms of updating material on the site.

The second problem is assigning responsibility for responding to e-mails. Websites often include an e-mail address for questions from site users. Often these questions may be wide ranging and beyond the ability of the web master. Some procedure must be established to address how these e-mails will be handled and how quickly. The Nevada Attorney General noted that this was a problem until a procedure was established for prompt routing of inquiries[4].

Another problem arises in terms of management. Administrators can have websites in this stage developed with little effort on their part. However, policies developed at this stage may have long-term effects on future on-line services. Privacy and confidentiality statements, the handling of e-mail requests and questions from users, multi-language requirements, and web accessibility features are examples of those managerial issues that must be addressed early on by administrators, not webmasters.

2.2. Stage II: Transaction

As government websites evolve, officials as well as citizens come to realize the value of the Internet as another service channel for citizens and want to exploit it. Citizens demand to fulfill government requirements on-line instead of having to go to a specific location after completing the required paperwork and standing in a line to submit the paperwork to someone behind a counter. Electronic transactions offer greater efficiencies for both the customer and the agency than simply "cataloguing information." In addition, such capabilities provide the opportunity for a broader democratic process by holding interactive conversations with constituents who are reluctant or unable to attend public hearings.

There is no question that fully functional e-government will make service delivery more efficient and increase savings both for government and for citizens. This second stage is the beginning of e-government as a revolutionary change in the way people interact with their government. Transaction-based e-government empowers citizens to deal with their governments on-line at anytime, saving hours of paperwork, the inconvenience of traveling to a government office and time spent waiting in line. Registering vehicles or filing state taxes on-line is only the beginnings of such transaction-based services [1].

2.2.1. Types of functionality

At this stage, citizens can be served on-line by 'e-government'. Whilst the cataloguing stage helps citizens' in fact-finding processes, this transaction stage e-government presents government on the other side of the Internet as an active respondent. It is the beginning of two-way communication. Citizens transact with government on-line by filling out forms and government responds by providing confirmations, receipts, etc. More importantly, citizens move from a passive to active role by not only conducting transactions on-line, but also participating through on-line forums and communities that allow citizens to talk directly to government officials or take an active role in public hearings or complete citizen surveys on any number of issues [1].

The First Annual Report of the United States Working Group on Electronic Commerce stated "that fewer than 10 million people were using the Internet in 1995, and that more than 140 million people world wide were using the Internet in 1998" [10:1]. This report also projects that more than one billion people worldwide will be using the Internet in the first decade of this century [10].

With this increasing number of citizens connected by and through the Internet, governments at all levels have no other choice but to take e-government seriously both externally and internally as a service channel. Internally, the following services could be administered with the help of the Internet: personnel services, benefits administration, payroll and timekeeping functions, supply ordering, travel services, conference arrangements, and on-line training, at the least. Response time will be reduced on the agency's part. Consequently, forms can be completed interactively on-line with intelligent agents – if designed well – helping on-line.

Most likely at this stage, a government portal will be conceptualized and the citizen-customer enters through the portal that guides the service needs of the customer as opposed to requiring the citizens to traverse numerous sites to find the information needed. This one stop on-line help center will be available through a portal, similar to that developed by the federal government through its FirstGov.gov (http://www.firstgov.gov).

2.2.2. Challenges

From this stage, e-government begins to deal with active and live databases. As online transactions could be recorded and histories could be maintained, stand alone databases will be built separately for different services and functions. The technical issue of transaction fulfillment is eminently critical and database design problems would rise to the surface. A lot of questions need to be answered for e-government to succeed at this stage. Would the customers be connected to the production server? What would link the transactional database to the main one? Will such databases be updated daily, hourly or weekly? Should fulfillment be outsourced? How will the responsiveness and quality of the on-line system compare to the off-line system?

The issue of database integration comes onto the scene. Governments must answer questions like "should the web interface be integrated with existing functional systems?" If not, what kind of legacy system information is necessary to support the on-line activities? When and how are on-line and off-line systems going to be integrated? How expensive will the integration be? How long will it take? As much of the information collected by governments may be politically sensitive, installation of appropriate security mechanisms may be an important technical consideration. At the same time, many other policy issues need to be resolved, such as authentication and confidentiality.

Organizational challenges are much greater in this stage. Existing electronic databases must be redesigned and reprogrammed to handle such changes, requiring internal committees to assess user demands and user interfaces of the current systems. Issues of confidentiality and security must be addressed by the organization as a whole. This requires study of existing legislation to determine how public or private the database is for the agency. Although many public applications were no doubt upgraded during the year 2000 crisis, many legacy systems still remain. It may not be possible to provide an interface for the citizen-customer without considerable investments at this stage.

2.3. Stage III: Vertical integration

As the number of information islands increases exponentially within the government sector during the second stage, the focus moves towards fundamental transformation of government services. Making government electronic is not simply a matter of digitalizing current processes and transferring these processes to the web. Information islands naturally reveal redundancies and inconsistencies as digitalization progresses, and people begin to see the value of integration. Customers may begin to complain that what appear to be similar services are handled by different agencies and they must run from one agency to another agency in order to perform a transaction that could be performed by one agency point. On a physical plane, as opposed to an electronic one, many local governments have established one stop style service point in which customers can have their building plans reviewed by all the required agencies in one location. This one location stops the complaints of citizens and businesses that must run from the planning departments to the building department to public works department, etc. On an electronic plane, similar complaints arise when one electronic form for completing a local business license has to be completed and another electronic form with the same information is also completed for a state business license. To achieve more efficient and effective service processes, what should and will be happening in the government is reviewing the processes themselves and possibly the level of government of that process. Just as electronic business is redefining private business and society in terms of processes and product, e-government initiatives should be accompanied by re-conceptualization of the government services itself. In the long run, the full benefit of e-government will be realized only when these services talk to each other in terms of processes and their databases are integrated, at least at the conceptual level. Also, this requires organizational and social changes to be complete.

After on-line transaction services become prevalent and mature, citizens' expectations will increase. Most transaction stage systems are localized and fragmented. A natural progression will be the integration of scattered systems at different levels (vertical) and different functions (horizontal) of government services. Agencies often maintain separate databases that are not connected to other governmental agencies at the same level or with similar agencies at the local or federal level. For example, a state business license database is often separated from a local business license database. Further, that state license system is probably not connected to the state vendor database.

It is expected that vertical integration precedes the horizontal integration. Integration within function will precede integration across function. Integration within function but across different levels of government will precede the integration across different functions at the same agency or at the same level of government structure. Many state agencies already interact more closely with their federal and local counterparts than other agencies at the same level of government. Integration across different functions will require much more intense level of service reengineering including organizational and structural changes.

At stage three where the focus is on vertical integration, federal, state and local counterparts are expected to connect or, at least, communicate to each other at the system level and at the database level. While some jurisdictions' websites currently provide links to other governmental agencies at different levels, vertical integration goes beyond this simple interconnection. If a citizen conducts a transaction with a state agency, the transaction information will be propagated to local and federal counterparts in a vertically integrated system. These various systems at agencies of different levels are connected and talk to each other so that results of transactions [1] from one system can be transmitted and logged at other systems. Physically, this may be integrated as a central database or a connected web of partitioned databases communicating with each other.

2.3.1. Types of functionality

According to a survey by the Momentum Research Group, citizens prefer to access information through their local portal because they are most familiar with the services offered by the local government [11]. However, not all community services are directly offered by the local authority. The citizen-user still should be able to access the service at the state or federal level from the same entry in the local portal, because the local systems are connected to upper level systems, directly or indirectly in the vertically integrated e-government.

One application of vertical integration could be the business license application process. In many states, a business must obtain both a local and a state business license. Under the scenario of stage three, a citizen would file for a business license at the local government transaction server, and the local server by accessing the state database would check state and federal databases, retrieve corresponding records, propagate changes, and calculate the total license fee. The reverse could also occur. The state could check local licensees to make sure locally licensed companies also had a state license. One example of this "vertical" integration can be found on the Washington State website, in which a federal employer identification number (FEIN) can be requested through the same process as a state business license (http://www.wa.gov/dol/bpd/startbus.htm#Aret). Since citizens often do not know where to start looking for a particular service, vertical integration would resolve much of that search.

Perhaps at this stage, more important than citizen-customer interactions are what might be considered "business to business" or "government to government" transactions. It is expected at this stage that many national level databases will emerge as a centralized database. These databases may not be located physically at one place or be physically one, but by talking to each other, the connection will become more and more transparent to citizens. For example, truckers who become licensed in a state would also become a part of a national database of truckers at the federal level, and this vertical integration would ensure a trucker who lost a license in one state would not be licensed easily in other states.

The target of vertical integration is to seamlessly integrate the state's system with federal and local systems for cross referencing and checking, and it has an effect of linking states to other states. Automated fingerprinting systems and felony arrests are examples of such databases. However, most of these systems are currently law enforcement accessible only, and are not available to the citizen.

2.3.2. Challenges

Beginning in stage three, communication and integration oriented technologies will become more important. As stage three targets to integrate agencies in state governments with their local and federal counterparts, technically, a web of remote connections is a prerequisite and stovepipe type databases will emerge at the national level. For remote connections and virtual transactions, several technological issues emerge: signal authentication, format compatibility, exposure level of internal legacy system to outside, quality of information, etc. The scope of vertical integration will also become a critical issue. Does the entire vertical 'value chain' need to be integrated and how fast? As systems in federal, state and local governments become vertically integrated, boundaries at different levels of government become less distinguishable as the lines between them blur and functions move back and forth between what was once federal and the state from a citizen's perspective. As these databases are integrated, compatibility of database models as well as database language and format will also become challenges to be overcome.

Accordingly, the role played by government employees will change. In the old traditional off-line government, many government employees are responsible for processing localized governmental transactions. Once systems are integrated and automated, most transactions are automated, and government employees now become more an overseer of the process than a simple task-oriented assembly-line worker. The scope of activities performed by each employee will extend beyond functional department boundaries.

Vertical integration is not a new concept. State universities and local school districts have worked together for years by having high school students take university level classes. A number of localities have automated fingerprint identification systems, which send data to the state fingerprint system based on certain criteria. Various types of criminal data are sent from the local government to a state repository that collects and summarizes the data and submits reports to the FBI.

Stage three does require various levels of government to allow some flexibility in the development of their databases that meet not only their needs. Agencies have to become less proprietary about their information. The 1988 Family Support Act required each state to develop a statewide automated data system that had the capability to control, account for, and monitor all processes for determining paternity and collecting children support [12]. By the 1997 deadline that represented a two-year extension of the original 1995 deadline, six states still did not have a system. All states complained that they could not transfer another state's system because the existing State systems they tried to transfer "did not meet the diverse needs of individual states and counties" [13:14]. Similar types of issues may greatly constrain vertical integration.

Even though stage three may provide improved efficiencies, privacy and confidentiality will also emerge onto the surface as more critical than ever. According to a report from the Intergovernmental Advisory Board, the "foremost" issue when developing such systems is "ensuring the privacy of the citizen requesting the service" [1:6]. A conceptually centralized database might be viewed with alarm as opposed to only increasing efficiencies. The Intergovernmental Advisory Board report suggests that privacy notices should be posted for the use of any information collected. One suggestion is: "An on-line form should have a clear and specific purpose and be directed to specifically authorized entities. Governments must consider the appropriate balance between the privacy of personal information and the right of individuals to access public records" [1:6].

2.4. Stage IV: Horizontal integration

The full potential of information technology, from the citizen's perspective, can only be achieved by horizontally integrating government services across different functions (or "silos"). Typically, citizens requiring assistance from governments need more than one functional service. For example, those requiring housing also need governmental assistance for education, food, medical attention, etc. To overcome this problem, some local authorities provide one stop service centers where, for example, the homeless can come and obtain information about jobs, clear any outstanding warrants, obtain medical assistance, etc. Governments continually fight the battle of getting services to the people who need them the most. The horizontal integration of stage four will considerably improve those efforts.

In the horizontally integrated e-government, databases across different functional areas will communicate with each other and ideally share information, so that information obtained by one agency will propagate throughout all government functions. Currently, two "Access America" sites, one for senior citizens (http://www.seniors.gov) and one for students (http://www.students.gov/index.html) locates multiple services available to these two groups at all levels and at all functions of government, although databases are not currently shared [1].

Citizens could conduct business across a wide variety of government services. As an example, when a citizen applies for a driver's license after moving to another state, the basic residence record could be propagated to different functional service branches of government such as the Social Security Administration and the local election department so that the citizen does not have to fill out a personal record form for each governmental agency. Horizontal integration refers to system integration across different functions in that a transaction in a department at one local agency can lead to automatic checks against data in other functional areas in other agencies at other levels of government.

2.4.1. Types of functionality

There is no current and complete example of e-government at stage four. However, there is movement in this direction as witnessed by the Access America sites mentioned above. Particularly interesting are the efforts of the US Department of Education, Veterans Affairs (VA) and the Department of Labor on the students.gov site (http://www.students.gov/index.html). This site will allow students to access financial aid transactions and register locally through campuses or on-line, using a digital signature and an assigned account code (ePIN) [1].

The horizontal integration of government services across different functions of government will be driven by visions of efficiency and effectiveness in using information technology, but pulled by citizens' demands on an 'inside-out' transformation of government functions to more service oriented ones. The stage four e-government offers the best hope for improved efficiencies through administrative reform because of both its vertical and horizontal integration. Such integration will better allow "one stop shopping" for the citizen. Each organization may have to give up power that they already have to move on to this stage.

2.4.2. Challenges

Technically, integration of heterogeneous databases and resolving conflicting system requirements across different functions and agencies are major stumbling blocks for any government to reach this stage. Data and process requirements in health systems may not be comparable to the requirements in transportation systems. Also, as in vertical integration, quality problems of information bases that each information island may have will be amplified as more databases are integrated. Even information for the same entity may be registered using different names and different metadata which may not be a visible problem in an isolated island but when integration becomes immediate, this will present a huge technical challenge.

It is not only a technical challenge but also a management challenge. Horizontal integration requires a change in the mindset of government agency directors. When thinking in terms of information needs or transactions, many directors perceive their department as most important and disregard, unintentionally, other agencies. This 'silo' structure may have worked well in settings in which functions and services are specialized for economies of scale and specialization. However, with the support of the Internet, the government processes defined by specialization may not be efficient, effective or citizen-friendly. The concept of governance and management of government staff may be subject to re-evaluation from the perspective of e-government. Functional specialization may not be suitable as a governing structure in e-government.

Robert Denhardt echoes this argument in discussing the future of public administration:

> *"In our view, these emerging trends will turn public management both inside out and upside down. Public management will be turned inside out as the largely internal focus of management in the past is replaced by an external focus, specifically a focus on citizens and citizenship. Public management will be turned upside-down as the traditional top-down orientation of the field is replaced, not necessarily by a bottom up approach, but by a system of shared leadership"* [14:285].

In many respects, horizontal integration will provide much benefit to citizens, businesses and society. It would be much easier for citizens to deal with government with more transparency, ease of access, and convenience. Ubiquitous computing described in many science fiction movies assumes complete horizontal integration in which transactions are propagated throughout the system where individuals are easily identified and serviced. However, this type of integration will also present the biggest challenges. It is important that the horizontal integration should not be directed as the beginning of Foucault's panoptical society in which the electronic data collected is used to glean information about the individual [15], or as the 'Big Brother' described by George Orwell in 1984. Individuals need to remain in control.

3. Discussion

Four developmental stages of e-government are presented here based on observations of current practices. Technological and organizational challenges have been discussed for each stage. Currently, e-government initiatives at federal and state level are rapidly evolving, but many challenges are still to be met. Among these challenges, following three issues are fundamental ones governments have to take into consideration if they want to evolve into efficient and effective e-government in support of citizens' demand: (1) universal access, (2) privacy and confidentiality; and (3) citizen focus in government management.

3.1. Universal access

The omnipresent nature of the Internet may be misleading in that any service can be accessed by anybody from anywhere anytime. Although the Internet population has grown exponentially recently, there is a portion of the people who may not be able to access e-government for various reasons [1]. The concept of e-government is very persuasive in increasing efficiency and effectiveness of government; however the service should be available to one hundred percent of citizens for e-government initiatives to be successful. Universal access is still a mirage. Similar services must be maintained outside the web, such as physical service facilities and automated telephone response systems. Governments may want to provide Internet access through public terminals as a part of their universal access efforts.

3.2. Privacy and confidentiality

Another critical obstacle in realizing fully functional e-government is the citizens' concern on privacy of their life and confidentiality of the personal data they are providing as part of obtaining government services. The word-of-mouth guarantee by government will not suffice unless accompanied by technical solutions, transparency of procedures and possibly independent auditing. Privacy and confidentiality has to be highly valued in establishing and maintaining websites. Data should be collected in a secure fashion, privacy notices on websites will be mandatory and independent auditing groups composed of citizens' representatives will also help in soliciting participation of citizens [1].

This issue is directly connected to the possible panoptical phenomenon. As technology itself is neutral, integration itself cannot be the goal. It should be taken as a step or a work-in-progress on which the ubiquitous uses of information technology in government services are built. Integration is not only a technical issue, but a societal and organization issue as well. Polices and procedures both external to the integrated governmental structures as *well* as internally within the organizations making up those structures must be developed to guard against using customer data in a manner unintended by the customer.

3.3. Citizen focus in government management

Practical realization of e-government requires re-conceptualization of government. As e-government becomes more prevalent, the public sector organizational structure will change accordingly and it will happen in two aspects: internally and externally. The focus of change will be on, internally, the system efficiency, and externally, the citizen as customer. Internally, the power conflicts over departmental boundaries and control of services will surface as integration progresses. Externally, government processes will be organized for citizens' convenience instead of the convenience of the government [16].

In other words, the integration should not be driven by efficiency and effectiveness alone. Focusing on efficiency and effectiveness will lead the e-government initiatives into a "Big Brother" government if it loses citizens' focus. It may be necessary to allow citizens to have the option of deciding whether or not they want information to go to another agency beyond the one with which they are dealing. A check box might be a good enough solution. Similar to the current concept which asks a user if they do not want advertising from other companies to "check the box," a citizen would have the same option in allowing other governmental agencies to access the information entered. As systems becoming more integrated, citizens' review boards may be established in order to review and observe how system integration occurs and its impacts.

4. Conclusion

It is suggested here that e-government is an evolutionary phenomenon going through stages of growth and therefore initiatives on e-government should take these stages into consideration. A four stage model of e-government is posited as cataloguing, transaction, vertical integration, and horizontal integration.

However, it should be noted here that this growth model does not assume saturation or maturity as suggested in other growth models. In other words the government services including e-government may grow beyond the four stages presented here as technology develops. Nor do governments necessarily "begin" their e-government efforts at the first stage. They could actually begin at a later stage, using other governments' experiences to guide them.

The stages of growth in e-government initiatives presented here offer a path for governments to follow. Challenges as well as the type of functionalities suggested here provide a reference framework for government to follow both in terms of the organization and technical aspects. It is important that this growth model is not meant to present the final destination of e-government. Rather, it should be considered as a work-in-progress as technology and society advances progresses. This stage model emphasizes citizens as customers of government services, and from this perspective, the transformation of government to an electronically based one necessitates major rethinking about how governments provide services, and how these services are organized. Universal access, privacy and confidentiality, and citizen focus management are suggested as critical issues involved in future e-government initiatives. However, just like the stage model presented here as an evolving tip of an iceberg, these issues may also be a tip of an iceberg which represents challenges to be met in achieving fully functional e-government in the near future.

Endnotes

1. Statement of David McClure
2. Statement of Clas Fornell, Director of the National Quality Research Center at the University of Michigan and founder of the American Customer Satisfaction Index (ACSI) as quoted in "E-Government Satisfaction Stalls," *PA Times*, 28 (April 2005), 4, 2.
3. Darrell West [3] notes that "many" government websites do not have a privacy policy; U. S. General Services Administration [1] also sees privacy as an issue.
4. Unpublished interviews conducted with department directors and elected officials in the State of Nevada by the authors during March-April, 2000.

References

[1] U.S. General Services Administration, Intergovernmental Advisory Board, *Integrated Service Delivery: Governments Using Technology to Serve the Citizen*. Online. Office of Intergovernmental Solutions. Available: http://policyworks.gov/intergov/reportsframe.html (August 1999).
[2] G.N.L. Stowers, Becoming Cyberactive: State and Local Governments on the World Wide Web, *Government Information Quarterly*, **17**, 1 (2000), 113-114.
[3] D.M. West, *Assessing E-Government: The Internet, Democracy, and Service Delivery by State and Federal Government*. Online. The Genesis Institute. Available: http://www.insidepolitics.org/egovtreport00.html (September 18, 2000).
[4] K. Layne and J. Lee, Developing Fully Functional E-Government, *Government Information Quarterly*, Summer 2001.
[5] J. Hiller and F. Belanger, *Privacy Strategies for Electronic Government*, (January 2001), available on-line at http://www.businessofgovernment.org/main/publications/grant_reports/details/index.asp?GID=60. Accessed May 14, 2005.

[6]   United Nations On-line Network in Public Administration, available online at www.unpan.org/e-government/stages.htm. Accessed May 14, 2005.

[7]   The World Bank, *The E-Government Handbook for Developing Countries*, The World Bank, Washington DC, 2003.

[8]   Gartner Group, *Gartner's Four Phases of E-Government Model*, Research Note Tutorials, 2000 (www.gartner.com).

[9]   Nevada State Governor's Office, press release dated March 8, 2000. Online. Available: http://egov.state.nv.us/ExecOrdSilvers.htm (last update November 28, 2000)

[10] U.S. Department of Commerce, United States Working Group on Electronic Commerce, *First Annual Report*, (November 16, 1999): 1.   Online. U. S. Commerce Department. Available: http://www.ecommerce.gov/usdocume.htm.

[11] Momentum Research Group, *Benchmarking the eGovernment Revolution*, p 3.

[12] U.S. Congress, P.L. 100-485, 1988.

[13] Department of Health and Human Services, Office of the Inspector General, *Implementation of State Child Support Certified Data Systems* (April, 1997), p. 14. Online. Available: http://www.acf.dhhs.gov/programs/cse/stsys/cserpt.htm.

[14] R.B. Denhardt, The Future of Public Administration, *Public Administration and Management,* **4**, 2 (1999), 285. Online. Available: http://www.pamij.com.

[15] J.F. Blanchette and D.G. Johnson, Cryptography, Data Retention, and the Panopticon Society, *Computer & Society,* **28**, 2 (1998), 1-2.

[16] E-government Satisfaction Stalls, *PA Times*, **28**, 4 (2005), 1.

Developments in e-Government
D. Griffin et al. (Eds.)
IOS Press, 2007

Local Public Administration in the Age of the Web: The Case of Spain

J. Ignacio CRIADO and M. Carmen RAMILO[1]
Department of Political Science and International Relations
Autonomous University of Madrid
Department of Political and Administrative Sciences, Basque Country University

1. Introduction

Public sector reforms using ICTs, including the Internet, have been the subject of considerable academic and public discussion in recent years; this chapter undertakes an approach to one specific aspect: websites in local public administration. Studies on ICTs addressing public sector organizations have flourished under the rubric of e-government; in particular, the World Wide Web (WWW) is one of the sub-areas that different authors have tackled in specialized books, reports, chapters and journal articles. The importance of web technology is its rich potential as a new channel for public sector organizations to contact with and provide information and services to citizens and the profit and non-profit sectors. In that regard, city councils are among the most active users of websites in order to improve their response to user needs, however, not all city councils have performed in the same way, nor have they developed the same kind of websites' features.

This chapter focuses on website application in the Spanish local level of government. It aims to build on the emergent area of local electronic public administration studies, identifying new ways deployed by city councils to respond to their customers using websites and management problems related with current use. In so doing, the authors have examined city councils' websites in two Spanish regions to measure the use of different dimensions and indicators. This work is supported with a revision of the most recent literature that has studied the WWW in local public administration and the authors' experience with web based research during the recent years in different contexts. Hence, this article is a systematic and comparative analysis of the diffusion and uses of web technology in this tier of government.

This chapter is organized into four sections. First, it describes the growing importance of the study of web technology in public administration. The second section presents the analysis of city councils' websites in Spanish municipalities; then, it shows a typology of website developments addressing different dimensions and indicators and provides some proposals about how to approach initiatives and advances in research. The conclusion summarizes the main results of this chapter.

2. The study of the World Wide Web in public administration: A review

Studies about websites in public administration have been increasingly extensive in the literature since the late 1990s. Some WWW innovations have been adopted in public administration, specifically related to electronic service delivery and provision of information to the citizens; even if some skepticism exists about long term results and promises, less than ten years after the first public sector websites were established there is no doubt about the importance of this specific technology, at least, as a new channel to reach the citizenry by public administration. In that vein, first evaluations, generally focused on the content available within the websites, have underlined the variety of design approaches, differences in general development, and thus expected benefits. At the same time, the most innovative local public administrations are using this technological innovation addressing specific needs for this tier of government, basically related with the idea of proximity that is in the core of their existence.

2.1. The scope of the web

Among the wide range of resources offered on the Internet, the WWW is just one. From a technical point of view, websites involve a graphic environment, based on the hypertext concept, consisting of multimedia presentations that offer text, graphics, sound, data, and animation resources, between different computers with a friendly user interface, through the hypertext transfer protocol which operates on the Internet [1]. The importance of the WWW originates from the fact that it is the service that prompted the social and political diffusion of the Internet in the early 1990s, because at its genesis during the 1960-70s the Internet was a network of computers used by small communities of scientists, universities and libertarian groups [2, 3]. Its diffusion as it relates to governmental websites websites has also been impressive: La Porte, Demchack & de Jong [4] detected the web in 101 countries and in 1,000 ministry-level organizations in 1999, growing considerably since then. More important is that:

> *"the WWW is a useful vehicle to evaluate public organizations "openness". It is a growing facet of the public face of government, and it increasingly instigates and reflects internal structural and procedural dimensions of organisations' non-electronic existence"* [4:413].

In recent years, different analyses of public sector websites have been undertaken; however they have almost exclusively addressed the potential for public service delivery. Reports and studies from various sources have generated rankings of e-government developments and efforts in groups of countries, regions, or municipalities using website content analysis, sometimes in an incomplete form, especially those from the consultancy domain (see for example, [5, 6, 7]), but not exclusively [8, 9, 10, 11]. In general, these studies tend to focus on comprehensive censuses of the content included in an organization's website, examining the ability to provide electronic public services using this new electronic channel. This kind of approach has concentrated on observations of how company websites have performed; nevertheless, the extent of progress is more questionable within the public sector [12, 13]. Even if those limitations are real, it is interesting to explore the systematic analysis of websites, as an innovative technology in politics and public administration, especially in order to identify the variables behind different levels of performance. In that regard, the local tier of government has been a fertile target, holding promise for comparative analysis, as it was in the past for the *informatization* literature [14, 15, 16, 17].

In recent years, local public administrations around the world have faced a common problem, if not an imperative: developing a website. This general statement implied different things for different local public administrations in different countries; nevertheless there has been an almost universal agreement about some capacities related with websites, above all, the ability to distribute information about local affairs in a cheaper and faster manner and delivering electronic public services continuously [18]. At the same time, the easy access, permanent availability, and friendly presentation of websites provide a clear effect on the possibilities for city councils to distribute information about local issues, making it potentially available for citizens and businesses 24/7 [19]. In fact,

> *"several factors have clearly promoted the rapid growth of the Internet and diffusion of web browsers (in city councils). The development of Mosaic, the original web browser, significantly simplified the use of the Internet. Newer HTML-authoring tools ease creation of and experimentation with websites, hit counters and web-tracking software enable the webmaster to observe closely how the technology is used. These characteristics of web technology are common to all cities"* [20:9].

On the other hand, through public websites governments can also involve citizens as partners in the public policy-making process, if mechanisms of information, consultation and active participation are available and are used by the citizens. Potentially, this participation channel can help to gather the suggestions of the citizens in order to improve policy-making, generate transparency and trust in governments, and improve the links between governments and citizens affording better democracy [21]. In that regard, even if participation using websites has been seen as limited, it offers possibilities worth exploring (as some local authorities do), in order to engage groups of Internet users traditionally reluctant to interact with political institutions (e.g. young people) [22]. However, not all local public administrations have provided the same answers to these challenges, nor have they looked for the same kind of prospects when adopting a website. These are the kind of results delivered by studies of city councils in various contexts, such as those of Ho [23] and Moon [24], in the United States, Dunleavy & Margetts [12] and Horrock & Humbley [25], in the United Kingdom, or Melitski *et al* [26], with a global focus.

2.2. Gathering evidence from Spanish city councils

This study of web technology as applied to local public administration is fairly recent in Spain. There are more than 8,000 city councils in Spain with a population of up to 43 million people, which implies a problem of size in order to promote some policies and, specifically, developments of technological innovations. At the same time, the diffusion of the web in some city councils has produced successful experiences receiving international awards in terms of electronic governance, as those of Barcelona or Jun [27, 28]. Differences among regions is another feature in Spain, where some advanced groups of city councils stand out, particularly in the Basque Country, Catalonia, Madrid and Valencia Regions, while others seriously lag behind. This does not imply the impossibility for comparison; what is more, previous works have stimulated interesting approaches in order to facilitate generalizations [29]. In that regard, this chapter focuses on a recent analysis of two of the most developed regions cited above (*Basque Country* and *Region of Madrid*), in order to report comparatively advances of their city councils on the web and suggest some conclusions potentially plausible for generalization in other contexts.

Empirical data provided in this chapter is based on direct observation of city councils' websites in the *Basque Country* and the *Region of Madrid* [4]. These regions are two of the most advanced *comunidades autónomas* (regional level) in economic terms, but also experienced in using ICTs, within the Spanish local tier of government [30]. The *Basque Country* is divided into three provinces (*Alava, Guipúzcoa* y *Vizcaya*); their governments have their own ICT policies, and mainly support their development within a territory with 250 municipalities made up of 2,115,279 people. The *Region of Madrid* has no provinces; its regional government plays a strong role within a territory divided in 179 municipalities of 5,804,829 people.

The *methodology* of this study involves the comparative analyses of city councils' websites in two different administrative settings that share some features of Spanish city councils. In that regard, this chapter presents results employing descriptive statistics, to show frequencies of appearance of each indicator observed in each group of municipalities, thus the authors sought to obtain primary data to compare complex contexts generating findings and an analysis to facilitate future studies of different regions in Spain and other countries. Data collection was supported on direct observation of websites using a common research protocol. Data was gathered during 2003 through direct observation of 244 existing websites in both regions, 140 in the *Basque Country* and 104 in the *Region of Madrid*. URL addresses were collected through personal interviews with city managers and contact with different engineers on the Internet, or using information from different governmental agencies, such as the Ministry of Public Administration, Regional Government of Madrid, Regional Government of the Basque Country, city councils' associations, and websites of three provincial governments of the Basque Country (*Álava, Vizcaya* and *Guipúzcoa*).

Four dimensions of website analysis were used: *content, participation, management* and *style*. The first, relates to types of information that city councils make available on the web, and their level of interaction with citizens; the second concerns the intention to promote public engagement between local political institutions and citizens using websites; the third expresses attention to maintenance and direction; and the fourth addresses website presentation and the kind of tools used to facilitate content access. Table 1 summarizes the dimensions and groups of indicators addressing their importance for website orientation to the citizens.

The primary purpose of this study is to address the orientation to the citizens of the websites analysed. The authors developed some dimensions (*content, participation, management* and *style*) and a number of indicators in order to gather knowledge about websites usage as a new tool increasingly deployed in different stages depending on the level of interaction with the citizens: information, interaction/processing or transaction. At the time that this analysis was conducted, a preliminary stage of ICTs deployment within city councils was presumed, mainly focused on information, rather than on citizen needs or actual usage. Another objective of this analysis is to identify the characteristics of these new means undertaken by local administrations to focus on their customers and the resulting management problems related to website use. This aspect implies that results about each dimension provided opportunities for comments about specific facets of website development with interest for building and improving future projects. Finally, this analysis sets up the basis for future work looking for reasons to explain differences in website development at the local level of government. In that regard, this research examines a set of variables, drawn from the most recent literature, in order to find out more about diffusion of technological innovations in the local public sector. This is the tenor of following sections.

Table 1. City council website dimensions and orientation to the citizens in city councils

Dimensions	Groups of indicators	Orientation to the citizens
1. Content Information and services and their level of interaction with users	- General information of the municipality	**
	- Council-institutional and internal organisation	**
	- Services and functions (area)	*****
	- Urban services and functions	****
	- Services and functions (groups of inhabitants)	****
2. Participation Information, interaction and active participation tools among Governments and citizens	- Relational information	**
	- Feedback tools	****
3. Management Tools to develop and maintain websites	General Indicators (*access to website designers, latest news,uUpdate, feedback opportunities*)	*
	- Domain management	*
4. Style Website presentation and tools to facilitate content access	- Accessibility (*use of other languages, disabled persons accessibility, readiness-subject, font size-background contrast*)	*
	- Usability (*search engine, website map and overview diagram*)	*

Source: Criado [31]

3. The web presence of the Spanish local level of government

In this section the authors analyse data from direct observation of the websites of all city councils in the Spanish regions of the *Basque Country* and *Region of Madrid*. The results of this study point out the nature and scope of the websites in relation to different dimensions. First, the *population* of the municipalities is described; then, this analysis measures website orientation to the citizens of the *Basque Country* and the *Region of Madrid* local governments addressing four dimensions: *content, participation, management* and *style*.

The diffusion of websites is over 50 per cent in the *Basque Country* (56 per cent) and the *Region of Madrid* (58.1 per cent) (see Table 2). Web technology follows in both regions a typical S-shaped diffusion curve: first, a new technology is adopted by a small group within an organizational population, then diffusion is accelerated because a growing number of them intend to benefit from the potentials of that technology and costs of experimentation decrease; finally, diffusion slows down [32]. City councils are now in the ascendant point of the curve, when an increasing number of them are looking for the immediate promises and diverse benefits of implementation. However, the idea of coercive and isomorphistic pressures from the administrative context is present, which implies that it is increasingly necessary to have a website and the best one possible, to deliver the idea of being a modern organization [33].

Table 2. Diffusion of web technology in Spanish regions

	N	No. City councils with a website (%)	No. City councils without a website (%)
Basque Country	250	140 (56.)	110 (44)
Region of Madrid	179	104 (58.1)	75 (41.9)

In order to improve comprehension of the nature of websites and their relationship with municipality size, they have been divided into two groups (the rest of the analysis considers both together). First, *council websites*, which offer information, not only about the municipality, but also the different services, buildings and organisations that councils and municipalities offer to local citizens and visitors. On the other hand, *municipality websites* are managed by other public administrations, at the provincial or regional level, (this is the criteria to distinguish them), but it was also observed that they usually give more general information about the municipality, focusing on the least strategic categories, in political and managerial terms. They are less complete in core dimensions and interaction with citizens is more difficult to find. In the *Basque Country* 20 per cent (28) of the cases are *municipality websites*. *Region of Madrid* presents 41.9 per cent (55) of sites within this group (see Table 3).

Table 3. Types of websites

	N	No. Council websites (%)	No. Municipality websites (%)
Basque Country	140	112 (80)	28 (20)
Region of Madrid	104	49 (58.1)	55 (41.9)

Addressing size criteria, the bigger the cities, the more probable their presence on the Internet. The *Basque Country* represents an extreme case where only 20.9 per cent of municipalities with less than 500 inhabitants have a website. The cause of these differences derives from municipality's size [20]: some of them do not have personal or material resources to maintain their own websites and, in this regard, the local tier of government is widely fragmented in Spain (see Table 4).

In summary, collaboration between different levels of governments and agents settled in the local area, but also, the participation of profit and non-profit organizations may provide the smallest councils with the opportunity to access the benefits of the Internet network. Recent studies about city councils have pointed out different institutional constraints to develop websites, including the lack of human and material resources, cultural decoupling with bureaucratic values and aspects related to security [34]. Where local level of government is composed of small city councils, as in Spain, collective action of institutional agents may develop a usual path to solve problems such as those of scope, particularly where human and material resources are lacking. In fact, this institutional variable, size of public administration, serves to explain differences in Website developments, as was made clear by Musso, Weare and Hale [34] or Moon [24].

Table 4. City councils population and types of websites

	Council websites				Municipality websites				Total City councils			
	Basque Country		Region of Madrid		Basque Country		Region of Madrid		Basque Country		Region of Madrid	
	N	%	N	%	N	%	N	%	N	%	N	%
< 500	9	13.4	2	4.7	5	7.5	14	32.6	67	100	43	100
501-2000	32	37.6	3	6.8	8	9.4	21	47.7	85	100	44	100
2001-5000	23	67.6	7	21.9	7	20.6	11	34.4	34	100	32	100
5001-10000	13	59.1	8	36.4	4	18.2	7	31.8	22	100	22	100
10001-50000	28	80	16	69.6	4	11.4	2	8.7	35	100	23	100
50001-100000	4	100	6	85.7	0	0	0	0	4	100	7	100
>100001	3	100	7	87.5	0	0	0	0	3	100	8	100
TOTAL	112	44.8	49	27.4	28	11,2	55	30.7	250	100	179	100

3.1. Content

Website *content* is the core dimension of this analysis, because it offers an overview of the governmental proximity to the citizens, in the sense that it provides insights about the type of information that governments make available on their websites, and their level of interaction with citizens. It is assumed that at one end of the spectrum are councils which consider websites like a mimetic and herd issue without reflection about their meaning and possibilities. At the other extreme there are councils using websites to deliver information, services and functions to the customers, simplifying processes and making relationships easier between government and citizen. In this study, different types of content are addressed: *general information of the municipality*; *council-institutional and internal organisation;* and *services and functions of the council*.

Before focusing on concrete groups of indicators, an aggregated summary of results from categories under analysis is presented. The most frequent category on the city councils' websites is *general information of the municipality*, with at least one of its indicators displayed in all of them, followed by information about *council-institutional and internal organisation* and with the least presence are the categories of information more oriented to the citizens: on services and functions by area, urban and focused on groups of inhabitants (see Table 5). The following sub-sections offer a brief resume of data about all of them.

3.1.1. General information of the municipality

This category reflects the most symbolic and miscellaneous information. At least one of the indicators considered is presented in 100 per cent of both regions websites, including generic data about some general areas related to the municipality, from an economic, social and historic view: *flag/symbol*; *history*; *museums, sights and buildings*; *socio-economic information*; and *access to town* (see Table 6). Some indicators have less presence; however this category presents more frequency of appearance than any other in this analysis, which provides a preliminary idea of the kind of content that city councils make a priority in the cyberspace.

Table 5. General presence. Types of information (%)

	General information of the municipality	Council-institutional and internal organisation	Services and functions (area)	Urban services and functions	Services and functions (groups of inhabitants)
Basque Country	100	86.2	47.8	45.7	64.5
Region of Madrid	100	89.4	92.3	76.9	43.3

Table 6. General information of the municipality (%)

	Accommodation	Leisure features	Museums, sights and buildings	Socio-economic information	Flag & Symbol	Access to town	Map	History
Basque Country	59.3	60.7	82.1	55.7	90.0	76.4	77.9	89.3
Region of Madrid	35.6	33.7	34.6	81.7	76.0	74.0	32.7	43.3

3.1.2. Council-institutional and internal organisation

This category refers to political and administrative aspects of the councils' organisation (86.2 per cent *Basque Country* and 89.4 per cent *Region of Madrid*), such as *budget*, *local government structure*, *organisational flow chart*, *human resources*, internal and external *regulations* and *council current activities*. Interactivity increases: there are examples from a mere compilation of public representatives to promote contact with them through e-mail, even chat rooms. The remaining categories offer good examples of interaction addressing possibilities of downloading PDF documents or reports. There are decreasing percentages of presence, significantly in the *Region of Madrid*, where only two indicators exhibit over 35 per cent of appearance (see Table 7).

3.1.3. Services and functions of the council

This is the core dimension related to website *content*. It focuses on information offered by the councils about the services and functions they deliver to citizens. In order to understand the complete range of categories, they are presented in three groups addressing different goals (*functions and services* attending *areas*, *urban* issues, and *groups of inhabitants*) and three levels of citizen interactivity (*information*, *interaction* and *transaction*).

Table 7. Council institutional and internal organisation information (%)

	Current activities of the council	Internal regulations of the council	Human Resources	Budget	Organisational flow chart	Local government structure
Basque Country	50	47.5	35.6	46.6	16.1	74.6
Region of Madrid	12.5	27.9	29.8	33.7	84.6	76.9

3.1.3.1. Services and functions (area).

In general, this is the group of services and functions with the strongest presence in the local councils websites (47.8 per cent Basque Country and 92.3 per cent Region of Madrid). In the Basque Country, this group is formed by social services, socio-economic development, culture and sports (see Figure 1a). In the case of the Region of Madrid, tourism, culture, sports, education, socio-economic development, social services, health, are among the most extended categories in the websites (see Figure 1b). In this group of indicators there exists a higher orientation towards the citizens: it is possible to find services which offer fully interactive relationships with citizens and businesses, including services delivered on line in areas such as census, socio-economic development, employment or social services. Unfortunately, the presence is lower than in previous categories, which confirms our initial assumption about the weakness of website interactivity: these three groups of functions and services are the most important regarding interactivity and transactional orientation, but they are the least developed among the websites.

3.1.3.2. Urban services and functions.

Indicators addressed here are relevant to local government in terms of social impact and budget expenses: *town planning, public transport, public works, maintenance, housing, police,* or *environment* (45.7 per cent *Basque Country* and 76.9 per cent *Region of Madrid*). It has been discovered that attention has been given to indicators such as *town planning, public transports, environment, police* and *public works*, however, the results are modest in the majority of the cases (see Figures 2a & 2b).

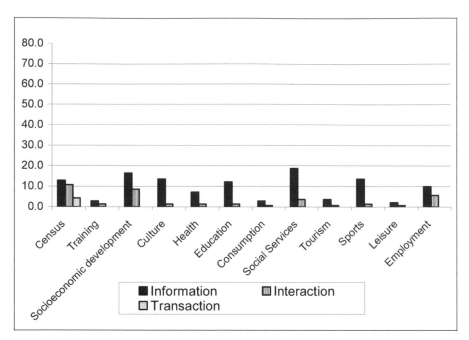

Figure 1a. Services and functions per area (Basque Country) (%)

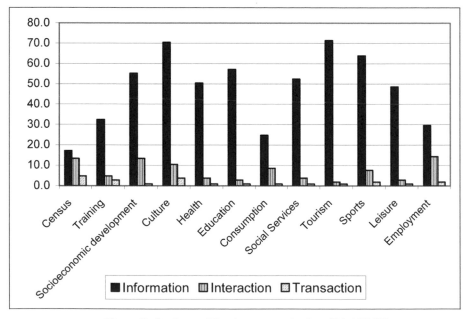

Figure 1b. Services and functions per area (region of Madrid) (%)

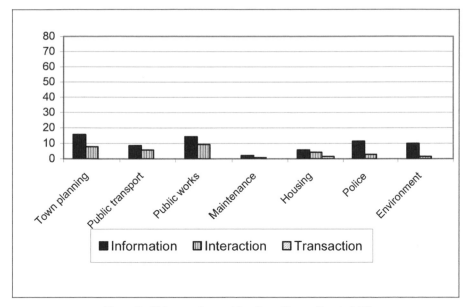

Figure 2a. Urban services and functions (Basque Country) (%)

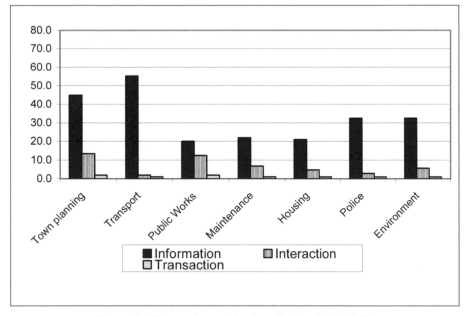

Figure 2b. Urban services and functions (Region of Madrid) (%)

3.1.3.3. Services and functions (groups of inhabitants).

Using groups of people is another way to present information and services on the website. This is a horizontal approach in which they are presented with profiles addressing groups of citizens with specific needs: *children*; *youth*; *women*; *elderly*; and *disabled persons* (64.5 per cent *Basque Country* and 43.3 per cent *Region of Madrid*). It is possible to find services completed on line in both regions in different categories (*youth, elderly, disabled persons* and *immigrants*) (see Figures 3a & 3b). In fact, it is remarkable the strong effort of some municipalities to inform and promote issues relevant to women, elderly or disabled persons, discriminated or underrepresented in our societies by different means, discrimination that also can be distinguished in website technology in terms of use, content and orientation.

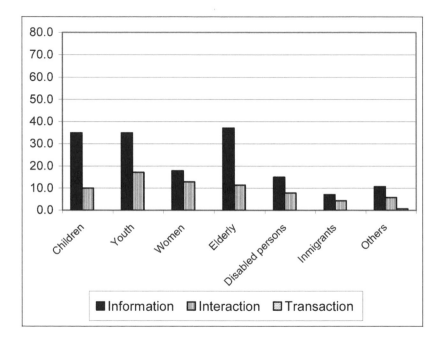

Figure 3a. Services and functions (groups of inhabitants) (Basque Country) (%)

In summary, information about public services offers different and bounded results. It is predominately arranged into content by the area and groups of inhabitants' categories, which implies that the web has not completely superseded the traditional organisation of the city councils. On the other hand, once websites are on line, they usually start with an acceptable range of information, but this does not mean that they promote delivery on line, as observed above, because interaction with citizens tends to finish with processing experiences, even if some transactional cases provide basis for *bench learning* in the future [35].

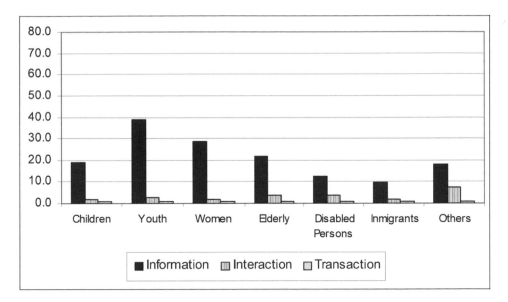

Figure 3b. Services and functions (groups of inhabitants) (region of Madrid) (%)

3.2. Participation

Relational information and *feedback tools* complete a wider vision of information, interaction and active participation means that are available on the web. Both groups of indicators may imply a limited focus on participation issues, however there are some cases in which websites are being used with participatory purposes, because they provide an inexpensive new channel for public authorities and a familiar tool for citizens to interact with each other. Here this potential use is addressed by examining two different groups of indicators.

3.2.1. Relational information

The first category reflects websites ability for linking citizens with council organisations and it is measured using indicators for *e-mail* and other *links* offered by the council (see Figure 4). Data interpretation assumes that websites provide contact with the closest public administrations, municipal actors or internal entities of the council, less importance is given to interaction with other levels of government that seem to be more distant, such as the Spanish central government or the European Union institutions.

Despite some councils being online, this does not guarantee successful use of their websites by citizens. Municipalities have to interact and be linked with other levels of government and with local agents (individuals, companies, or other municipalities) in order to ensure an effective position and use of the Internet. At the same time, as governments promote technologies within public administration, future analysis of websites becomes more difficult because of these networked relations. Different public departments and organisations may participate in shared responsibilities, processes and results, hence the strategies to analyse this digital part of the organisation should pay attention to these new arrangements.

3.2.2. Feedback tools

Public websites are used in most cases to publish organizational information or interact with other entities through *e-mail* and *links*; however participation practices are less frequent. The lack of citizens' voice on the Internet is not a technological problem, but a political and cultural one; technologies allow different applications in order to introduce them into the policy process, however, information is a prerequisite for participation. Bearing this in mind, websites offer an opportunity for politicians and senior civil servants to enhance participation in order to design policies and solutions to problems in a more complex and interdependent society.

Further than previous categories, a small number of websites include *news* and *newsletters* to registered users offering a proactive approach (see Table 8). Full active participation tools considered in this analysis, such as *surveys* to measure preferences of citizens, *forums* to identify their ideas and priorities, or *chatrooms* to interact on line with them, are now in a very preliminary stage of development, which implies that promises of e-democracy, positive or negative, are far from being accomplished through the web.

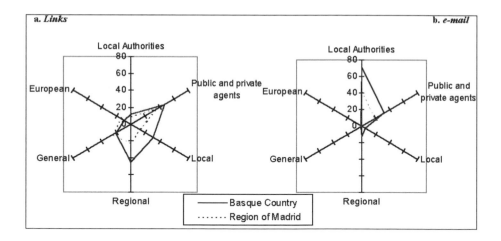

Figure 4. Engagement to other organisations (%)

3.3. Management

This dimension measures how websites are conducted in terms of content. Websites, as a new system to communicate and give information to the citizens, need to be maintained and adapted to fresh realities and impacts. Citizens demand greater government accountability; however websites seem to be fuzzier than other structures of the public sector management. Regarding this assumption, do websites enhance transparency or are they merely a shop-front providing nothing new?

Table 8. Feedback tools (%)

	Newsletters	News	Forums	Surveys	Chats
Basque Country	2.1	0	17.1	8.6	1.4
Region of Madrid	6.7	26.9	5.8	7.7	1.9

3.3.1. General indicators of management

A first group of indicators within this category should be clearly present on the websites: direct *access to website designers*; existence of categories with *latest news*; *feedback opportunities* for the citizens; and *date of last updating*. Data analysis suggests modest presence of the majority of indicators; especially *access to webmasters*, the tool with more possibilities for feedback within this dimension, presents the less favourable results (see Table 9).

These results support our idea that city councils in the *Basque Country* and the *Region of Madrid* do not assume websites as an actual competence of management. New abilities and extra resources for public ICT projects should be displayed in order to

Table 9. General indicators of management (%)

	Access to website designers	Latest news	Update	Feedback opportunities
Basque Country	38	60.7	-	65
Region of Madrid	26	36.5	56.7	-

obtain results; this seems to be one of the tasks for the next few years. Here, there are two ideas; first, websites are considered as another area of management within public organisations. Second, websites require investment and trained personnel to become a reality: attention to the development of feedback and diary management facilities should to be first step.

3.3.2. Domain management

A domain is a translation of a numeric IP address into an alphanumeric formula, easier to remember and write for human beings. Domain management includes two levels of analysis, on the one hand, first level domains, such as, *.com*, *.org*, *.net*, *.info*, etc., and on the other, second level domains, where formulas selected are flexible, even if they usually try to identify organizations, so we keep them out of this analysis.

Differences between the *Basque Country* and the *Region of Madrid* in first level domains are evident. Addressing *.es* as national domain of Spain, a third of city councils in the Region of Madrid have adopted this option to identify their website domain, whereas in the *Basque Country* this criteria is broadly rejected, due to political reasons, which is an evidence of the implications and importance of this kind of decision (see Table 10). Neither in these two regions, nor in the rest of Spain, is there a clear tendency within city councils to develop common guidelines to identify first level domains in cyberspace. Obviously, it is an open decision for city councils to adopt any formula; however, addressing the new wave of first level domains, it could be interesting for them to identify with their national state in order to avoid confusion with other city councils with similar names in other Spanish-speaking areas of the world and to facilitate location in search engines.

3.4. Style

Style suggests public policy terminology and addresses website presentation and the kind of tools used to facilitate content access. The analysis is completed with this dimension because even if the websites have interesting and high quality information, give opportunities for feedback and interaction with citizens and businesses or complete services on line, problems with style can decrease previous advantages making access and understanding difficult for the diverse groups that will visit the site. Data about two different groups of indicators is presented: *accessibility* and *usability*.

Table 10. Management of first level domains (%)

	.es	.org	.net	.com	.info
Basque Country	0	24.8	57	16.8	1.3
Region of Madrid	32	31	4	33	0

Table 11. Indicators of accessibility (%)

	Use of other languages	Disabled persons accessibility	Readiness-subject	Font size-background contrast
Basque Country	22	46.7	72.3	82.3
Region of Madrid	3.8	69.2	87.5	94.2

3.4.1. Accessibility

Website *accessibility* points out physical skills needed for accessibility and the ease of attaining the information. Here, it is addresses indicators related to content comprehension for different groups of people and the process of loading: *use of different languages* to give an international view; attention to *disabled persons accessibility* with tools for blind people; *readiness - subject* or use of basic tools to write on the Internet; and *font size – background contrast* addressing ease for reading text on the screen (see Table 11).

The results indicate more development of readiness instruments than physical accessibility ones. The core idea is that websites encourage users with different needs (potential world wide visitors) and public managers should challenge problems with inequality in educational (levels of education), economic (types of computers or connections), even cultural (languages or interests) terms, in order to make access to websites universal.

3.4.2. Usability

Website *usability* addresses logic design and ease of mental comprehension for users, indicators about tools used to facilitate navigation information effectiveness are analysed. The group, *search engine, website map* and *overview diagram*, is composed by tools that can be implemented in an easy way giving advice regarding internal organisational structure (see Table 12). This group of indicators is based upon previous studies of website usability within public and private organisations [36].

Results describe scarce attention to navigation tools facilities. Indicators have low percentages of presence (only the *overview diagram* in the *Basque Country* reaches the 50 per cent), all of them provide a good opportunity for enhancing website *usability* for the citizens with a classical and easy web toolkit. *Usability* means easy access to content. At present, the web is only available to a minority of citizens, however during the next few years of expanded use of websites, the promotion of effective instruments to improve *usability* will be of paramount importance.

Table 12. Indicators of usability (%)

	Search Engine	Website Map	Overview Diagram
Basque Country	39	33.3	75.9
Region of Madrid	14.4	14.4	43.3

4. An assessment of results

4.1. A typology of website development for city councils

Results addressing the dimensions analyzed in this chapter have provided a basis to classify websites into groups. In general, it is accepted that there are different stages of development determined by the level of interaction between government agencies and citizens or other public or private agents [37, 38, 39, 40]. Here a classification is offered which considers three main stages of website development: *information, interaction/processing* and *transaction*. The objective of this typology is to introduce criteria for future practice within this singular reality at the local tier of public administration and a framework to conduct research in the future [5] (see Figure 5).

4.1.1. 1st level. Information. One way websites

This first stage includes websites in which the prevailing *content* is passive and about general issues of the municipality. On-line services for citizens are not included and information is posted following a departmental and hierarchical view. *Participation* is understood as providing e-mail addresses or links to other public organizations or entities. Website *management* does not exist at all; these websites develop the classic administrative division of public organisations; there is no staff to manage websites; and they have not been updated from the moment when they were published on the Internet. Finally, there is no *style* in them or clear definition. They provide total disintegration and they are difficult to use. In this stage, departments and agencies use the World Wide Web to post information about them and, even if the information is easily accessible with relatively few clicks of the mouse, the site is passive and does not provide a service as such. For the reasons pointed out previously, website orientation to the citizen in this first stage is low. A majority of such one way communication websites are up and running in the municipalities of the *Basque Country* and the *Region of Madrid* due to the impact of various organizational reasons (e.g.. lack of human resources and budget for ICT, the absence of a strategic vision about technologies in public management, etc.) or sociological variables (i.e. population size, young demand, etc.) [24].

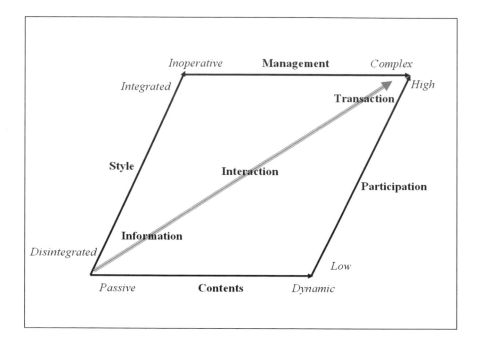

Figure 5. Websites dimensions and stages

4.1.2. 2nd level. Interaction/processing. Two ways websites

4.1.2. 2nd level. Interaction/processing. Two ways websites

These websites present a step further in the exchange between governments and citizens. First of all, *content* is more centered towards the citizen, focusing on needs and functions rather than on the department or agency that provides the information or services. Information about governments is gathered with instruments such as e-mail or box files integrated in the sites: it is not necessary to phone or write a letter to contact the government. Requests for service can be submitted on-line and subjected to basic editing and validation before being stored for off-line processing. Services which involve a set fee, for example renewing a license, paying a fine or enrolling for an education course, can be completed on-line. In this second stage, *participation* tools have a more pro-active and interactive approach through suggestions forms or forums in order to obtain citizens' opinions and impressions. Website *management* improves with its periodic updating and the use of various tools, links and feedback possibilities in order to make civil servants more accessible to citizens. Finally, in terms of *style*, the design of systems is more coherent, incorporating logic tools, presenting information in a manner which reflects the institutional view, and catering for different languages and disabilities such as blindness and deafness. City councils at this level have more resources and experience of using technology in their organizations. Fewer websites from the municipalities of the *Basque Country* and the *Region of Madrid* are included in this second level, with a medium orientation to the citizens.

4.1.3. 3rd level. Transaction . Transactional websites

This final stage is much more than a simple website. Rather, it is a collection of websites accessible via a portal that integrates the complete range of government services and provides citizens with seamless access to more than one agency. Different dimensions (*content, participation, management* and *style*) are integrated providing a global view of a virtual or digital organization. *Content* addresses citizen and business needs by offering a complete range of dynamic information and services on-line, while seeking to extend services as a consequence of improved technical and human resources. *Participatory* channels are more oriented to the service provision rather than to the policy-making process. But improving public services, by considering citizen participation through their comments, also means improved policy-making. *Management* of the websites allows users to interact fully with government. It is a complex, growing system, rich in data, transactions and multimedia. It is this third transactional stage which will have the most impact on service delivery both in terms of greatly enhanced access and functionality for users, and restructuring of government departments and internal management. Privacy and security are required in order to assure that the exchange with the users through telematic channels is carried out with guarantees. The *style* of transactional websites tries to guarantee the usability and accessibility to them. Users' opinions are considered in order to improve the management and content. This stage, with a high website orientation to the citizens, has been reached only by limited number of pioneer city councils in the *Basque Country* and the *Region of Madrid*. These municipalities are characterized by a wide experience and tradition in the extensive use of ICT in their organizations in order to improve internal management and communication.

Even at the early information and interaction stages, where there is an approach to provision of information to the customers, some reorganization of work and re-conceptualization of the role of the agency may be needed. Major change is undertaken within the third stage. But, in spite of this organizational change required by a strategic design of websites, what happens in the city councils of the two case study regions? In general, websites present an initial stage of development and a low orientation to citizens addressing different dimensions, closer to passive, disintegrated and inoperative features than the other extremes. Governments speeches, promises and commitments are some steps further than effective implementation of ICTs in order to improve public management and service delivery and, as it is suggested by some authors, this is a reality in different cultural and political atmospheres world wide [41, 42, 43, 44]. However, once it is clear that website performance is different in specific groups of city councils, it is also important to look for explanations for such differences.

4.2. Speculations about differences in city councils' website development

The findings of this study implies that, despite promises regarding the Internet in organisations, it can be assumed that, at the least, websites are not producing drastic changes and benefits in the core structure of government or the institutional basis of their activity. However, what is beyond doubt is that there will be effects caused by an extensive use of ICT in local public sector management and that such changes have implications in the way that they interact with citizens. On the one hand, this chapter has suggested a low orientation from the government to citizens through websites, in that sense, it is unclear whether or not traditional organisations are being challenged by digital ones, in order to create more flexible structures of government, and problems with the digital divide are not being addressed to provide easier access for specific groups of people. At the same time, the most experienced and innovative local governments are promoting a range of services through their websites including, for example, delivery systems integrated with life events, on-line payments and, what is more, negotiations with other levels of government in order to generate one stop shops and engage activities in an horizontal way that can overcome institutional arrangements and increase expectation about other likely changes in the future. Why those extreme differences between city councils? Which variables are behind that phenomenon?

In this theoretical speculation the position adopted by the authors does not imply neutrality about ICT diffusion, but a complex (not deterministic) relationship with the organisations in which they are embedded. Diffusion of technologies needs to have regard for the countries, regions and municipalities in which they are implemented, and reflects different institutional, social, political, economic and cultural differences. In particular, city councils may provide different approaches and lead to distinct institutional arrangements; for example, this chapter has demonstrated that organizational size collaborates as a variable with importance to explain diffusion of websites. Also, recent literature suggests a set of other institutional features to explain developments of this technology in city councils [4, 45, 20]: existence of a central unit for ICT management, strategic planning of e-government plans, existence of personnel devoted to website maintenance, content management using feedback from different units of the organization, use of and compatibility with previous technologies, or time of experience with websites are between them. In practical terms, this supposes that city councils have opportunities to adjust, to some extent, the diffusion of web technology, even if some of the institutional arrangements mentioned above are difficult to transform.

At the same time, the context in which city councils are embedded could promote different website development patterns. Variables addressing socio-economic aspects of municipalities may explain not only the private use of the Internet and the WWW, but also the progress of city councils' websites, especially, aspects such as average age, per capita income, levels of urban residents, percentages of graduates and professionals, or political participation [23, 24, 20]. In practical terms, this means that the local tier of government also should have a say in the process of ICT diffusion, bearing in mind contextual variables. In this case, the potential control of city councils includes not only focusing on an increasing use of technologies within public management, but also on providing knowledge, vision and leadership; particularly by addressing the facilities of the WWW to create local networks between institutions, developing public-private partnerships, to enhance governance, promote public service delivery or foster citizen participation, all of them in an open perspective highly oriented to the citizenry. However, not all these variables are under the control of city councils.

5. Conclusion

This chapter has provided an approach to web technology in local public administration. Theoretically, different authors have underlined the growing importance of the study of the WWW in government in general and city councils in particular. Websites are increasingly a point of reference of internal structural and procedural dimensions of organisations' existence and this is the reason why analysis of site content has been the core subject of a number of reports and studies about e-government developments in groups of countries, regions, or municipalities world wide. The case of city councils has offered a fertile example for analysis. In that regard, two of the most advanced Spanish regions in terms of diffusion of ICT, *Basque Country* and *Region of Madrid*, have been selected to gather and analyze data from direct observation of city councils' websites using a common protocol about three dimensions (*content, participation, management* and *style*), and almost one hundred indicators. At the time of this analysis, there was a preliminary stage of website development within city councils, mainly focused on information, rather than on interaction with citizens, even if new means have been undertaken by local administrations to focus on their customers and overcome the arising management problems related to website use. City councils' websites have been classified intro groups, building a typology which considers three main stages of development: *information, interaction/processing* and *transaction*. This typology creates a solid framework for future practice within this singular reality. Last, but not least, this chapter developed some final theoretical speculations looking for reasons to explain differences in website development. Some institutional and contextual variables related to city councils have been suggested in the literature of technological diffusion in order to elaborate explanations about this phenomenon and, even if those hypotheses are not tested in this chapter, they are proposed for future research in this field.

In summary, the debate concerning feasible results of new technologies in public administration has been hindered by the WWW. It was a common place to find in the literature extreme visions about possible effects of the technologies before the Internet growth in the 1990s. The massive use of the web has changed the terms of the debate, as suggested in this analysis, in the sense that even if impacts are more moderate than expected, nobody now doubts the social, political, economic or organizational implications of ICT. For instance, this implies that citizens will have opportunities to be better informed and it also has implications for government accountability. This analysis has attempted to move away from the old debate, between deterministic utopian and pessimistic, in order to describe and analyze a limited set of changes, insert on a broad public management reform agenda, due to the web technology. This implies a much more complex relationship between technologies and organisations. Governments and public administrations have the challenge to deal with these new informational and communicative policies in a strategic way or leave key decisions in the hands of other private interests [46]. These decisions are not technological, but political, and the effects and results of them will lead to different scenarios which will be very interesting to research in the future.

Endnotes

1. Authors' names are ordered alphabetically; their contributions were equally important. We are very grateful to anonymous referees and to Clara Maria Chu (University of California, Los Angeles) and Rebeca Coriat (London School of Economics and Political Science) for their valuable comments in order to improve the text.

2. Browsers (such as Explorer, Firefox, or Opera) are client software programs used for searching and viewing various kinds of Internet resources such as websites [47].

3. In recent times, website research has faced serious criticisms. One type of criticism is based on this argument: not all public organizations provide information or services directly to the citizens, in other words, some of them cannot use websites to improve their relational tasks because they do not contact directly with the public (i.e. regulatory agencies) [12]. Other criticism underlines the importance of international benchmarking in order to understand what and how perform public administrations on the web, with the implicit idea being: '*if you measure it, they will score*' [13]. As international benchmarks have tended to provide more importance to service delivery (this vision is deeply rooted on private company processes, with consultants as major supporters), getting around other spheres closer to the political dimension of government, public sector organizations have adopted this approach in order to guide their presence on the Internet, taking for granted it and without reflection about its potential consequences and effects.

4. This chapter is based on a second website analysis, with the previous time reported in an article [30]. This research aspires to gather longitudinal data about this phenomenon in order to examine the evolution of this technology and its growing implications for local politics and public administration. In that regard, authors will be glad to provide more information about methods, if required to develop a comparative perspective.

5. This kind of stages model can be complemented with other principles when the analysis in centred in different agencies or units within the same public administration. In these cases, the stages delineated here seem to confuse issues about type of agency being analysed with the separate questions of how sophisticated that agency's e-government or digital public services strategy is. For example, some units or agencies within one single public administration do not undertake individual transactions with citizens because of their fundamental role [12].

References

[1]   T. Berness-Lee, *Weaving the Web. The Original Design and Ultimate Destiny of the World Wide Web, by its Inventor*, HarperCollins, New York, 1999.
[2]   M. Castells, *The Information Age: Economy, Society and Culture*, (3 vols.), Blackwell Publishers, Oxford, 2000.
[3]   M. Castells, *The Internet Galaxy*, Oxford University Press, Oxford, 2001.
[4]   T.M. La Porte, C.C. Demchak and M. de Jong, Democracy And Bureaucracy in the Age of the Web: Empirical Findings and Theoretical Speculations, *Administration & Society*, **34**, 4 (2002), 411-446.
[5]   Accenture, *e-government Leadership: High Performance, Maximum Value Fifth Annual Accenture eGovernment Study Reveals Governments at a Crossroads*, Accenture, 2004. Available: http://www.accenture.com/xd/xd.asp?it=enweb&xd=industries%5Cgovernment%5Cgove_egov_value.x ml. [18/01/2005].
[6]   Cap Gemini Ernst & Young, *Overall Report Oct 2001 - Oct 2002. On Line Availability of Public Services: How Does Europe Progress? Web-Based Survey on Electronic Public Services*, European Commission, Brussels, 2003.
[7]   Economist Intelligence Unit – IBM, *The 2003 e-Readiness Rankings*, The Economist, London, 2003.
[8]   European Commission, *Top of the Web - User Satisfaction and Usage, Survey of eGovernment services*, European Commission, Brussels, 2004. Available: http://europa.eu.int/information_society/activities/egovernment_research/doc/top_of_the_web_report_20 04.pdf. [18/01/2005].
[9]   M. Holzer and S-T. Kim, *Digital Governance in Municipalities Worldwide. An Assessment of Municipal Websites throughout the World*, University of New Jersey & Sungkyunkwan University, 2003. Available: http://www.andromeda.rutgers.edu/~egovinst/Website/Report%20-%20Egov.pdf. [18/01/2005].
[10] D.M. West, *Urban eGovernment 2003*, Center for Public Policy, University of Brown, 2003. Available: http://www.insidepolitics.org/egovt03city.pdf. [18/01/2005].

[11] United Nations, *UN Global E-government Readiness Report 2004*, United Nations, 2004. Available: http://unpan1.un.org/intradoc/groups/public/documents/un/unpan019207.pdf. [18/01/2005].

[12] P. Dunleavy and H. Margetts, *Government on the Web 2002,* National Audit Office, London, 2002.

[13] D. Janssen, S. Rotthier, and K. Snijkers, If you Measure it they Will Score: an Assessment of International eGovernment Benchmarking, *Information Polity*, **9** (2004), 121-130.

[14] J.N. Danziger and K.L. Kraemer, *People and Computers. The Impacts of Computing on End Users in Organizations*, Columbia University Press, New York, 1986.

[15] K.K. Guthrie and W.H. Dutton, The Politics of Citizen Access Technology: the Development of Public Information Utilities in Four Cities, *Policy Studies Journal*, **20**, 4 (1992), 574-598.

[16] N. Kazama, The Regional Informatization Policies of the Local Government in Japan. Why They Fail to Increase Communication with Citizens, *Information Infrastructure and Policy*, **5** (1996), 279-289.

[17] A. Northrop, K.L. Kraemer, D.E. Dunkle and J L. King, Payoffs from Computerization: Lessons over Time, *Public Administration Review*, **50**, 5 (1990), 505-514.

[18] L. Chaty and C. Girlanda. Towards an Electronic Administration? Local Information Systems, or the Web Modernization of Local Administration, *International Review of Administrative Sciences*, **68**, 1 (2002), 25-43.

[19] C. Scavo and S. Yuhang, World Wide Web Design and Use in Public Management, In G. D. Garson, (Ed), *Information Technology and Computer Applications in Public Administration: Issues and Trends*, Publishing Idea Group, Heshey, 1999.

[20] C. Weare, J. Musso and M. Hale, Electronic Democracy and the Diffusion of Municipal Web Pages in California, *Administration & Society*, **31**, 1 (1999), 3-27.

[21] OECD, *Citizens as partners. OECD handbook on information, consultation and public participation in policy-making*, OECD, Paris, 2001.

[22] D.M. West, E-Government and the Transformation of Service Delivery and Citizen Attitudes, *Public Administration Review*, **64**, 1 (2004), 15-27.

[23] A.T. Ho, Reinventing Local Governments and the e-Government Initiative, *Public Administration Review*, **62**, 4 (2002), 434-444.

[24] M.J. Moon, The Evolución of e-Government among Municipalities: Rhetoric or Reality?, *Public Administration Review*, **62**, 4 (2002), 424-433.

[25] I. Horrocks and N. Hambley, The Webbing of British Local Government, *Public Money and Management*, **18**, 2 (1998), 39-44.

[26] J. Melitski, M. Holzer, S.-T. Kim, C.-G. Kim and y S.-Y. Rho, Digital Government World Wide: an e-Government Assessment of Municipal Websites, *International Journal of Electronic Government Research*, **1**, 1 (2005), 1-19.

[27] M. Castells and E. Ollé, *El Model Barcelona II, L'Ajuntament de Barcelona a la Societat Xarxa*, Universitat Oberta de Catalunya, Barcelona, 2004. Available: http://www.uoc.edu/in3/pic/cat/pdf/PIC_Ajuntament_0.pdf. [18/01/2005].

[28] J.I. Criado, *Construyendo la e-Administración Local*, EuroGestión Pública, Madrid, 2004.

[29] Fundación Retevisión, *eEspaña 2004. Informe Anual sobre el Desarrollo de la Sociedad de la Información en España*, Fundación Retevisión, Madrid, 2004.

[30] J.I. Criado and M.C. Ramilo, e-Government in Practice. An Analysis of Website Orientation to the Citizens in Spanish Municipalities, *International Journal of Public Sector Management*, **16**, 3 (2003), 191-218.

[31] J.I. Criado, Modernización administrativa y difusión de innovaciones tecnológicas en el sector público, *Revista Internacional de Sociología*, **39** (2004), 63-105.

[32] D.F. Norris, Leading Edge Information Technologies and Their Adoption: Lessons from U.S. Cities, In G.D. Garson, (Ed), *Information Technology and Computer Applications in Public Administration: Issues and Trends*, Publishing Idea Group, Hershey, 1999.

[33] J.E. Fountain, *Building the Virtual State*, Brookings Institution Press, Washington D.C., 2001.

[34] J.A. Musso, C. Weare and M.L. Hale, Designing Web Technologies for Local Governance Reform: Good Management or Good Democracy?, *Political Communication*, **17**, 1, 1-19.

[36] C. Leitner, and J.I. Criado, Aprendizaje organizativo y cambio institucional a través de buenas prácticas europeas de e-Administración. Una aproximación a los premios de e-Europe for e-Government, *Revista Vasca de Administración Pública*, **71** (2005), 139-172.

[36] J. Nielsen, *Designing Web Usability: the Practice of Simplicity*, New Riders Publishing, Indianapolis, 1999.

[37] European Commission, *eEurope 2002 Final Report*, European Commission, Brussels, 2002.

[38] K. Layne, and J. Lee, Developing Fully Functional E-Government: a Four Stage Model, *Government Information Quarterly*, **18**, 2 (2001), 122-136.

[39] C.G. Reddick, A Two Stages Model of e-Government Growth: Theories and Empirical Evidence for U.S. Cities, *Government Information Quarterly*, **21**, 1 (2001), 51-64.

[40] Economist, *A Survey of Government and the Internet*, 24 June, 2000.
[41] C. Bellamy and J.A. Taylor, *Governing in the Information Age*, Open University Press, Buckingham, 1998.
[42] R. Heeks, (Ed.), *Reinventing Government in the Information Age: International Practice in IT-Enable Public Sector Reform*, Routledge, London, 1999.
[43] C. Leitner (Ed.), *e-government in Europe: the State of Affairs*, European Institute of Public Administración-European Comisión, Maastricht, 2003.
[44] H. Margetts, *Information Technology in Government: Britain and America*, Routledge, London, 1999.
[45] A. Peled, Centralization or Diffusion? Two Tales of Online Government, *Administration & Society*, **32**, 6 (2001), 686-709.
[46] J.W. Ross and M. Weill, Six IT decisions your IT people shouldn't make, *Harvard Business Review*, **80**, 11 (2002), 84-91.
[47] E. Lawrence, B. Corbit, J. Fisher, J. Lawrence and A. Tidwell, *Internet Commerce. Digital Models for Business*, 2nd Edn. , John Wiley, New York, 2000.

Developments in e-Government
D. Griffin et al. (Eds.)
IOS Press, 2007

73

Critical Review of e-Government Benchmarking Studies

Kris SNIJKERS, Sabine ROTTHIER and Davy JANSSEN
Public Management Institute, Katholieke University, Belgium
Hogesschool, Gent, Belgium and University of Antwerp, Belgium

1. Introduction

e-Government benchmarking has received a lot of attention during the past few years [1]. In the first section we will look at the concept of 'benchmarking'. Benchmarking is a technique that originally took shape in the private sector but, during recent decades, is more and more used in the public sector as well. We will explore what benchmarking is and what we, theoretically, can do with it.

In the second section we will provide an analysis of 18 e-government benchmarks. We will discuss the focus of the benchmarks, their definition of e-government, the way in which they compare across time and space and the indicators that were used. We classified the indicators into four categories: input, output, usage, impact and environment.

In the third section, based on the analysis of benchmarking practices, we will draw some lessons for the future use of e-government benchmarks. We will describe two recent benchmarks that took a very different approach than the benchmarks from our analysis. We will discuss whether these benchmarks can provide a solution to the shortcomings of most of the e-government benchmarks. We conclude the third section with an analysis of the difference between a quantitative and a qualitative way of benchmarking.

2. Benchmarking: origin and growth

To explain the concept 'benchmarking', several authors refer to Japan [2, 3, 4]. During the 1950s, Japanese entrepreneurs visited trade fairs in the United States and Europe. They had a great interest in the products that were built by Western companies. In the first instance, Japanese companies copied products. Secondly, they made visits to Western companies. The Japanese did not only want to copy products, they also wanted to obtain knowledge about the work processes behind a product. Thirdly, the Japanese took another step: they not only copied work processes, they also improved these processes. In this way, during the 1970s, Japanese companies were able to produce better and cheaper products than Western companies.

In this context, the concept of 'benchmarking' was introduced by Xerox [5]. This American company became aware of the Japanese competition on the market of copiers in the 1980s. Although Xerox did well in terms of productivity, suddenly,

Japanese companies were able to build a qualitatively better copier at a much cheaper price than Xerox could. The management of Xerox then sent engineers to Japan to compare their products and work processes. From this moment on Xerox started a large benchmarking-program to continually improve its own work processes.

There are several definitions of benchmarking [3, 6]. They all have some elements in common. First, benchmarking is seen as an iterative process. Benchmarking is not something you do once; you have to do it on a continuous basis. Second, benchmarking is a search for best practices. Third, it is not only useful to find and to describe best practices; you also have to understand them. Fourth, you have to implement the things you have learnt from the best practices.

Waalewijn, Hendriks, and Verzijl distinguish three different forms of benchmarking [7]. The first one they call 'reverse engineering'. This is the simplest method of benchmarking: analyze the product of your competitor. This is what the Japanese engineers did during the 1950s: copy and imitate products. The second form of benchmarking is called 'operational benchmarking'. This method of benchmarking is aimed at the operational processes. In this way, the attention shifts from the product itself to the process behind the product. The difference between these two forms of benchmarking is the focus of the benchmarking activities: do we study the result or the processes? The third form of benchmarking is 'strategic benchmarking'. Strategic benchmarking wants to explore and reveal the way in which a company reached a certain competitive advantage. Through strategic benchmarking a company does not want to obtain an incremental improvement of its processes, but a radical redesign of its processes. This is what McNair and Leibfried call a 'quantum leap' [5:21] or, in the words of Bendell, Boulter and Goodstadt [2:9] a 'breakthrough improvement'. According to Waalewijn, Henriks, and Verzijl it is difficult for a company to reach these forms of improvement on its own. For real, radical, improvements a company needs benchmarking. A company needs to find a best practice, study it, understand it, and implement it. The search for a best practice does not have to be limited to organizations in your own sector [5]. Innovative solutions are often found in other sectors. Then, to understand a best practice, it is not only necessary to describe products or processes in a quantitative way like a lot of consultants do [2]. A quantitative analysis can help you to learn your strong and weak points, but does not teach you why you have these strong or weak points and what you can do about them.

Although benchmarking has its origins in the private sector, public sector organizations also are making more use of this technique [8]. Public sector organizations experience pressure to perform better. Just like private sector companies, public sector organizations will have to make 'quantum leaps' of 'breakthrough improvements'. In a public sector context benchmarking can be used to compare for example different local authorities or different agencies with each other. However, for public sector organizations, it can also be interesting to benchmark processes from the private or not-for-profit sector. In this way, new technologies or work processes can be discovered. In the area of e-government a lot of these benchmarks were published during recent years. However, there are a lot of differences between these benchmarks on the level of their approach as well as on the level of their results.

3. An analysis of 18 international e-government benchmarks

In this section we will present an analysis of 18 international benchmarks that were published in the period 2000-2003. We will look at the focus of the benchmarks, their definition of e-government, their comparison across time and space and the indicators that are used.

3.1. The focus of the benchmarks

The benchmarks could easily be divided into four groups with a clear difference in focus (this is shown in Table 1). A first cluster of benchmarks can be called the supply-oriented e-government measurements. Half of the benchmarks (1-8) inventoried fall into this group. The focus is on the supply of e-government applications, and the success of a country's e-government is measured by counting the amount of visible applications. A second group of benchmarks (9-11) takes an opposite approach and evaluates the demand side of e-government. These are benchmarks that see e-government success in terms of actual levels of usage ('take-up' levels) or levels of customer satisfaction with online services. A third group of benchmarks (12-16) has the Information Society as a focus. These benchmarks evaluate countries, not only in terms of e-government efforts, but also according to their broader policy for (creating enabling conditions for) the Information Society and/or the Knowledge Economy. A fourth and final cluster (17-18) contains two meta-benchmarks in which criteria and indicators for the measurement of e-government are sought and proposed.

Although the segmentation of benchmarks into four groups provides for a first categorization, differences in country rankings cannot be solely attributed to differences in focus, for even within each category country rankings vary considerably. Rankings should not necessarily be interpreted as 'good-better-best' qualifications. The aim of a benchmark is not always to see who has the 'best' e-government. Other rationales for e-government benchmarking include:

- Finding out if lessons can be learned from other country's e-government policies;
- Measuring e-government progress compared to other countries;
- Identifying and learning from best practices in other countries;
- Discovering global trends in e-government;
- Measuring of underlying e-government concepts to identify points of leverage.

This diversity of underlying goals and focus has its effect on the approach and the outcome of each benchmark. One of the issues that has to be decided from the outset is the construction of a definition of e-government

3.2. The concept of e-government

A crucial step in the activity of measuring e-government is a clear demarcation of the concept itself. E-Government definitions abound, so it is crucial to realise that country rankings from different benchmarks are probably based on different definitions of what is being measured. It is not our intention to formulate yet another definition of e-government. We merely give a descriptive account of how e-government is defined in the benchmarks themselves. These definitions can be placed on a continuum with the following extremes: 'service delivery on the internet' (narrow definition) and 'the use of ICT in the public sector' (broad definition). Table 1 shows that the supply benchmarks indeed mostly define e-government quite narrowly as online service delivery. The demand benchmarks mostly take a somewhat broader perspective, often including aspects of e-participation. The Information Society benchmarks do not measure e-government in a narrow sense, but in some way look at the enabling environment for ICT, thereby often including e-government as one aspect of a broader scale of policy measures. The two e-government indicator benchmarks, finally, are looking at indicators to monitor broader aspects of ICT development.

Benchmarks that limit their view to online service delivery will obviously take into account different indicators than benchmarks that include aspects of process change, back-office development and e-participation. It seems that the inclination to limit the definition of e-government might partly be explained by the difficulties of gathering the information necessary for a broader conception of e-government.

The meagre attention for e-participation in the benchmark studies may also be the result of the narrow focus of most e-government initiatives on service delivery. Citizens can be seen from different perspectives: as subordinated to the law, as consumers of public services, and as partners and co-producers of new policies [9] [10]. Yet, most e-government projects seem to focus on the role of citizens as consumers of public services, and less on the possibilities of ICT to improve the interaction with citizens to develop new policies [11].

Concerning data gathering strategies, it has to be said that most of the benchmarks under consideration use existing, secondary, sources such as studies, national statistics, country reports, website analyses and so on. Again, it seems that –besides the choice of a definition of e-government– also the choice of e-government indicators is often based on the information sources that are easily available.

3.3. Comparing across time and space

Most of the benchmarks under consideration were commissioned out of a concern for comparisons, be it a comparison with one's own position at a previous point in time or be it a comparison with another country or organisation. The benchmarks under consideration are mostly cross-country comparisons that also have a temporal character because of the recurrent (yearly or bi-yearly) replications of the research. Table 1 shows the variety in the number of countries included. Apart from the two meta-benchmarks and the two demand-benchmarks, all benchmarks compare countries, with a pool of countries varying from 6 to 196.

3.4. Indicators for the measurement of e-government

For each of the benchmarks under consideration an inventory of the indicators used

Table 1. The concept of e-government

Focus of the benchmark	Benchmark	Concept of e-government	Number of countries compared
Supply	(1) Accenture [12]. e-government leadership: engaging the customer.	Online service delivery	22
	(2) ASPA, UN division for Public Economics and Public Administration [13]. Benchmarking E-government: A Global Perspective. Assessing the Progress of the UN Member States.	Online service delivery + infrastructure component + human development component	190
	(3) Bertelsmann Foundation [14]. Balanced e-government.	Online service delivery + e-participation component	Separate cases from Canada, USA and Europe
	(4) Central IT unit UK [15]. Benchmarking electronic service delivery.	Online service delivery + back-office (qualitative study, indicators)	13
	(5) Cap Gemini Ernst & Young [16]. Online availability of public services: how does Europe progress?	Online service delivery	17
	(6) Kable [17]. Europe's readiness for e-government.	e-gov = 'when the public sector digitises its processes and interactions'	15
	(7) The office of the e-envoy UK [18]. e-Government. Benchmarking electronic service delivery.	Online service delivery + back-office (qualitative study, indicators)	13
	(8) Worlds Markets Research Center [19]. Global e-government Survey.	Online service delivery	196
Demand	(9) Dialogic Innovation and Interaction [20]. E-government: the demand side. An inventory of the wishes and expectations of citizens on electronic government.	Service delivery + participation	Not applicable, intra country demand
	(10) Dialogic Innovation and Interaction [21]. Let the citizen speak. Judgments and complaints about electronic government.	Service delivery + participation	Not applicable, intra country demand
	(11) Taylor Nelson Sofres [22]. Government Online: an international perspective.	Service delivery	31
Information society	(12) National Office for the Information Economy [23]. The current state of play. Australia's scorecard.	Infrastructure + usage	14
	(13) Booz, Allen & Hamilton [24]. International e-Economy benchmarking. The world's most effective policies for the e-Economy.	Use of ICT to advance social and/or economic development	9
	(14) Harvard University [25]. The networked readiness of nations.	ICT environment	83
	(15) Ministry of Interior Affairs (Netherlands) [26], International ICT benchmark 2002.	ICT environment	6
	(16) The Economist Intelligence Unit [27]. The 2003 e-readiness rankings.	ICT environment	60
e-Gov indicators	(17) Final report of the feasibility study for an ICT-monitor in Flanders [28].	Indicators to measure ICT environment	Not applicable, metabenchmark
	(18) Benchmarking Ireland in the Information Society [29].	Indicators to measure production and use of ICT	Not applicable, metabenchmark

was made. A global comparison of indicators led to the following categorisation of Indicators:

- Input indicators
- Output indicators
- Usage/Intensity indicators
- Impact/Effect indicators
- Environmental/Readiness indicators

Input indicators try to measure the resources countries have invested in e-government. Output indicators do not measure financial resources but instead measure the amount of e-government applications realised. Usage indicators do not measure the amount of applications but their actual usage by citizens/businesses. Impact indicators then, try to measure the impact e-government has had, for example concerning changes in processing time or waiting time. Finally, environmental indicators try to assess the degree to which a country is 'ready' for the Information Society and its consequences.

3.4.1. Input indicators

Examples of input indicators
• Amount of financial resources devoted to e-government. Absolute figures, per capita figures.
• IT/e-government spending as % of GDP
• Amount of resources devoted to research and development
• Amount of public resources devoted to internet infrastructure

In the benchmarks under consideration input indicators seldom get a lot of attention. Most benchmarks limit themselves to a statistic of public IT spending, per capita or as a percentage of GDP. It is often not quite clear how these statistics emerge: how can one separate IT and e-government spending? How can one take into account countries where most IT spending is done in decentralized governments? How can one compare accounting systems of countries that deal differently with IT investments (or instead see them as costs)? One can only conclude that if a statistic is found, it is never entirely comparable with statistics found in other countries.

3.4.2. Output indicators

Examples of output indicators
• Number of online services for citizens
• Number of online services for businesses
• Percentage of government departments that have a website
• Percentage of government websites that offer electronic services

Benchmarks that make use of a broad set of output indicators are mostly those with a limited definition of e-government as online service delivery. The indicators used try to measure the online presence and complexity of services. Complexity is often measured with the categories information, interaction, transaction and integration. Electronic service delivery indeed is one of the most salient features of e-government, so the output indicators are in no way unimportant. There is a danger though that those governments that base their strategy on benchmarks that only include output indicators tend to forget that e-government is more than online service delivery. When governments try to score in those benchmarks they can often do so by 'digitalizing' as many existing services as possible, thereby neglecting the more fundamental process of redefining service delivery in an online environment: you might be better off with less but better services. Pro-active service delivery and so-called zero-stop government might be ingenious ways of approaching government in the information age; output indicators do not value them as they are used in the benchmarks under consideration. A country that has a nice website where citizens can apply for some document online gets higher scores than a country that has improved its back-office and was thereby able to abolish the document (and the need for citizens to apply for it).

3.4.3. Usage indicators

Examples of usage indicators
- Number of individuals that have made use of electronic services offered
- Number of businesses that have made use of electronic services offered
- Percentage of citizens that has visited government websites to search for information
- Number of businesses that have made payments online
- Percentage of internet traffic that pertains to electronic service delivery

Usage indicators try to measure the actual usage or 'take-up' of electronic services offered. In more recent benchmarks, there seems to be an acceptance of the critique on output indicators. The main critique concerns the fact that countries get good grades for making lots of applications but that it does not matter if these applications are actually used by citizens. This is being corrected more and more by the use of usage indicators and by weighing them together with output indicators. This seems to make sense as the result is an evaluation of both the supply of and the demand for e-government in a country.

The usage indicators furthermore, provide for a good monitoring instrument for governments to evaluate the success of different applications and make corresponding strategy decisions. To arrive at a nuanced view of usage, there are often indicators for information seeking, information provision, and transactions.

3.4.4. Impact indicators

Examples of impact indicators
- Reduction of waiting time at government counter x by y %
- Decrease in case processing time at government organisation x by y %
- Citizen/business satisfaction levels concerning e-government
- Survey-type questions, e.g.: 'do you feel more positive to your government, now that you can contact it by email?' 'Has your government become more efficient, now that you can perform services online?'

The use of usage indicators described above already resulted in an overview of actual usage patterns per online service. Impact indicators go even further down the demand side and are used in benchmarks that measure end user satisfaction, but also in benchmarks that evaluate government organisation's efforts. They try to establish some form of impact, be it citizens that are 'happier' or waiting lists that are shorter because of the introduction of e-government. Only a few benchmarks deal with these kinds of indicators. They are, of course, also the hardest to put into practice and require primary data gathering: interviews with citizens, overall evaluations of organisation's efforts. They do measure in a much more direct sense than usage indicators (which represent 'consumer power') the actual satisfaction of end users, or more generally the way that things have been improved because of e-government.

3.4.5. Environmental indicators

Examples of environmental indicators
• ICT penetration rates (pc, internet, mobile phone) private households, work, schools
• Indicator that measures 'fear of invasion of privacy'
• Online shopping rates as an indicator of trust in online environments
• Indicator that measures 'quality of legislation concerning the information society'
• Telephone tariffs, GSM tariffs, Internet access tariffs

The environmental, or 'readiness'-indicators do not measure e-government as such, but instead measure some of the preconditions of a successful e-government. They are indicators of the e-society that is the surrounding environment of e-government, and mostly have to do with ICT infrastructure, ICT skills, trust in ICT and the legal environment. ICT infrastructure is one of the basic requirements of online government and can be measured by indicators such as internet penetration rates, broadband penetration, internet access tariffs, amount of public access points, and so on. ICT skills have to do with the way a country's population is able to handle computers and ICT. A further categorisation here distinguishes ICT skills among citizens, businesses, and civil servants. Another indicator that is sometimes used here concerns the presence of scientific or academic institutions that excel in ICT knowledge.

A third group of environmental indicators indirectly measure trust in online environments by measuring the presence and success of e-business and e-commerce. A final group then, focuses on a country's legal environment and assesses this in the light of the requirements of the information society, dealing for example with the juridical value of an e-mail and with the issues of online identification, online safety and online privacy.

4. Alternative approaches to e-government benchmarking: qualitative versus quantitative methods

The analysis of e-government benchmarks teaches us that a lot of attention is paid to output indicators. Countries are ranked according to the amount of services that are put online. While the front-office is at the center of attention, back-office reforms remain a blind spot. In the perspective of our theoretical framework on benchmarking we can conclude that most of the e-government benchmarks are product-benchmarks. Countries look at the products that are produced by other countries (in this case the amount of online service delivery) and try to copy these products, in order to rise in the next e-government benchmark. As we have seen in the first section of this chapter, this is the first stage of benchmarking. What has happened with the other two stages of benchmarking: the analysis of processes and the improvement of processes? Recently, this lack of interest in back-office processes of e-government has been acknowledged. In this section we will discuss two interesting, although very different, initiatives. The first approach is this of Kunstelj and Vintar from the University of Ljubljana (Slovenia) [30]. These authors developed a quantitative approach to measure progress of the back-office integration of e-government projects. The second approach is a study by Millard *et al* of the Danish Technological Institute and the German Institute für Informationsmanagement of the University of Bremen [31]. This is a qualitative approach. We will briefly discuss these two different approaches and try to learn some lessons about the value of both quantitative and qualitative methods of benchmarking back-office processes.

4.1. Quantitative study of back-office processes

Kunstelj and Vintar draw the conclusion that the slow development of e-government is caused by the lack of attention for back-office reforms [30]. Due to the focus of benchmarking studies on front-office solutions, governments give priority to front-office quick wins over the re-engineering of back-office processes. In an attempt to solve this problem Kunstelj and Vintar propose an alternative method of e-government benchmarking. Their approach has a double goal. First, they want to present a comprehensive method for the evaluation of e-government initiatives that not only focuses on front-office solutions but also takes into account back-office reforms. Second, their model has to be a source for the development of guidelines for the implementation of e-government.

The model proposes indicators at four levels: the environment, the back-office, the front-office and the impact of e-government. Compared to the benchmarking studies from our analysis, the indicators concerning the back-office processes, in particular, are important. To measure the development of the back-office several indicators are proposed. For example the availability and use of information systems in the back-office and the informatization of databases. Also, a method has been developed to quantify the progress of back-office integration. In order to measure back-office integration the approach focuses on service delivery as well as on process reform. For both these aspects, the level of development and the level of integration is measured in a quantitative way. The level of development of a service or a process refers to the level of informatization. Is a service or process carried out manually or automatically (for example pro-active services or a fully automated process)? The level of integration refers to one way in which services and processes are dispersed or integrated. Are services and processes scattered over a lot of different administrations or are they linked to one another? Each dimension is broken up into several stages with a hierarchic structure. The higher a particular service or process is placed in the hierarchy of stages, the higher its score will be. For example, to measure the level of process development a five-stage model was designed: a process can be carried out manually (0 points), partially electronic (1 point), through a workflow with separate information system (2 points), electronically (3 points) or automatically (4 points).

This method goes further than the first stage of benchmarking we mentioned in the first section of this chapter: the benchmarking of products. The method not only looks at products (front-office solutions) but also at the processes behind these products (back-office process reforms). Beside the interest for back-office reforms the method also states clearly that one of its objectives is to be a source of guidelines for the development of e-government. So, processes are not only measured, there is also an attempt to learn from these processes and to transfer knowledge about them. However, the authors are not quite clear about the way in which this knowledge has to be transferred.

4.2. Qualitative study of back-office processes

Millard et al start from a similar position as Kunstelj and Vintar. They argue that there has been little attention for back-office reorganization in general, and for the relation between back-office reorganization and the quality of public services in specific [31]. The objective of their study is threefold. First they want to present good practices of back-office reorganization. Second, they try to demonstrate the relation between back-office reorganization and the quality of public services. Third, attention is paid to the transferability of knowledge about good practices.

Although Millard et al start from the same point of departure as Kunstelj and Vintar, they took a different approach. Whereas Kunstelj and Vintar propose a quantitative benchmark, Millard et al propose a qualitative benchmark. They started with a detailed study of 29 cases spread over different countries and different service clusters. Information was collected by web-research, telephone interviews and face-to-face interviews. Findings from these cases are presented in two ways. First, five management issues are identified (for example the management of change or the way in which user needs are met). For each management issue best practices are described. Second, the cases are presented according to the type of service delivery. In this way, for a certain type of service delivery (for example electronic tax filing) different best practices are elaborated.

The analysis of 29 cases results in the formulation of eight possible back-office reorganization strategies. Millard et al distinguish (1) the digitalization of an unchanged back-office, (2) the reorganization of a back-office, (3) the centralization of the back-office combined with the decentralization of the front-office, (4) a back-office clearing house, (5) generic types of interaction between user and agency, (6) the creation of portals, (7) pro-active services and (8) the creation of user control [31]. The authors describe each strategy and give examples and evidence from their case studies.

Special attention is given to the transfer of knowledge. Because of the qualitative description and analysis of the best practices, practitioners can obtain a detailed and nuanced view on back-office process reorganization. In this way, you do not only identify best practices, but you can also understand them.

Although this benchmarking initiative, at the first glance, seems to be the odd one out in the large pile of benchmarking initiatives, it may very well come the closest to what a real benchmark is supposed to be. According to Waalewijn, Hendriks, and Verzijl the best form of benchmarking is strategic benchmarking. This form of benchmarking focuses on the way in which another company has obtained a certain competitive advantage [4]. So, strategic benchmarking does focus on the products, the processes, and tries to learn from these processes. This is exactly what Millard et al try to do: identify e-government best-practices, try to understand these best-practices and formulate strategies that can be of help for other governments to realize a higher quality of public services.

4.3. Quantitative and qualitative benchmarking: two sides of the same medal

To end this chapter on e-government benchmarking we want to analyze the difference between a quantitative and a qualitative approach of e-government benchmarking. The most important criticism that emerged from our analysis was that most of the benchmarks do not pay attention to back-office reforms. Now, the two benchmarks mentioned above do both specifically pay attention to the back-office of an e-government project. However, the first developed a quantitative approach while the second developed a qualitative approach. What is the best way? Probably a combination of both.

A quantitative approach poses some severe problems. A first problem is the risk for goal-displacement [5]. When a quantitative benchmark has been established, the risk exists that countries do not focus on the best strategy to develop their e-government program, but on the way in which they can rise in a ranking. So, the goal of improving public services is displaced by the goal of doing well in a ranking. A second problem with quantitative benchmarks is their impossibility to give a nuanced view on e-government developments. Because all countries are measured with the same (rather general and abstract) instrument, differences between countries, administrations or services are not taken into account. A third problem is the lack of explanatory power of a quantitative benchmark. A quantitative benchmark can tell you which country is doing better or worse than another, but does not explain the reasons why.

A qualitative benchmark can give an answer to the shortfalls of a quantitative benchmark. In, for example, case studies of different e-government initiatives a lot of attention can be paid to the context and the particularities of a project. A qualitative benchmark has a lot more explanatory power than a quantitative benchmark has. However, a qualitative benchmark has its own weaknesses. A great advantage of a quantitative benchmark is the pressure it puts on organizations to perform better. This is a very important characteristic, especially in the public sector were there often is no, or little, external pressure on public administrations to perform better. Public sector organizations often have a monopoly and citizens often are compelled to make use of a public service (for example paying income taxes) [32]. As this is the case, there is no battle for customers for a lot of public sector organizations, as there is for private sector organizations. A quantitative benchmark, with a ranking, can function as a substitute of these forms of pressure: it can create competition between different administrations to improve the quality of their service delivery.

As both quantitative and qualitative approaches of e-government benchmarking have their advantages and disadvantages the best way to benchmark e-government practices is a combination of both methods.

5. Conclusion

We can distinguish several forms of benchmarking: the benchmarking of products, processes and strategies. When we translate this distinction to e-government benchmarking we see an interesting evolution. During the period 2000-2003 a lot of e-government benchmarks looked at the products of the e-government policy: the front-office presence of a government in the form of a website or electronic service delivery.

Benchmarks measured mainly the amount of services that were put online, but had limited attention for the processes in the back-office.

Recently more attention is paid to the back-office processes and strategies. In 2004 two initiatives were undertaken in which the back-office processes were at the center of attention. These benchmarks did not only look at the front-office products of e-government, but also at the back-office process improvements. The question that these benchmarks try to answer is not only what and how many services are available on-line, but how can one innovate the processes behind these services? In a next step these benchmarks try to deduce strategies for a good e-government policy. Which strategy does a government follow to obtain a radical improvement of its on-line service delivery and back-office processes? Which strategies seem to be the most successful?

Although both benchmarks focused at the understanding of processes, they had a different approach: one benchmark was quantitative while the other one was qualitative. Both methods seem to have advantages as well as disadvantages. However, the disadvantages of a qualitative approach can be overcome by the advantages of a quantitative approach and vice versa. In this way, the best way to benchmark e-government probably is a combination of a qualitative analysis of process improvement and strategy formulation, combined with a quantitative analysis that can put pressure on governments to improve their e-government policy.

References

[1]   D. Janssen, S. Rotthier, and K. Snijkers, *Benchmarken van eGovernment (Benchmarking of eGovernment)* Steunpunt Bestuurlijke Organisatie Vlaanderen, Leuven, 2003.

[2]   T. Bendell, L. Boulter and P. Goodstadt, *Benchmarking for competitive advantage* Financial Times Pitman Publishing, London, 1998.

[3]   R. Camp, *Benchmarking. Het zoeken naar de beste werkmethoden die leiden tot superieure prestaties (Benchmarking. The search for industry best practices that lead to superior performance,* Kluwer, Deventer, 1992.

[4]   Ph. Waalewijn and B.W.C.M. Kamp, *Strategische benchmarking. Wie durft de vergelijking aan? (Strategic benchmarking. Who dares to be compared?),* Erasmus Universiteit Rotterdam. RIBES, Rotterdam, 1994.

[5]   C.J. McNair and K.H.J. Leibfried, *Benchmarking. A tool for continuous improvement,* Harper Business, New York, 1992.

[6]   J. Prins, *Zoek, rapporteer, vergelijk en verbeter! (Find, report, compare, and improve!),* Stichting Moret fonds, Rotterdam, 1997.

[7]   Ph. Waalewijn, A. Hendriks and R. Verzijl, *Benchmarking van het benchmarking-proces (Benchmark the benchmark process),* Erasmus Universiteit Rotterdam. RIBES, Rotterdam, 1996.

[8]   G. Bouckaert, N. Thijs and S. Vandeweyer, *Kwaliteit in de overheid (Quality in the public sector)* Academia Press, Gent, 2003.

[9]   E. Vigoda-Gadot, From responsiveness to collaboration: governance, citizens and the next generation of public administration, in E. Vigoda-Gadot and A. Cohen (Eds.), *Citizenship and management in public administration,* Edward Elgar, Cheltenham, 2004.

[10] R. Maes, Political and administrative innovations as a social project: the Belgian case, in A. Hondeghem (Ed.), *Ethics and accountability in a context of governance and new public management,* IOS Press, Amsterdam, 1998.

[11] S. Zouridis and M. Thaens, Reflections on the anatomy of E-Government, in V. Bekkers and V. Homburg (Eds.), *The information ecology of e-government* IOS Press, Amsterdam, 2005.

[12] Accenture (2003). e-government leadership: engaging the customer

[13] UN Division for Public Economics and Public Administration (UNDPEPA*), Benchmarking E-government: A Global Perspective. Assessing the Progress of the UN Member States.*

[14] Bertelsmann Foundation, *Balanced eGovernment, 2002.*

[15] Central IT Unit, *Benchmarking electronic service delivery,* UK, 2000.

[16] Cap Gemini Ernst & Young, *Online availability of public services: how does Europe progress?*, 2003.
[17] Kable, *Europe's readiness for eGovernment*, 2000.
[18] The Office of the E-Envoy, *Egovernment. Benchmarking electronic service delivery*, UK, 2001.
[19] Worlds Markets Research Center (2001). Global *e*Government Survey.
[20] Dialogic Innovation and Interaction, E-*government: the demand side. An inventory of the wishes and expectations of citizens on electronic government*, 2001.
[21] Dialogic Innovation and Interaction, *Let the citizen speak. Judgments and complaints about electronic government*, 2002.
[22] Taylor Nelson Sofres, *Government Online: an international perspective*, 2002.
[23] National Office for the Information Economy, *The current state of play. Australia's scorecard*, 2002.
[24] Booz, Allen & Hamilton, *International e-Economy benchmarking. The world's most effective policies for the e-economy*, 2002.
[25] Harvard University, *The networked readiness of nations*, 2003.
[26] Ministry of Interior Affairs (Netherlands), *International ICT benchmark 2002*.
[27] Economist Intelligence Unit, *The 2003 e-readiness rankings*
[28] Final report of the feasibility study for an ICT-monitor in Flanders.
[29] Benchmarking Ireland in the Information Society.
[30] M. Kunstelj and M. Vintar, *Evaluating the progress of e-government development: critical analysis of current approaches,* Paper presented at the EGPA 2004 annual conference, Ljubljana, 2004.
[31] J. Millard, J.S. Iversen, H. Kubicek, H. Westholm, and R. Cimander, *Reorganisation of Government Back Offices for Better Electronic Public Services - European Good Practices. Final report to the European Commission,* Danish Technological Institute en Institut für Informationsmanagement GmbH, University of Bremen, Brussels, 2004.
[32] A. Scheepers & C. Kommers. De overheid als dienstverlenende instelling (The government as a service provider), in A. Zuurmond, J. Huigen, P.H.A. Frissen, I.Th.M. Snellen and P.W. Tops (Eds.), *Informatisering in het openbaar bestuur (Informatization in the public sector,* Vuga Uitgeverij, 's-Gravenhage, 1994.

Part 3

Impact on Democracy and Accountability

Developments in e-Government
D. Griffin et al. (Eds.)
IOS Press, 2007

e-Democracy: An "e" Too Far?

Dan REMENYI and Diana WILSON
Trinity College, Dublin, Eire

1. From e-government to e-democracy

There is no doubt that we are on an intellectual treadmill and that it is a full time job to keep up with some of the ideas related to the Internet and the web which are being produced today.

As we have come to terms with e-government and we have started to really appreciate the opportunities and challenges this technology has offered us, a new set of ideas provided by the application of the Internet and the Web or other aspects of ICT march out of the intellectual production line. This new set of ideas and concepts, which is of special interest to those who are concerned with the application of technology to government, is referred to as e-democracy and in some circles it is believed that this will be even more important to our society than e-commerce and e-business ever was. And if e-democracy does succeed it will certainly have a major impact on our society.

Although sometimes mistakenly regarded as being the same as or at least very similar to e-government, e-democracy is really quite different[1]. Whereas e-government addresses the way the Internet and the Web facilitates the administration of our society as government both central and local affects it, e-democracy concerns itself with the facilitation of political processes. Political processes in democracies involve the changing of our rulers, the creation and administration of laws, and the formulation of policy. Thus the political processes and not the services offered by government are the focal point of e-democracy. But despite the differences between e-government and e-democracy there are links between these two concepts. In the first place it is probably that before the citizenry would take up the use of e-democracy, whose benefits may be rather intangible, it will be necessary for there to have been some clear successes in e-government, whose benefits are certainly more tangible. As is well known, success with e-government is quite patchy with there being many e-government systems and not that many e-government users. There is also the fact that there is potentially a much larger number of citizen activities and processes who could benefit from e-government than from e-democracy. In the e-government arena many citizens need to interface on a fairly regular basis with tax collectors, health services, education authorities to mention only three government departments. The need to vote is a much less frequent requirement – maybe once every other year if we include national and local elections[2].

It is also clear that from the point of view of a government Information Systems manager the development of e-democracy systems will be regarded as yet another set of e-government software. It is also correct to say that the implementation of laws and policies created by a government is influenced by the type of democracy that they have. Thus for these three reasons it can be argued that there is, at least some overlap between e-government and e-democracy.

2. Ideas of democracy

Those who read this paper will hardly need reminding of the difficulties in defining democracy and in understanding its various manifestations. As Nugent [1] pointed out "There is no single accepted definition of what a healthy democracy ..... should look like". We refer to the political processes in the USA and the United Kingdom as both being democratic, although in many ways they are really different. We describe the voting system (first passed the post) in Great Britain as being democratic as we also describe the Irish system (proportional representation with a single transferable vote in multi-seat constituencies). We say that the Swiss system, which relies on regular referenda or plebiscites, and the British system, where these populist events are virtually once in a lifetime happenings, are both democratic. In thinking about the meaning of the word democratic it is also worth mentioning that it has sometimes been hijacked and applied in countries such as the German Democratic Republic (or in Germany the Deutsche Demokratische Republik[3]- the old East Germany) and South Africa under apartheid (by defining black people to be aliens in their own land apartheid leaders argued that their government was democratic) which could hardly be considered democratic by any objective observer[4].

In this paper we use the word democratic to refer to a political process that normally leads to a government that has the best interests of the majority of the people at heart[5]. This is much the same as the description of government articulated by Abraham Lincoln at Gettysburg when he referred to government of the people, by the people and for the people. This implies an environment where the rule of law prevails; civil rights are important; government, police and soldiers are held to account; governments can be changed without resort to *coup d'etats*; there is an independent judiciary or separation of powers; where there is freedom of speech and freedom of faith and the right to organize new pressure groups including political parties.

Underlying these characteristics of democracy is the fact that they all work most effectively when appropriate information about our society is freely and rapidly available. It has often been said that democracy thrives on information. In fact information fuels democracy. When information is cut off or when dis-information is spread about the democratic process cannot function properly. The concept of the 'informed electorate' can be traced back to Plato and reaches its apogee in the 'Jeffersonian Ideal' whereby just such an informed populace makes its decisions based on the free exchange of sound information and thoughtful deliberation. Too much information can be a liability and that is perhaps a separate issue. But modern sophisticated democracies do need some ability to focus the enormous amount of information available and be able to interpret relevant facts from fatuous gossip.

Making information readily available is of course to a considerable extent where the "e" comes in the democratic equation and we find ourselves needing to come to terms with the concepts of e-democracy.

Nor is a simple matter to define e-democracy. According to Steven Clift [2:1]:

> *"e-democracy represents the use of information and communication technologies and strategies by democratic actors (governments, elected officials, the media, political organizations, citizen/voters) within political and governance processes of local communities, nations and on the international stage. To many, e-democracy suggests greater and more active citizen participation enabled by the Internet, mobile communications, and other*

*technologies in today's representative democracy as well as through more
participatory or direct forms of citizen involvement in addressing public
challenges."*

This wide-ranging description of e-democracy certainly gives some feel for the
fact that the subject may be seen to have a very broad scope.

3. The processes of democracy

The actual processes of democracy involve *inter alia* debating, campaigning and
canvassing, lobbying and of course voting. These processes can all apply to local or
city government, regional, national and even trans-national government. The amount of
value e-democracy will deliver will depend upon how enthusiastically these systems
are welcomed by the citizens and residents. But each of these processes at each of these
levels can be facilitated by the use of the Internet and the Web, which is now
extensively used in many democracies.
Let us consider these issues one at a time.

3.1. The challenge of e-debating

It is clear that political debate at its best needs to be conducted face to face. The great
debates between politicians standing of 'soap boxes' in front of mass audiences during
the last part of the 19th and the early part of the 20th century epitomized debate at its
best. These days are certainly gone. Today we only see our politicians debating on
television in a very contrived and orchestrated manner.
It is no longer easy to attend a political debate and even if one does there is no
guarantee that members of the audience will be given adequate time to present their
views. This is where e-debating can come in. e-debating can open up the discussion to
a much larger group of people, independent of location and time and directly facilitated
by tools such as chat rooms, e-conferences, e-mails and posting of information to web
pages. The Internet and the Web certainly has the potential of opening up debate so that
those who have difficultly in traveling to a debating venue at a particular time can still
participate [1]. But will many people be prepared to become engaged in this type of
non-face-to-face forum [3]? There is no doubt that some people will. But it is unlikely
that e-debating will ever become a significant element in political discourse. There are
various reasons for this including the fact that for many people communication in
writing is simply no substitute for the entertainment or maybe emotional value of the
type of argument which occurs when political opponents face each other in a verbal
confrontation. There is also the considerable problem that e-debating as it currently
stands mostly requires the use of a keyboard and this is seen as a major obstacle by
many people - there are still large sections of the population who are not keyboard
competent and who have no intention of ever becoming such.
Through Voice Over Internet Protocols (VOIP) it is possible to obtain very
inexpensive telephone links, which will allow conversations to take place at a fraction
of normal cost. Cost of telephone conferencing is also on the decline. This may attract
more people to enter the political debate but it is not entirely clear how effective this
type of discussion really is.

There may be a more specific role for e-debating in special circumstances. For example at this time an e-Debate between the Minster for Education, the heads of the universities and other stakeholders including student leaders could offer a useful forum in which to discuss student fees. e-debating can certainly deliver a group who cannot directly attend a meeting but it is not at all clear whether this will be an effective way of debating and whether it will actually be used by the citizenry. Bulletin boards, Special Interest Groups and Blogs can be described at this moment as platforms for self-expression (as opposed to genuine interaction to understand the points of view of others) at one end of the spectrum or full interaction and debate, albeit by a minority of participants, at the other. But having said that the use of these arenas as interactive discussion in political discourse is certainly on the increase and perhaps this will be the way forward for interesting debates in the future.

3.2. e-Consultation to get closer to the citizen

e-Consultation is another way of employing the technology. Some pundits of how the government will absorb ICT claim that e-consultation will be one of the most important applications. The supporters of this view believe that the technology allow ideas to be expressed in a much less threatened environment when it is conducted impersonally across the Internet. This is said to be especially true when very sensitive issues are being addressed such as drugs, child abuse or violence within the family.

The counter argument to this points out that very sensitive subjects such as these mentioned above require the presence of a sympathetic person before any of the real issues are aired.

It would seem that there is probably some sense in both of these views and that e-consultation will not replace the personal touch. Furthermore, in countries with a strong and long tradition of 'clientilism[6], the 'personal touch' which serves the mutual interests of both the elected and electorate at a local level, it will take some time to accept the idea of the 'digital parish pump'. With regards the other issues related to e-consultation one of the worries is that the cost of the technology which is still too high will disadvantage certain groups in our society.

Another term which is sometimes used in connection with e-consultation is e-participation. The logic behind this is that if citizens are being consulted then they are at least to some extent participating in the democratic process. But the point is that consultation is definitely a necessary condition for democracy, but it is hardly a necessary and sufficient condition. Participation implies much more than simple consulting and perhaps here lies one of the rubs. ICT will not in any way guarantee participation, even of those for whom the technology is completely and easily available.

3.3. Will e-canvassing work?

Campaigning and canvassing can certainly be conducted with the help of the Internet. In addition politicians are increasingly using their own web pages to promote themselves. It is interesting to note that Google.com found 726,000 web references when Irish Politicians was entered and it found 3,870,000 web references when British Politicians was entered. Given the relative difference in the size of the population this suggests a much greater interest in using the website by politicians and those interested in political comment in Ireland than in England.

When it comes to campaigning and canvassing, this is a matter of voters being contacted by candidates and their supporters with requests to vote for them or the person that they represent. Under this heading we can also include the creation of websites that contain information concerning the policies of the candidate as well as details of his or her track record. This type of website would reinforce traditional brochures and paper pamphlets. It is however not likely that e-campaigning and e-canvassing will ever have anything like the same impact as the real thing. The candidate's physical presence and his or her ability to appear empathetic to the voter is what really counts.

An example of using the Internet for e-canvassing was provided by Bill Jones in the 2002 California Governors election. The following is an extract from an e-mail sent out by Bill Jones:

"This is a new and unique experiment. For the first time in history I am trying to make the Internet the vehicle to provide information to the people of California - NOT 30 second TV ads.

I believe that Democracy is enhanced when the voter has factual information instead of propaganda and that the Internet has the power to transform politics and political campaigning.

So while other candidates for Governor are spending over $10,000,000 dollars on 30 second TV ads, I am trying something new. What's new is this? I am only going to provide you with the facts on my record. Please go to my website and check it out for yourself."

However this e-mail was not appreciated by everyone who received it and the following is some correspondence to this effect.

"I was sort of shocked to find TWO emails in my box from two different "spamming" email addresses in regards to Bill Jones for governor. First, I don't live in California. Second, I hate spam. Third, I hate getting the same spam more than once. And fourth, whatever my political affiliations, I wouldn't like ANY politician spamming me. Call me crazy, but don't we all get enough unsolicited email?

Perhaps Mr. Jones needs to have a chat with his campaign managers in regards to this new way of harassing voters?[7]"

Clearly it is so easy and so inexpensive to dispatch e-mails it will be quite important to use this type of canvassing approach very sparingly as unsolicited e-mails, as demonstrated above will be regarded as Spam [4] and may well have the effect of deterring voters from supporting the candidate. In fact it is not difficult to imagine mischief being done to a candidate's campaign by his or her opponents flooding voters with unwanted Spam purporting to come from the other candidate/s[8]. This is a form of identity theft which is on the increase and which is not easy to halt. However the law is taking this crime increasingly seriously with substantial penalties being handed down (http://news.bbc.co.uk/1/hi/world/americas/4163237.stm). Unfortunately it is virtually impossible to prevent this type of activity. Of course election complaint procedures may be put in place and penalties can be imposed on candidates who violate the rules if proof can be determined.

3.4. Is e-lobbying the way forward?

When individuals come together on a particular topic, whether it be Pigeon Fancying for Cat Owners or Supporters for Global Warming, two things seem to happen; they share and grow information and they raise the awareness and interest of others who are not in their group. Statistics show [5] that people who are members of groups are more politically aware and informed; they have to be, because eventually on various levels, political decisions, whether local or national, will affect them. Due to their clout, or potential clout, they may be courted by politicians and officials. Therein lies a teasing contradiction: the phenomenon of the single issue against the collective ideology. As it becomes difficult to see the differences between the various political parties' policies and ideals (indeed, as politicians seem increasingly reluctant to espouse any at all) and they all homogenize into a type of 'lowest-common-denominator politics' [6], the Internet allows for millions of diverse, heterogenic, and fragmented voices to be heard.

Websites are also lobbying tools and e-lobbying will continue to grow to be a substantial industry of its own. Websites such as www.ash.org (Action on Smoking and Health), www.greenpeace.org and www.foei.org (Friends of the Earth) are three well-established examples of lobbing websites. But of course making the information available about the issue is only part of the lobbying process and like campaigning and canvassing the personal touch will always be required. Nonetheless, informative and engaging websites will become an increasing part of the lobbying process and as high bandwidth becomes increasingly available these e-lobbying websites will increasingly contain attractive graphics and video[9].

e-lobbying will also increasingly be done by e-mail. In the words of President George W Bush:-

> *"See I believe in the power of the people. I truly do. I do. I believe that that when you e-mail a congressman or a senator it makes at difference. It makes a difference*[10]*."*

However it is not all that clear how much the congressmen and senators are supportive of this type of communication as the potential to be overwhelmed by e-mail is very real[11].

Another aspect of e-lobbying is the ability to use this technology for the purposes of expanding the opportunity for consultation[12] and this would seem to be an area in which there has already been some success [7].

3.5. e-Voting – the central issue?

To some e-voting is a primary objective of e-democracy. According to Robin Cook [8] in the consultation paper on a policy for electronic democracy there are two main issues, which are e-participation and e-voting. And there are many who hope that e-voting will be able, some how, to revive the waning interest in democracy in the western world[13]. In the last general elections in the Republic of Ireland in 2002 only 65% of the population entitled to vote actually bothered to so do. In the United Kingdom in the 2001 general election it was only 59% who turned out to vote. According to the Electoral Commissions Website (http://www.electoralcommission.gov.uk/your-vote/)

"There has been much talk about 'voter apathy'. But we believe that the reasons for low rates of participation in elections are more complicated than this. Research shows that people do not vote for a number of reasons - including lack of information, distrust of politicians and inconvenience."

Members of government as well as politicians hope that the provision of e-voting with its obvious convenience, to some members of the community, will bring voters back into the democratic process[14]. But it is not clear how realistic this expectation is. It appears to be likely that e-voting will actually develop quite rapidly. This technology will be used as one of the mechanisms for electing representatives at local, regional, national and trans-national levels. Of course it is most unlikely that e-voting will ever become the sole means whereby an individual will state his or her preference for a party or a candidate [9]. In fact it is unlikely that more than a relatively small percentage of the electorate will choose to use this means of voting [10]. But e-voting will to some extent speed up the counting [11], reduce errors and possibly eventually reduce costs which is always important in democracies. It has been suggested that e-voting will have an effect on reducing voter apathy, but this is questionable. It is very easy to let the imagination run away when speculating on the impact and the benefits of the Internet and the Web and it may be that this suggestion of apathy reduction is to some considerable extent wishful thinking. The convenience of being able to vote from one's office and/or one's home or from a hotel room may induce a few additional voters who have found it difficult to get to a polling station to cast a vote. But the majority of those who currently do not vote are not likely to flock to e-voting just because of the convenience factor. The reduction in the popularity of voting is probably a reflection or a result of a process of deep disillusionment, which is not directly linked to the inconvenience of the process of "manual" voting. Many who do not vote are of the view that the differences between the candidates is not material and that their participation in the political process has no effect on the outcome or the policies, which will be implemented. This is referred to by Angell [12] as the sameness of the current democratic system. Angell [12] also talks about the "false opposites" of the system.

There are many reasons why the numbers flocking to the polls to vote are on the decline. Many worry about the sincerity and perhaps even the integrity of the political establishments. The cash for honours scandal (http://news.bbc.co.uk/1/hi/uk_politics/4918388.stm) which currently plagues the United Kingdom is only the current manifestation of questionable conduct of politicians. Leading politicians like Geoffrey Archer (http://news.bbc.co.uk/1/hi/talking_point/1448486.stm) and Jonathan Aitkin (http://news.bbc.co.uk/1/hi/uk_politics/593724.stm) have actually "spent time at Her Majesty's pleasure". Neil Hamilton was disgraced over accusations concerning the cash for questions dispute but was not prosecuted (http://news.bbc.co.uk/1/hi/uk_politics/1485089.stm). These types of scandals do not encourage the population to esteem the political process and this results in declining votes.

And there is a darker side to e-voting. The current system which required citizens to go to a private voting booth ensures privacy and confidentiality i.e. a secret ballot. Most countries consider this to be a major platform on which democracy is built. Voting in the home or in the office will automatically reduce the degree of privacy and confidentiality and the secret ballot will go out the window. This would be a very poor development in the process of democracy as parents, husbands and wives, brothers and sisters as well as bosses and colleagues could try to directly interfere in the voting preferences of individuals who were not sufficiently confident or assertive to remain uninfluenced. There is also something 'affirming and humbling' [6:100] in physically going to a community polling station to vote.

> *"And yet when I stand in the voting booth, facing choices I'd rather not have to make and cast a vote in an election that will turn out the same if I exit the booth without voting, the fact that I am merely one person in a land of other people is humbling and affirming. I am merely one, but I **am** one"*[6, p100].

In the age of 'bowling alone' and 'cocooning', this rare opportunity to connect physically and visually with our neighbors in a collective act should perhaps be welcomed and encouraged and maybe even protected.

It is also thought in some quarters that e-voting will lead to a plethora of formal referenda and plebiscites[15] , but this does seem to be rather unlikely as the use of these populist approaches to measuring public opinion are highly culturally based and the availability of new technology will probably have little or no impact on the frequency with which they are used. It is possible however that the e-voting technology will allow politicians to have, if they so wish, continuous access to public opinion through online opinion polls or even focus groups. It is not clear how popular this would actually be with politicians, as they tend to be suspicious of opinion polls and generally give them more attention only when they support their policies[16]. Thus it is not clear that this would be an important feature of e-democracy. In any event in our society it is well established that we want a gap for reflection between public opinion and law and policymaking. Few people would consider it "a good thing" if our politicians were continually pressurized by online opinion polls. If our politicians were to simply follow public opinion it is likely we would be hanging murderers until they were dead[17]. But when we reflect on this matter we generally agree that capital punishment is not really a satisfactory way to handle such crimes. Frequently the error potential inherent in our criminal justice system is just too great for such drastic punishment.

3.6. e-Democracy and enhanced decision making

It is also said in some circles that the tools provided by e-democracy will lead to enhanced decision making. This is one of the drivers of the e-Cabinet initiative. Whether computer aided decision-making leads to better or more efficient or effective courses of action is a highly contentious matter and the different schools of thought on this subject argue robustly. Certainly the application of artificial intelligence as a decision making device, except in the simplest environments, is in such an embryonic state that it is not worthy of serious consideration now and this technology is unlikely to be perfected even in the medium term. Decision support systems, which have been on the corporate agenda since the 1970s are not universally agreed to have been all that satisfactory and there is no reason to believe that they will be anymore successful in supporting democratic processes. Of course group decision support systems have some potential to help in decision-making but it is possible that in political circles these types of tools, which have been designed for anonymous voting among executives, will not be popular, especially as far as party bosses are concerned. Thus as an aspect of e-democracy computer facilitated decision-making or problem solving is not likely to deliver enormous value in the short term.

3.7. Major challenges

These five or six primary aspects of e-democracy - that is e-debating, e-campaigning and e-canvassing, e-lobbying, e-consultation and e-voting all offer major challenges if they are to work in a satisfactory way. The technology is available to deliver these applications. However in a matter as important as e-voting it will be essential that the systems be highly secure. This will mean additional protection against hackers and viruses and other attempts to disrupt these systems. Protecting these systems is expensive. But without adequate security an e-voting system will not have an appropriate level of confidence and would then be unlikely to be used. Perhaps even worse if an e-voting system was used and then it was shown to have been compromised there could be several different types of political crises and the need to revert to manual systems. It is easy to imagine Ukrainian type re-elections being needed because the population had lost confidence in the e-voting mechanisms.

It will be necessary to impose strict rules relating to acceptable behavior in e-debating, e-canvassing and e-lobbing.

With regards to the skills required by the citizen it is not intrinsically difficult to master the Internet and the Web but the challenge of encouraging the use of these systems by a substantial number of citizens should not be underestimated. There are still many people who are cyber-phobic and will remain so for the rest of their lives. For a lot of citizens it will take time to really appreciate the value of e-democracy. In many circles there is a deep rooted suspicion of the Internet and Web technology. There is concern about trusting what one sees on web pages. Especially there are worries about confidentiality. In democracies it is generally held that secret balloting is very important if not essential[18] and it is not clear how credible this is using Internet and Web technology. Thus there are many non-technical issues, which will have to be addressed, and solutions will have to be found. Making e-democracy work will need a lot of hard work with citizens of all ages and all classes. Nonetheless with the right will and some perseverance these problems will be overcome – they surely should not be underestimated.

4. Summary and conclusion

The jury on e-democracy is definitely still out. It could go either way. It is certainly not going to be easy to make e-democracy work. It is not by any means certain that the application of "e" technology to this aspect of our lives will actually succeed. e-democracy could be just a pipe dream of the cyberphiles i.e. it could be an application too far and it might just flop – fall on its face. The 'ease and speed' with which the electorate can engage with its elected representatives is increased indeed; but so too is the potential for the government to monitor and use surveillance on its electorate. The recent flight of the Airbus 380 has been hailed a great success but at the same time it has also been proclaimed as the biggest commercial risk ever undertaken. It is quite possible that it is no bigger a risk than all those governments and all those vendors and consultants who have invested in e-democracy. The challenges e-democracy faces are truly substantial. Amongst other things a thorough risk analysis needs to be performed.

On the other hand e-democracy can be seen as just another step towards the information society, which many believe will bring a greater level of welfare to our communities. Of course there is still some debate as to what actually constitutes an information society. In our view an information society is one in which citizens and other residents have increased opportunities for education, health, careers, leisure, security etc., through the greater provision of access to and use of information. An information society implies the availability of suitable computer hardware and software, the ease of access to appropriate telecommunication lines and a population sufficiently computer literate and information savvy to be able to take advantage of the benefits of this technology. It also implies a wide range of e-business, e-government and perhaps e-democracy activities. Before a country can claim to be an information society it is necessary for a substantial majority of the population to be in a position to use this technology and have a wide range of applications at its disposal. It is also necessary that malware[19] be brought under control.

It seems that we have already made considerable progress with e-business and e-government. By introducing systems which facilitate e-democracy it is hoped that we will effectively be moving further towards an information society and that this is why many are enthusiastic about initiatives to launch e-democracy at the various levels from local government to trans-national government. However from the above it is clear that the Internet and the Web will not, *per se*, change the democratic processes themselves, or make a great impact on how politics are regarded. We are very unlikely to have massively more referenda or plebiscites, nor will we have a surge in the rate of turnout for voting because the old paper and pencil system has been replaced by e-voting. The voters will come back to the polls when they have some person and some issues for which they feel strongly.

However there are benefits to be gained by the use of this technology and if it is implemented carefully these may certainly be obtained.

Endnotes

1. Not all authors would agree that e-government and e-democracy are distinctly different issues. Vedel [13:227] suggest that e-democracy began in the 1950s and describes their function as "powerful tools to process big amounts of data".

2. The boundaries of e-government and e-democracy are actually quite tricky. It has been suggested that it might be possible to extend the "e" of government activities by even moving to an e-Parliament. In the United Kingdom this would certainly go someway towards removing or limiting the club nature of the current institution. Of course an e-Parliament might not suit the Government Whips. In the Republic of Ireland an e-Cabinet initiative has been launched and we await with interest to hear of progress for this project.

3 Of course the leaders of the German Democratic Republic would have argued strongly that their form of government was democratic and in terms of their worldview and their definitions, indeed they would have considered their political processes as such.

4. It has been pointed out that the proportion of white people who dominated the South African political process under the apartheid system was greater than the proportion of the population who participated in Athenian democracy. This does not justify referring to apartheid South Africa as democratic but rather wondering about the claims of ancient Athens to have been democratic. Relative to Sparta of course, Athens was indeed democratic which leads us to the conclusion that democracy is, perhaps, a relative term.

5. There would be some debate or even dispute about this type of description of democracy as there would be those that argue that the best we can expect is a government which is responsive to interest groups in the society. Some would say that in a democracy the government should implement the will of the people. Certainly the events in the United Kingdom which lead up to the 2nd Gulf War demonstrate that the government did not follow the will of the people.

6. "Clientelism refers to a form of social organization common in many developing regions characterized by "patron-client" relationships. In such places, relatively powerful and rich "patrons" promise to provide relatively powerless and poor "clients" with jobs, protection, infrastructure, and other benefits in exchange for votes and other forms of loyalty including labor". http://www.uwsp.edu/cnr/gem/ambassador/what_is_clientelism.htm

7. More details of this correspondence are available at: http://www.cipherwar.com/news/02/bill_jones_spam.htm

8. A positive e-canvassing website can be found at http://www.dail-eireann.com/cand_new.asp

9. It is worth mentioning that e-lobbying has been developed by a number of groups who have wanted to bring the negative aspects of businesses to the worlds attention. http://www.mcspotlight.org/ points out that "McDonald's spends over $2 billion a year broadcasting their glossy image to the world. There are actually 53,200 anti McDonalds references in google.com and some 296,000 anti Disney references. This is a small space for alternatives to be heard." http://www.untied.com performs the same function for United Airlines. The anti-Livingston (Mayor of London) site is also worth mentioning and this is at

http://www.sod-u-ken.com/ . One can well imaging a glut of these websites being created to encourage gossip about politicians when e-democracy really gets going.

10 These words are at http://www.vote.com/ on the audio link.

11 At a round table discussion at the International Conference on e-Government at the University of Pittsburgh on 12-13 October 2006, the problems of receiving 10,000 or perhaps even 20,000 e-mails was discussed. Such volumes overloads the system and the impact of the e-mails is effectively lost. E-Mailing a Representative or a Senator is seen by many to be a pseudo or wasted communication.

12 Queensland Government: e-democracy policy framework, available at http://www.qld.gov.au/edemocracy, accessed May 20, 2003

13 The 2004 US Presidential election produced a very high turnout with Bush obtaining nearly 61 million votes against Kerry's 58 million. Some argue that when the election is about important differences then the electorate is not apathetic.

14 The term e-voting is being used to cover a wide range of electronic devices which can facilitate the recording and the counting of votes. The Direct Recording Electronic (DRE) voting system purchased for use in Ireland is produced by a British-Dutch conglomerate called Nedap/Powervote. See http://www.election.nl/bizx_html/IVS-GB/. Another supplier in the USA is Diebold see http://www.forbes.com/2006/10/17/election-security-fraud-tech-security-xx_ll_1017voting.html?partner=tentech_newsletter

15 It has also been suggested that there will be a mass of informal referenda and there are two ways of seeing this. One perspective says that it will be a good thing to allow individuals to canvass support for their ideas and in so doing discover how much or how little support there is for their ideas. The other view is that we may be inundated with fatuous statistics on obscure subjects.

16 There is little doubt that institutions such as the media will increase the use of on-line voting to determine the popularity of policies of both the government and oppositions.

17. In England when a high court judge, dressed in his red sash, sentenced someone to death he would put a black cap (known as the doomsters cap although it looked like a black handkerchief) on his head and said something to the effect of "You will be taken from this place to another and there you will remain until the appointed date and time until you are hanged by the neck until you are dead".

18. In the United Kingdom the present system of voting allow ballot papers to be traced back to individual voters. The following comment was received from an informal reviewer concerning how the British government has used this ability to know which way people have voted in the past:- You also wrote "In democracies it is generally held that secret balloting is very important". Not in the UK it isn't. Before I emigrated, on two separate occasions I was told by Special Branch officers how I had voted in a general election. I don't know the details of the UK e-voting trials, but I am willing to bet money that they will not compromise the ability of the state to know how every citizen votes."

19. Malware is the current buzz word for viruses, spams, scams and spyware.

References

[1]   J.D. Nugent, If e-democracy is the answer, what's the question?, *National Civic Review*, **90**, 3 (2001), 221 – 233.

[2]   S. Clift, *Top Ten e-democracy 'To Do List' for Government Around the World*, 2000, Available at http://www.e-democracy.org/do

[3]   J.W. Cavanaugh, (2000), e-democracy: Thinking about the Impact of Technology on Civic Life, *National Civic Review*, **89**, 3 (2000), 229 – 234.

[4]   D. Remenyi, Spam and Viruses, *2ⁿᵈ European Conference on Information Warfare and Security*, Reading University, June 30-1 July, 2003.

[5]   P. Levine, Can the Internet Rescue Democracy? Toward an On-Line Commons, in R. Hayduk and K. Mattson(eds), *Democracy's Moment: Reforming the American Political System for the 21ˢᵗ Century*, Rowman and Littlefield, Lanham MD, 2002.

[6]   D. Weinberger, *Small Pieces Loosely Joined: a unified theory of the web*, Perseus Publishing, USA, 2002.

[7]   S. Coleman, *In discussion in the School of Systems and Data Studies*, Trinity College Dublin, March 6, 2003.

[8]   R. Cook, http://www.socitm.gov.uk/nr/egovindex/crosscutting/citizen/democratic.html

[9]   L. Lerer, Is Your Vote Safe, *Forbes Magazine*,

[10] J. Holyer, Identifying the right barriers to e-voting, *New Media Age*, August 2002, 18 – 19.

[11] D. Wilson, P. Fyffe, M. Dunne, A. Gogan and D. Remenyi, Reflections on e-voting in Ireland: Misunderstanding both Democracy and Technology?, *2ⁿᵈ International Conference on e-government*, University of Pittsburgh, October 12-13, 2006.

[12] I. Angell, *The New Barbarians*, Kogan Page, London, 2000.

[13] T. Vedel, The Idea of Electronic Democracy: Origins, Visions and Questions, *Parliamentary Affairs*, **59**, 2 (2006), 226-239.

Developments in e-Government
D. Griffin et al. (Eds.)
IOS Press, 2007

Holding e-Government to Account
Renovating Old Forms of Public Accountability and Creating New Ones

Albert Jacob MEIJER
Utrecht School of Governance, The Netherlands

1. Introduction

Public accountability is a key concept in public administration and embodies the central value of accounting for delegated authority. In political theories on democracy, accountability plays a crucial role in ensuring that government acts according to the will of the people. How can we ensure that government officials do not abuse their power? Additionally, public accountability serves as a mechanism for collective learning. Does the public sector function adequately? Or are adjustments needed to improve the performance of public sector organizations?

Discussions on e-government tend to focus on public service delivery and access to public information. One-stop-shops and government portals are widely debated and implemented forms of e-government. ICTs, so it is argued, are to be used to facilitate interactions between governments and citizens. These debates, however, often only focus on one role of the citizen: the citizen as consumer of government services. The role of citizens, and their representatives and institutions, as a forum for public debate and control of e-government has received much less attention.

Research on e-government indicates that ICTs do not only have the potential to improve service delivery and access to information, but can also enhance public accountability. ICTs can be used to support traditional forms of internal and external accountability. The transparency of government increases and thus the quality of reconstructions of government behavior and decision making can be improved. Additionally, ICTs may also facilitate new forms of accountability. Direct accountability to citizens seems to be an important addition to existing forms of accountability to political representatives and legal institutions.

In this chapter I will explore how governments can be held accountable in the information age. I will first briefly discuss the concept of public accountability and indicate that five key forms of internal and external accountability can be distinguished. Then I will describe these forms and, on the basis of empirical research, I will discuss the effects of the use of ICTs on accountability. I will end this chapter with a discussion of general trends and a plea for a new conceptualization of public accountability that fits the network society. I will argue that public accountability concerns accountability for public affairs and these affairs are not only dealt with by government.

2. Public accountability: a key concept in democratic governance

Democracy remains a paper procedure if those in power can not be held accountable in public for their acts, decisions, policies, and expenditures. As a concept, however, 'public accountability' is rather elusive. It serves as a synonym for loosely defined political desiderata, such as transparency, equity, democracy, efficiency and integrity [1, 2, and 3]. Bovens [4] defines public accountability as a social relationship in which an actor feels an obligation to explain and to justify his conduct to some significant other. The actor, or *accouter*, can be either an individual or an agency. The significant other, which we will call the *accountability forum* or the *accountee*, can be a specific person or agency, but can also be a more virtual entity, such as the general public. The *object of accountability* is the conduct, often decision making, of the accouter. This conduct is then compared to certain *standards*, or criteria, which the accountability forum uses to evaluate the conduct of the accouter.

The relationship between the actor and the forum, the account giving, usually consists of three elements or stages. First of all, the actor must feel obliged to inform the accountability forum about his conduct, by providing various sorts of data about the performance of tasks, about outcomes, or about procedures. Often, particularly in the case of failures or incidents, this also involves the provision of justifications. This then, can prompt the forum to interrogate the actor and to question the adequacy of the information or the legitimacy of the conduct. This is the debating phase. Hence, the close semantic connection between 'accountability' and 'answerability'. Thirdly, the forum usually passes judgment on the conduct of the actor. It may approve of an annual account, denounce a policy, or publicly condemn the behavior of a manager or an agency.

In passing a negative judgment the forum frequently imposes some sort of sanctions on the accouter. These sanctions can be highly formalized, such as fines, disciplinary measures or even penal sanctions, but often the punishment will only be implicit or informal, such as the very fact of having to give an account in front of television-cameras, or of having your public image or career damaged by the negative publicity that results from the process.

The obligation that is felt by the accouter can also be both formal and informal. Civil servants will often be under a formal obligation to give accounts on a regular basis to specific forums, such as their superiors, supervisory agencies, or auditors. In the case of unpleasant incidents or administrative deviance, civil servants can be forced to appear in court or to testify before parliamentary committees. But the obligation can also be informal or even self imposed, as in the case of press conferences, informal briefings, or public confessions.

Finally, the conduct that is to be explained and justified can vary enormously, from budgetary scrutiny in the case of financial accountability, to administrative fairness in the case of legal accountability, or even sexual propriety when it comes to the political accountability of Anglo-American public officials.

The quality of accountability can be evaluated from a democratic and a cybernetic perspective [4]. The democratic perspective stresses the importance of controlling the execution of government power. Citizens delegate power to fellow citizens but require that they account for their conduct. This type of accountability has a long tradition: in ancient Athens generals already had to account to all citizens for their conduct in warfare. In this perspective, accountability functions adequately if it ensures that government officials do not abuse their power.

A cybernetic perspective puts emphasis on the function of accountability for collective learning. Accountability is regarded as a feedback mechanism in a learning loop. Do policies result in the intended results? Or are adjustments required? Accountability creates room for reflection on government. Collective learning is sometimes regarded as the key to the success of democratic societies [5]. In the cybernetic perspective, accountability functions adequately if the performance of government is continually improved.

In the daily life of modern civil servants operating in a democratic system, there are at least five different sorts of forums that they may have to face up to, and therefore also five different types of potential accountability relationships, and five different sets of norms and expectations:

- Hierarchical accountability
- Professional accountability
- Political accountability
- Legal accountability
- Administrative accountability

Hierarchical accountability primarily takes place *within government*. This type of accountability shapes relations and information exchanges between managers and civil servants within government organizations. Professional, political, legal, and administrative accountability form a *linkage* between government organizations and the relevant environment of these organizations.

Civil servants have to deal with all these types of accountability. The introduction of ICTs in government organizations, however, has led to changes in the functioning of government. ICTs have influenced these five accountability relationships in different ways. In this chapter, I will have a look at each of these five accountability relationships and I will describe the influence of ICTs to understand both the changes within government and the changes in linkages between government and the environment.

3. Hierarchical accountability

The most important accountability relation *within* organizations is hierarchical. Through a chain of hierarchical relations, civil servants account to their superiors and, eventually, to the political leader. The superiors of civil servants, both administrative and political, will regularly, sometimes on a formal basis, such as with annual performance reviews, but more often in daily informal meetings, ask them to account for their assignments. This usually involves a strong hierarchical relationship and the accounting may be based on strict directives and standard operating procedures, but this is not a constitutive element. Senior policy advisors and project managers will often have a considerable amount of autonomy in performing their tasks, and yet may strongly feel the pressures of hierarchical accountability.

Strictly speaking, hierarchical accountability is not 'public' accountability, because the account itself is usually not accessible to the public at large. Nevertheless, this hierarchical accountability is the *sine qua non* for the other, external forms of public accountability. A political leader is presumed to be able to account for the actions of his civil servants since he is at the top of a pyramid of hierarchical accountability relations. This leads to an important question for the information age: will the use of ICTs strengthen or undermine this system of hierarchical accountability relations?

The impact of the use of ICTs on hierarchical accountability has been investigated by various researchers. Zuurmond [6] indicates that bureaucracy is transformed into an 'infocracy'. In an infocracy, control is not exerted through bureaucratic structures but through the information infrastructure. This information infrastructure controls the behavior of civil servants and also renders their behavior transparent to their superiors. The hierarchical accountability of civil servants is increased since superiors have more means to monitor their behavior and ask them to account for their behavior. At the same time, one can argue that there is less need for *ex-post* accountability since *ex-ante* control is increased, because civil servants can no longer escape from hierarchical procedures. The account giving has become less explicit and overt, because in the infocracy the behavior of civil servants is increasingly controlled *ex-ante*, through the information infrastructure, instead of ex post, through answerability to their superiors. An example illustrates the change from bureaucracy to infocracy.

In the Netherlands, civil servants used to have a fair degree of autonomy in deciding who was to get a student grant or loan. They used their discretionary powers to evaluate whether a student was in need of a grant and looked into the personal situation of the student. This was a source of professional pride but also of personal biases. Nowadays, the provision of public grants to students is fully automated. This expert system is based on the law concerning student grants and legal procedures have been encoded in computer programs. Civil servants only have to enter data in the system and the system then decides who will get a grant. Hierarchical accountability concerning the use of discretionary powers is no longer relevant [7].

In the example, the effects of ICTs on hierarchical accountability seem clear: ICTs strengthen hierarchical accountability. ICTs enable the creation of a perfect Weberian administrative machine which does exactly what its political leaders want. However, research by Meijer [8] indicates that the use of ICTs – in his case e-mail and text editors – may have the opposite effect on hierarchical accountability. He states that these ICTs hamper hierarchical accountability because these ICTs render the behavior of civil servants less transparent to their superiors. Superiors do not know who civil servants are communicating with and lack control over information storage. Meijer argues that these changes require a shift from hierarchical to professional accountability. These changes fit well within Hekscher's [9] ideas about post-bureaucratic organizations. Hekscher indicates that in these organizations individuals in network relations structure their actions according to the mission of the organization. An example illustrates the change from a bureaucratic to a post-bureaucratic organization.

At the Dutch Ministry of Foreign Affairs e-mail facilities are used for both business and personal communication. Business communication at the ministry follows official, functional lines and e-mail addresses are connected to functional mailboxes of embassies, consulates or directorates. In practice, however, little use is made of this form of communication. Civil servants prefer to use either the protected network, fax or snail mail. Apart from the functional e-mail addresses, civil servants also have a personal e-mail address. This personal address is used for both private and work related communication. Civil servants use personal e-mail according to their own standards and decide whether they need to preserve e-mail messages and in which form. Central management has no control over this use of e-mail [8].

The findings of Zuurmond and Meijer seem to be contradicting. A closer look at their research, however, indicates that the findings apply to different ICTs. Zuurmond focuses on the effects of large database systems whereas Meijer highlights the effects of e-mail and text editors. Another difference concerns the administrative processes that are supported by ICTs. The findings of Zuurmond concern the use of ICTs in large scale policy execution, Meijer studied the use of ICTs in policy development. These findings seem to indicate that hierarchical accountability is strengthened by the application of ICTs in policy execution and hampered by the use of ICTs in policy development.

This brings us to the future of hierarchical accountability. The transition from bureaucracies to infocracies may demand new forms of hierarchical accountability. The object of accountability has shifted from policy execution to the design and implementation of information infrastructures. In the terms of Mintzberg [10]: accountability in the technostructure becomes more important than accountability in the operating core. A question which remains unanswered is whether accountability relations in the technostructure will be of a hierarchical or rather of a professional nature. Will organizations set up information infrastructures in the technostructure to control the design and implementation of information structures in the operating core? Or will organizations rely on profession accountability to assure the quality of information structures in the operating core?

Another question for the future of hierarchical accountability is: what will happen to accountability concerning policy development? Will there be a turn-around and will political leaders reemphasize the need for hierarchical accountability concerning policy development? Or will government organizations continue along existing lines and look for new forms of accountability that fit post-bureaucratic organizations?

4. Professional accountability

Many civil servants are, in a technical sense, professionals. They have been trained as engineers, doctors, veterinarians, teachers, or police officers. This may imply that they do not only account to their superiors but also maintain accountability relationships with professional associations and disciplinary tribunals [11]. Professional bodies lay down codes with standards for acceptable practice that are binding for all members. These standards are monitored and enforced by professional bodies using oversight on the basis of peer review. This type of accountability will be particularly relevant for civil servants that work in professional organizations, such as hospitals, schools, psychiatric clinics, police departments, or fire brigades. Are these forms of accountability supported or inhibited by the use of ICTs?

In line with their findings on hierarchical accountability, Zuurmond [6], and Bovens and Zouridis [12] stress that professional autonomy is limited through the use of ICTs. Operating procedures are embedded in software and professionals cannot evade these procedures. This does not only apply to administrative professionals but also increasingly to doctors and police officers. Professionals have to register all their actions in information systems and hence render their behavior transparent to their superiors. These superiors increasingly ask these professionals to account for their actions with a strong focus on the efficiency of their work. This type of accountability slowly becomes more important to professionals in government than accountability to their professional peers. Use of ICTs leads to a process of 'deprofessionalization' in government and thus to less professional accountability.

Other developments, however, point to an increasing professionalization in government and thus to a shift in professional accountability. Use of ICTs may lead to accountability relations for occupational groups that hitherto were not recognized as professions. An interesting example of these new groups of professionals is the 'information professionals'. Electronic data processing auditors in the Netherlands, for example, have formed professional associations and standards for acceptable practice. This indicates that civil servants in public organizations try to improve their position by strengthening linkages with their – professional – environment and hence move away from hierarchical accountability.

Both developments I have described so far, maintain the traditional idea of professional accountability: accountability to peers in formal associations. One may wonder whether the new communities of information professionals will be at the same distance from the general public as classic professionals. It seems likely that in the near future (information) professionals in government will not only be held accountable by professional peers but – through the Internet – also by 'amateurs'. LINUX and the open source movement may provide interesting models for public forms of professional accountability in the information age [13, 14]. Professional accountability in the Open Source Movement is not based on membership of a professional association but on (informally) proven knowledge and experience concerning a subject. Translated to the public sector this could mean that, in the future, civil servants may increasingly be called to account by knowledgeable citizens.

5. Political accountability

For civil servants, accountability to political forums, such as elected representatives or political parties, can be very important facts of life. In parliamentary systems with ministerial responsibility and a general civil service, such as Britain and The Netherlands, this political accountability usually is exercised indirectly, through the minister. Increasingly, however, civil servants too have to appear before parliamentary committees, for example in the case of parliamentary inquiries. In the American presidential system, senior civil servants, heads of agencies for example, are often directly accountable to Congress. In administrative systems that work with political cabinets and spoils, as for example in the US, France, or Belgium, civil servants will also find they have an, informal and discrete, but not to be disregarded, accountability relationship with party bosses. Civil servants, especially those with a professional or legal background, often find political accountability difficult to handle, if not threatening, because of the fluid, contingent, and ambiguous character of political agendas. Is the threat of political accountability enhanced by the use of ICTs or do ICTs offer civil servants a 'shield' for public accountability?

Meijer [15] indicates that the use of ICTs increases the informational and the analytical transparency of government. Government organizations are opened up to their environment. The use of White House e-mail messages to investigate Irangate provides an interesting example.

In 1986, the Tower Committee investigated the Irangate affaire. The communication between Oliver North of the National Security Council and the

National Security Advisor John Pointdexter was of crucial importance to this investigation. These civil servants tried to prevent the use of their communication for the inquiry and deleted both their paper and e-mail correspondence. However, the system administrator of the White House preserved the back-up tapes with the e-mail messages. Therefore the Tower Committee could use the e-mail messages for the inquiry to reconstruct communications between White House officials [16].

Political forums can profit from the increased transparency of government, however, they may also be confronted with an information overload. Government agencies generate enormous amounts of information and it seems unlikely that elected representatives will be able to adequately deal with all this information. An example of the inability to use all relevant (digital) information is a Dutch parliamentary inquiry into the use of various methods of investigation by the police.

The Central Information Agency of the Dutch police is the central actor in exchanges of information concerning police suspects. To perform this task, this agency uses an elaborate database system to manage data about suspects. This database system can be considered as a rich source of information for evaluating the functioning of the Dutch police organization. However, these digital data were not directly used by the parliamentary enquiry committee. The committee limited itself to a paper report that showed numbers that were generated with the database system. In this case ICT created many opportunities for fact-finding, but these opportunities were left unused for lack of expertise and resources to analyze it [8].

How can political forums deal with this information overload? They may increase the capacity to process information. Political representatives may turn to citizens for help in dealing with the information overload. In the context of government and ICTs, direct accountability to citizens is the most debated form of political accountability [17]. Direct accountability could be an addition to – rather than a substitute for – indirect accountability. New technologies can facilitate 'digital agora' so that modern rulers can then be held accountable in the same way as Greek rulers.

ICTs, such as the Internet, are important for direct accountability: citizens can have direct access to information about the functioning of government agencies and use communication technologies for a public debate. Government organizations are thus not only opened up to the political environment but also to (individual) citizens. Northrup & Thorson [18] give the interesting example of the Korean government that enabled citizens to monitor the process of permit applications. They claim that this form of transparency enables accountability and reduces corruption.

6. Legal accountability

Although political accountability receives most attention in scientific and popular literature, it is not the only form of external accountability in government. Civil servants can be summoned by courts to account for their own acts, or on behalf of the agency as a whole. Usually this will be a specialized administrative court, but, depending on the legal system and the issue at stake, it can also be a civil or penal court. In most western countries, legal accountability is of increasing importance to civil servants as a result of the growing formalization of social relations [19]. Legal accountability is the most unambiguous type of accountability as the legal scrutiny will be based on detailed legal standards, prescribed by civil, penal, or administrative statutes or precedent. In contrast with political accountability, civil servants know exactly how legal forums will call them to account. The high degree of formalization seems to imply that this form of accountability will hardly be influenced by the use of ICTs.

Legal accountability of digital governments used to be a matter of debate for legal scholars. Can electronic information be admitted as evidence? What is the legal value of a digital signature? These questions, however, do not seem to be relevant anymore as courts in countries all around the world are granting digital information the same status as paper information. A few years ago, the use of an e-mail in court was an exception and was widely reported in the media. Nowadays, use of e-mail messages and other forms of digital information is considered to be as normal as the use of paper documents and oral testimonies.

This does not mean that the digitization of government does not have an impact on legal accountability. As I have already indicated, the use of ICTs increases both the informational and the analytical transparency of government. Fact-finding by legal forums is facilitated. E-mail messages have played a crucial role in a recent inquiry into corruption in Dutch government.

Moving away from the debate on transparency, one may even wonder whether there is still so much need for legal accountability. Empirical research seems to indicate that the legal quality of routine decision making has increased because of the use of ICTs [20]. Humans are likely to make more mistakes than computers. In that respect, the use of ICTs leads to a change from *ex-post* to *ex-ante* legal accountability.

The use of ICTs in routine decision-making also has a dark side to it. Legal checks and balances may not be adequate anymore since the power of government organizations over citizens has been increased by their use of ICTs. The net result of these developments may be that citizens have less legal protection against the abuse of power by government organizations. This 'accountability gap' has been described by De Mulder [21]. He indicates that ICTs can be used to pre-program decision-making in highly individual cases. Traditional forms of legal accountability are not capable of dealing with use of power since they were designed to evaluate individual cases. De Mulder therefore called for a new form of legal accountability that can check on 'mass customization' in government.

7. Administrative accountability

Next to courts, a whole series of quasi-legal forums, that exercise independent and external administrative oversight and control, has been established in the past decades. These forums vary from Ombudsmen, national or local audit offices, to independent supervisory authorities. They exercise regular financial and administrative control, often on the basis of specific statutes and prescribed norms. This type of accountability can be very important for civil servants that work in quangos and other executive public agencies.

The increase in the informational and analytical transparency of government organizations because of the use of ICTs also facilitates fact-finding by administrative forums. ICTs can increase the quantity and the quality of the information which they need for evaluating government policies and government decisions. The following example illustrates how the increased transparency of government facilitates administrative accountability.

In the Netherlands, the Ministry of Finance is responsible for collection of national taxes. A wide variety of information systems is used to execute this task. Additionally, the ministry advices the minister in developing tax policies. Data about income taxes in the Netherlands are gathered in a database system for policy analysis. As it turned out, this system was not only helpful for policy analysis but also for administrative accountability. The National Audit Office was able to use data from this database system to calculate the effects of certain legal arrangements. Without the digital application, this type of fact-finding would have been practically impossible. In this case ICTs created many opportunities to analyze data and can therefore facilitated fact-finding [8].

The development of more direct forms of accountability through ICTs – which I have mentioned as an addition to political accountability to representatives – may also change administrative accountability. Auditors and controllers may no longer function as separate forums, but may function as support mechanisms for direct accountability. Auditors and controllers can monitor the quality of the information which government agencies present to citizens and indicate whether this information is reliable and complete. This evaluation could take the form of a (required) hyperlink on government web pages. Auditors would then monitor the accountability of government organizations to the wider environment.

8. ICTs and public accountability: general trends

So far we have focused on effects of the use of ICTs on specific types of accountability. On the basis of empirical research we can also identify several general trends. These trends refer to changes in government that influence various types of accountability.

The first general trend is the blurring of boundaries between public organizations: "When informational domains entangle, it is quite difficult to find out where something has gone wrong. And, if information is shared and refined, where lies the right of ownership? Who is responsible for the use of new, virtual databases that are based on the combination and refinement of data which is stored in database management systems in different organizations with different jurisdictions [22:74]"? Blurring of organizational boundaries may have serious implications for the organizational jurisdiction which can be described as the exclusive authority of an actor as a unified entity to determine right and obligations of citizens in a task domain with (a certain degree of) discretion for which the actor is legally and politically accountable. This means that blurring of boundaries influences political, legal, and administrative accountability. It may also aggravate the problem of many hands [23, 24]. Who is to be held accountable? And who can provide the required information?

The second general trend is an increase in transparency. More data are recorded and there are more ways to retrieve these data. The use of ICTs leads to a more 'transparent state'. Meijer [15] indicates that the increased transparency may be the result of deliberate actions, but often results unintentionally from efforts to improve the execution and management of work processes. We have seen that this transparency facilitates fact-finding by all accountability forums.

The third general trend is an increase in the diversity of mechanisms for accountability. New mechanisms do not replace old forms of accountability but supplement the traditional mechanisms. The diversity of accountability practices increases: civil servants have to deal with a wider variety of information exchanges.

This increases the accountability and strengthens public control and may facilitate societal learning. A heavy burden of accountability may also lead to rising control costs and negative effects on the functioning of government organizations. The lack of protection of civil servants against harsh criticism from the outside world might result in paralysis, risk avoidance, goal displacement, and stressful working conditions [25].

These changes in the accountability relations of government require a new conceptualization of public accountability. The public consists of all kinds of other societal actors (journalists, societal groups, intermediaries, and so on). These societal actors increasingly add dynamic, informal and non-hierarchical accountability relations to the existing accountability relations through formal institutions. The only way in which we can get a grip on the accountability of government is by placing government in a network society. Northrup & Thorson [18] suggest that we should move the focus from e-government (the institutions of government) to e-governance (the larger web of formal and informal institutions). This transition means that public accountability does not relate to accountability relations between government agencies and society but concerns a wide range of horizontal accountability relationships between societal actors. Public accountability concerns accountability for public affairs and these affairs are not only dealt with by government.

This transition will affect all phases of accountability processes. In the information phase there will not be one single source of information. Information will increasingly be provided and contested by various actors. The debate phase will change with regard to participants and the structure of the debate: the debate will be open for many participants and will not always be structured according to formal procedures. Most actors will not dispose of formal sanctions. It seems probable that publicity and public exposure will develop into dominant sanctions and will play a crucial role in holding e-government to account.

Endnote

1. Previous versions of this chapter were presented at the European Group for Public Administration 2003 Conference in Oeiras and the E-government Workshop of JURIX 2003 in Amsterdam. A chapter on public accountability in an information age, which partly discusses the same developments but focused on 'information ecologies', has appeared in Bekkers & Homburg [26]. The author would like to thank Mark Bovens for his cooperation on earlier versions of this paper.

References

[1]   R. Mulgan, "Accountability": an ever expanding concept?, *Public Administration,* **78**, 3 (2000), 555-573.
[2]   R.D. Behn, *Rethinking Democratic Accountability*, Brookings Institution Press, Washington DC, 2001.
[3]   M.J. Dubnick, Seeking Salvation for Accountability, *Paper presented at the Annual Meeting of the American Political Science Association,* Boston, 2002.
[4]   M. Bovens, Publieke verantwoording. Een analysekader (Public Accountability: A Frame for Analysis), 2004, to be published.
[5]   C.E. Lindblom, *The intelligence of democracy*, Free Press, New York, 1965.
[6]   A. Zuurmond, From Bureaucracy to Infocracy: Are Democratic Institutions Lagging Behind? In: I.Th.M. Snellen and W.B.H.J. van de Donk (eds.): *Public Administration in an Information Age,* IOS Press, Amsterdam, 1998.
[7]   S. Zouridis, *Digitale disciplinering. Over ICT, organisatie, wetgeving en het automatiseren van beschikkingen*, University of Tilburg, Tilburg, 2000.

[8]   A. Meijer, *De doorzichtige overheid. Parlementaire en juridische controle in het informatietijdperk,* Eburon, Delft, 2002.

[9]   V. Hekscher, Defining the Post Bureaucratic Type. In: C. Hekscher and A. Donnellon (eds.): *The post-bureaucratic organization. New perspectives on organizational change,* Sage Publications, London, 1994.

[10] H. Mintzberg, *Structure in fives. Designing effective organizations,* Prentice Hall, Upper Saddlle River, 1983.

[11] H.L. Wilenski, The Professionalisation of Everyone?, *American Journal of Sociology,* **70**, 2 (1964), 137-158.

[12] M. Bovens and S. Zouridis, From street-level to system level bureaucracies. How ICT is transforming administrative discretion and constitutional control, *Public Administration Review,* **62**, 2 (2002), 174-183.

[13] E.S. Raymond, The Cathedral and the Bazaar, *First Monday,* **3**, 3 1998, (http://firstmonday.org/issues/issue3_3/raymond/index.html).

[14] A. Bonaccorsi and C. Rossi, Altruistic individuals, selfish firms? The structure of motivation in Open Source software, *First Monday,* **9**, 1, (2004) (http://firstmonday.org/issues/issue9_1/bonaccorsi/index.html).

[15] A.J. Meijer, Transparent government: Parliamentary and legal accountability in an information age, *Information Polity,* **8**, 1/2 (2003), 67 – 78.

[16] Blanton (1995)

[17] C.D. Raab, Electronic Confidence: Trust, Information and Public Administration. In: I.Th.M. Snellen and W.B.H.J. van de Donk (eds.): *Public Administration in an Information Age,* IOS Press, Amsterdam, 1998.

[18] T.A. Northrup and S.J. Thorson, The Web of Governance and Democratic Accountability. In: R. Sprague (ed.), *Proceedings of the 36ᵗʰ Hawaii International Conference on System Sciences,* Hawaii, 2003.

[19] L.M. Friedman, *Total Justice,* Russel Sage, New York, 1985

[20] M.M. Groothuis and J.S. Svensson, Expert system support and juridical quality. In: J. Breuker, R. Leenes and R. Winkel (eds.): *Legal Knowledge and Information Systems. Jurix 2000: The Thirteenth Annual Conference,* IOS Press, Amsterdam, 2000

[21] R.V. de Mulder, The digital revolution: from trias to tetras politica. In: I.Th.M. Snellen and W.B.H.J. van de Donk (eds.): *Public Administration in an Information Age,* IOS Press, Amsterdam, 1998.

[22] V.J.J.M. Bekkers, 'Wiring Public Organizations and Changing Organizational Jurisdictions'. In: I.Th.M. Snellen & W.B.H.J. van de Donk (eds.): *Public Administration in an Information Age,* IOS Press, Amsterdam, 1998.

[23] D.F. Thompson, Moral Responsibility of Public Officials: The Problem of Many Hands, *American Political Science Review,* **74** (1980), 905-916.

[24] M. Bovens, *The Quest for Responsibility: Accountability and Citizenship in Complex Organisations,* Cambridge University Press, Cambridge, 1998.

[25] A. Halachmi, Performance measurement: A look at some possible dysfunctions, *Work Study,* **51**, 5 (2002) 230-239.

[26] V. Bekkers and V. Homburg (eds.), *The Information Ecology of E-Government. E-Government as Institutional and Technological Innovation in Public Administration,* IOS Press, Amsterdam, 2005.

Developments in e-Government
D. Griffin et al. (Eds.)
IOS Press, 2007

How Does e-Government Innovation Affect Local Government's Accountability to the Public?

David GRIFFIN

Innovation North: Faculty of Information and Technology,
Leeds Metropolitan University, UK

1. Introduction

In the opening chapter of this book, Professor Bryant challenges e-government practitioners and academics to critically evaluate the contribution of Information and Communications Technology (ICT) to government. Too often the concern has been how ICT can be exploited to improve the current machinery of government. This has led to the development of new access channels for communications between government and its citizens but, predominantly, it continues with the established ways of working and governing. Bryant suggests a better critique might be obtained by questioning the nature of government, given the ICT facilities available for use.

This chapter makes an initial contribution to this debate. The underlying question in the discussion that follows is this: to what extent might the introduction of ICT lead to a paradigm change in the accountability relationship between government and its citizens? This chapter presents the results of an investigation of public accountability at the local level. Specifically, it studies how councils are, and might be, accountable to the public for their implementation of the e-government programme.

Public accountability has long been considered an important aspect of democratic society [1]. In the UK, all tiers of government, government agencies and other public bodies (graphically illustrated on Figure 2 in chapter 10) are expected to be accountable to taxpayers and other stakeholders for the funds they spend from the public purse. All councils in England and Wales operate one of three arrangements: a cabinet with a leader, a directly elected mayor with a cabinet or a directly elected mayor with a council manager. The executive is responsible for policy implementation and service delivery. All other elected members of the council have the responsibility of scrutinizing the decisions made by the executive. This separation of roles is intended to encourage improved public consultation and participation in council decision making [2]. Council scrutiny committees make a dual contribution to accountability: they act as agents of the public reviewing policy and executive decisions; through their meetings and investigations, they provide formal and informal opportunities for citizens themselves to hold the council cabinet to account. This chapter presents an initial framework for evaluating the public accountability enabled by the scrutiny committee structure. Further, it critically discusses the elements of this framework using empirical evidence from a study of local authorities.

2. The notion of public accountability

What is meant by 'public accountability'? At its most basic, it can be said to be a relationship between two parties, in which one party, the steward, is held to account for their performance by a second party, the principal [3, 4]. The steward may be obliged to give an account to certain parties which have power over it. This power is exhibited by the setting of performance objectives and measures and by applying sanctions when performance targets are not met. Sanctions take several forms, for example withdrawal of funding or, in the more extreme case, replacing the steward by another service provider. The steward may additionally feel accountable to other stakeholders who have an interest in its activities, but lack formal power over it [4]. In the local government context, these stakeholders may include the customers and clients of the service [5], local businesses and voluntary organisations [4]. It is likely that these three types of stakeholder will have differing values and differing views about the objectives and measures of public services [6]. They might not be well-equipped to scrutinize the activities of their local council [3]. For example, the quality of the information made available to external stakeholders is open to question [4].

In chapter 7 of this book, Meijer identifies five types of accountability relationships: hierarchical, professional, legal, administrative and political. The first of these is a form of internal accountability which exists within the bureaucracy of the organization. The Service Head in a local authority, for example, is answerable to the Executive of the council. The others can be characterized as forms of external accountability [7]. At the external level, there are numerous stakeholders to whom the council is responsible [8].

The Council structures through which transparency and accountability to external stakeholders are delivered have been recently re-engineered. The New Public Management (NPM) agenda is introducing private sector practices into public service delivery [9]. How is the citizen stakeholder perceived under NPM? Is the citizen merely a customer of council services [10]? Or does the citizen have a more complex role to play (Benyon-Davies and Williams, 2003)? One sense the citizen may be perceived as owner of the government service [11].

The restructuring of local government to separate service definition from its delivery has affected accountability. Professional discretion and accountability within the local authority has been replaced by central agencies setting objectives and monitoring service provision [6]. The monitoring mechanisms set for this, according to Mather [12], have developed into a costly and resource-consuming 'snoopocracy', tilting the emphasis of service activity towards target achievement rather than service improvement [13]. A further complication is introduced by the current move to introduce partnership working and joined-up public service delivery. This often includes a network of public and private organizations [14]. According to Ling [15], this is typified by the blurring of boundaries between functional areas and less hierarchical relationships between organizations. As a result, structures may be merged, budgets shared and joint teams formed from the partner organizations [16]. As a result, it becomes more difficult to identify the contribution for which each individual partner is accountable [6].

Table 1. Composition of the survey

Type of council	Sample size	Number of respondents (response rate)
Metropolitan borough	24	8 (33%)
London borough	16	1 (6%)
District council	10	1 (10%)
County council	8	0
Unitary council	3	0
TOTAL	61	10 (16%)

3. The empirical study

The empirical evidence that forms the basis of this chapter was collected in spring 2004. Here we shall present a summary of the methods employed in the study. Readers interested in a more complete account of the methodology are referred to Griffin and Halpin [17]. Interviews were held with council elected members and officers responsible for both e-government management and the transparency and public accountability of policy implementation. A sample of 77 English councils was selected from the index of local authority websites compiled by Tagish Consulting (www.tagish.co.uk), following the practice of previous studies that have used this as the sampling frame [18, 19]. The 61 councils from this sample, which providing contact details for the Scrutiny Manager, or other officer with a similar title, on their website, were emailed a short questionnaire. A response rate of 16 percent was achieved. Table 1 shows the composition of the survey and the responses achieved for each type of council.

Semi-structured interviews were held at six metropolitan borough councils from the sample. This tier of English authorities has unitary responsibility for all local government functions in a metropolitan area. The interviewees comprised of personnel with strategic, tactical and operational responsibilities in their council. The roles of the participants are shown in Table 2.

The interviews were supplemented by document analysis to provide an insight into the scrutiny of e-government. A number of reports were collected in preparation for,

Table 2. Participants in the interview sessions

	Role	Number interviewed
Elected member	Chair of Scrutiny Commission	1
Officer	Chief Executive	1
	Head of Scrutiny	2
	Principal Scrutiny Officer	2
	e-Government Manager	2
	Accountant and e-Government project manager	1

and during, the interview sessions. These included:

- the Implementing Electronic Government (IEG) statements for each Council
- the report of an Inquiry into Implementing Electronic Government
- notes of Scrutiny Board investigation meetings
- ICT Manager's report to the Scrutiny Board investigation team
- Chief Customer Services Officer's report to the Scrutiny Board investigation team
- Scrutiny Board report on developing customer-focused council services, in which aspects of e-government were considered
- minutes of scrutiny board meetings, open to the public, at which e-government was discussed

Finally, a public meeting of a scrutiny committee, at which e-government was reviewed, was observed.

4. A framework for evaluating e-government accountability

A review of the literature on public accountability has identified a number of significant issues. These issues are grouped into five components, forming the basis of the evaluation framework employed in this study (Figure 1).

These components are:

- The principal stakeholders involved with examining e-government performance
- The processes of scrutinizing the e-government agenda
- Sanctions that are applied for unsatisfactory performance
- The impact of partnership funding and working and joint service delivery
- The impact of politics and power relationships on e-government and scrutiny

5. Evaluation of the findings of this study

5.1. Principal stakeholders

Respondents to the questionnaire ranked external stakeholders according to their perceived significance in holding the council to account for e-government progress. The results are presented in Table 3. Local residents are identified as the key stakeholder for scrutinizing the implementation of electronic service delivery by councils. There is no evidence that the public share this view. Scrutiny meetings at which e-government has been discussed have not attracted public attendance. Moreover, there appears to be little public interest in scrutiny activity generally. As noted by one scrutiny adviser: "I have to be honest. We are disappointed with the amount of contact that we get from members of the public. It is very rare that we get responses in any way."

According to the interviewees, there are other mechanisms for disseminating scrutiny information to the public and for encouraging them to influence investigations. For example, local newspapers sometimes communicate the results of scrutiny investigations; some members of the public are corresponding with scrutiny committees over particular issues.

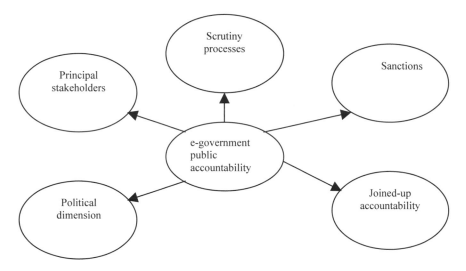

Figure 1. e-Government accountability evaluation framework

Table 3. Survey ranking of key stakeholders

Stakeholder	Ranking
Local residents	1
Local businesses	2
District Audit	3
e-Government partners	3
Central government	5

5.2. Scrutiny processes

e-Government progress has been examined by the scrutiny committees in two-thirds of the survey. Furthermore, this is not seen as a one-off activity. All of these authorities plan to review e-government again in the future, with sixty-six percent of them intending to review the programme bi-annually. The main reasons given by those who had not yet investigated e-government were higher priority matters to investigate and waiting for further e-government progress to be achieved.

The stimulus to investigate e-government has been varied. In one council, the inquiry had been initiated following elected members' complaints over their own email facilities and computer hardware. This had been widened to review the entire e-government programme. In another council, electronic service delivery had been considered as part of an overall investigation into customer services. In a third council, it was the IEG statement itself that had sparked scrutiny interest. This council had submitted an IEG statement that failed to meet the target set by the government. The scrutiny committee was eager to explore the reasons for not achieving the targets and the likely impact in terms of government sanctions.

Two councils mentioned the importance of benchmarking to internal scrutiny processes. During their investigations visits had been made to other local authorities to observe their use of ICTs in service delivery. Elected members also took the opportunity to inspect the websites of other councils to experience, at first hand, their rollout of the e-government programme. As one scrutiny official complained:

"There is a strong element of comparing. [Elected members] get on the computer and say 'look at X's site, look at what Y is doing on their site. Because it is accessible, you can actually see on your screen what other authorities can do. Officers don't get so excited. What X has done is window-dressing. You know the back-office stuff isn't necessarily as good as the front-office stuff".

The Chief Executive of one council broadened the discussion of benchmarking to consider the availability of information to enable members of the public to make comparisons. He explained:

"It would be very hard for people to make comparisons between one authority and another.. ..For a comparison to be made, they would also need to take into account how much you'd spent... It would be very difficult for the public to have full knowledge."

The e-government Manager in this council emphasized the need for consistency in measuring e-government progress across authorities. She felt that benchmarking was problematic for any stakeholder to undertake, given the lack of standardization and definition in some areas. The e-government Manager in another Council, which had already achieved the 100 percent electronic service delivery target, provided evidence to support this proposition:

"We like to think we are reasonably well advanced. Exactly how far is hard to say, really. Part of the way we hit the target was someone splattering electronic forms all over the place and some of them weren't particularly sophisticated."

5.3. Sanctions

Central government used the annual IEG statement to measure councils' progress towards the target of 100 percent electronic service delivery. The Government assembled a set of sanctions, of increasing severity, for poor performance. All councils making satisfactory progress on e-government were awarded a capital grant for the next financial year. Councils submitting an unsatisfactory IEG statement were required to make improvements and resubmit it. In the event that this version of the statement still did not meet government expectations, the final sanction was to withhold the following year's allocation of funds. As mentioned above, one of the councils visited in this study was required to reconsider their plans and revise the IEG statement. These changes included new e-government staffing appointments and the reallocation of priorities in the ICT services future work plan.

The ultimate sanction available to the public is the ballot box. If sufficient residents are concerned about council performance, they have the power to remove the controlling party. However, according to one interviewee, "that is such an obscure link to democracy because e-government is essentially a managerial process. It is not a political process; failure to achieve is not a political failure."

The activity of the scrutiny process, per se, however is unlikely to rally significant public interest in most issues. The interviewees all felt that e-government was not a burning issue for the public. They would not be interested in the outputs of the e-government programme, shrouded, as one interviewee commented, in the "dryness of the IEG priorities and all the techie stuff". The public are more likely to be concerned about the physical outcomes resulting from electronic service delivery, such as emptied bins, that do impact on residents' lives.

5.4. Joined-up accountability

Better collaboration between tiers of government, and more integrated working arrangements with other agencies, has been championed by governments throughout the last century in order to achieve the goals of public policy [20]. The ICT-based processes forming the e-government programme provide new opportunities for joined-up working: sharing information between distinct organizations, combining in joint teams to share information, building a joint website, etc. This change in approach to public administration represents 'a paradigm change in public policy' [21:61] and will take considerable political will to achieve [9]. The sample councils in this study, as evidenced by their IEG statements, have initiated, and are developing, areas of joined-up working with a range of partners: other councils, other local public agencies, the voluntary sector and private sector companies.

How is council accountability discharged in joined-up working arrangements? The Chief Executive in one council stated: "Clearly, anything that we are a party to, we are all jointly and severely liable for." However, in practice, he recognized that there were significant practical obstacles to achieving accountability for partnership initiatives, for example:

- The growing number of partnerships to monitor. His council was a member of thirty-three formal partnerships and more than one hundred informal partnerships.
- The cost of being responsible and accountable for partnerships. It was his opinion that this fragmentation of service delivery was particularly expensive to audit.
- The resource capacity needed for setting up governance and accountability arrangements for all partnership ventures.

5.5. Political dimensions

Politics and power relationships were apparent in several of the interviews.

5.5.1. Dependence on the executive for continuity of e-government scrutiny:

The interviews were held towards the end of the municipal year and scrutiny planning was on hold until after the June local elections. The principal scrutiny officer at one authority emphasized the significance of this:

> *"We will be in a state of flux after this month. The scrutiny boards aren't necessarily permanent fixtures. This has an impact on how we take forward the IEG scrutiny agenda. The Chair is very keen, but he is not entirely convinced the Board will remain the same. He is very keen that IEG scrutiny doesn't drop off."*

This particular committee was disbanded by the Executive shortly after this comment was made.

5.5.2. Balance of power between the executive and the scrutiny committee:

Are the two parties perceived as equals? The executive, as the decision-making body, appears to wield more power. In one of the councils, the respondent felt they were striving to achieve parity between the two. In another council, the head of scrutiny highlighted the role of key executive personnel in scrutiny decision-making:

> *"We've been satisfied with the IEG group that the council has put in place, with the deputy leader being personally involved. When he got concerned things weren't happening in certain areas, he got the chief executive involved, along with the director of resources and other strategic directors. So we've generally been satisfied that there has been a sufficient handle to secure this."*

One of the respondents highlighted the political maneuvering that can take place between the completion of an investigation and the publication of the scrutiny committee's findings. Although the committee had identified shortcomings in the exploitation of ICT in support of a particular service, several recommendations in this area were omitted from the final report. These actions had been sacrificed to ensure the retention of critical actions in other areas covered in the investigation.

6. Discussion

The modernization programme, of which e-government and the new democratic structures are constituent parts, aims to achieve democratic renewal and improved public accountability. All interviewees in this study reported difficulties in engaging citizens in the scrutiny of their e-government progress. They felt that e-government is not the type of issue likely to capture the attention of the general public. However, it might be of interest to certain 'communities of interest' [22]. Some councils provide facilities on their websites for members of such communities to register and be pro-actively informed when the issue is due to be investigated in the future. This limited evidence shows how ICT is being employed to efficiently disseminate information to citizens who register with the service.   There has been little change in the accountability processes of the scrutiny committee, or the accountability relationship between the committee and the residents, but ICT has enabled it to improve efficiency. Taking a more critical stance, we might return to the aim of improving public accountability, stated above, and question whether ICT might be exploited in order to change the very nature of the accountability relationship itself.   Prompt information dispatch to targeted citizens is merely a first step towards this more radical improvement.

One complication impeding public sector accountability is the difficulty of measuring performance [23]. e-government typifies this. Complications observed in this study include: monitoring the activity of numerous individual project teams with the potential for different measurement practices, summarizing their performance in a manner that fulfils the needs of all significant stakeholders, likely divergent definitions between councils as to the scope and boundary of their e-government programme. The perceived interest of the public in the outcomes from e-government, rather than its more measurable outputs, is another contributory factor to this problem.

The scrutiny processes investigated in this study took some account of benchmarking and comparison with similar councils. This practice has been adopted for a number of years by other public services, particularly in the health and education services.   These have tended to be compulsory benchmarking initiatives initiated by government agencies as distinguished from voluntary benchmarking that might be set up by councils themselves [1]. None of the participant councils provided benchmarking data to assist members of the public to scrutinize their e-government progress. However some comparative information was collected and was observed in the private working papers of one scrutiny committee.

The range of sanctions open to members of the public if they are unhappy with e-government progress is limited.   We distinguish between the formative and summative sanctions which were identified during this study. A formative sanction might be to make a complaint to an elected member. One interviewee used the term 'embarrassment sanctions' in this context. Other formative sanctions that might embarrass the council service provider include writing to the newspaper or protesting on the town hall steps. Of course, it might be argued that this interviewee cited examples of formative action that fall within the current received wisdom and have an impact that is within the comfort zone of members of the executive. ICT provides a mechanism which might permit a formative action to have a much embarrassing effect on the council's services and reputation.[1] A summative sanction might be to vote the majority party out of office. Formative action can be taken immediately. The feedback of summative action is delayed, as it is usually only available at four yearly intervals.

Stakeholder theory suggests that the key stakeholders to consider during the implementation of strategy are those with high interest and high power over its outcomes [24]. The sample councils considered members of the public to be the main party that should hold them to account for electronic service implementation. It is surprising that central government, which demonstrates its interest in e-government, by obliging councils to make an annual progress report, and its power, through IEG grant allocation and funding for projects of national interest, does not rate more highly. Is it realistic to consider a discretionary principal to have more significance than the obligatory principal, the government, which has the power to name and shame and to withhold future e-government funds? The current mantra of 'citizen-centricity' may have influenced the respondents somewhat. Do members of the public exhibit the desire to scrutinize e-government activity? One participant chief executive felt that residents would lack interest in what he perceived to be 'back-office stuff, predominantly.' The evidence gathered in this study suggests that the public are more likely to be interested in customer-facing services rather than the outputs from e-government. However, in one authority, the lack of visibility and presence of this "back-office" function was overcome by deploying kiosks around the borough, as a symbol of the e-government programme. Nevertheless, the councils surveyed consider local residents to be the principal stakeholder to whom they are accountable. If this is the case, it makes the role of the Scrutiny Committee, representing the public, more significant and necessary to ensure that councils are held to account for their e-Government progress. It is encouraging that two-thirds of the councils in this survey are subjecting this programme to scrutiny at least once a year by the relevant scrutiny committee.

The Local e-government Strategy [25] recommended that councils should consider how they could work with the full range of public and private organizations in the development of electronic services. This study has indicated the extent to which this joint working is contributing to the re-sourcing of e-government. It has also highlighted the potential for the partner organizations to take a narrower view of public accountability for the use of these funds. Respondents pointed out that internal accountability was achieved by project teams engaged in joined-up service development reporting to a joint board comprising of representatives from the partner organizations. They were less clear as to how their own scrutiny committees contributed to the external accountability for all joined-up working. Page (2004) identifies several reasons why difficulties occur in holding partner organizations to account, for instance, there may be disagreement between the partners over which outcomes to measure; underperforming partners might be less willing to be measured by others; partnership governance needs to be clarified to determine who is accountable to whom in the joined-up service delivery. The classic definition of accountability, presented in section 2 of this chapter, presents a model containing a single steward being accountable to one or more other parties for their performance. Joined-up service delivery complicates this definition. Should each of the stewards in the joint delivery partnership, which might include private as well as public organizations, be separately accountable for a slice of the service performance or should they be jointly and severally be responsible for their actions? If the stewards are unable to fathom out the intricacies of the web of relationships and accountabilities, what chance has the citizen of ultimately holding them to account?

7. Conclusions

This chapter has examined the notion of public accountability with reference to the electronic service delivery being implemented by UK local authorities.

The councils consulted in this research consider local residents to be the principal stakeholder to whom they are accountable for e-government progress. Following Kelly [3], we suggest that members of the public may not be equipped to scrutinize these activities. It is questionable as to whether they have the desire to scrutinize e-government implementation specifically. It is unlikely that local residents will be interested in the same set of performance data as the Government [8] and, as we have found in this study, there are complications associated with measuring e-government progress [23]. These factors limit the extent to which it might be possible to claim that ICT, such as Internet-based services and email, has contributed to a measurable improvement in public accountability.

In accountability theory, the principal partially legitimizes their power over the steward of the service by applying sanctions [4]. The present study clearly illustrates the lack of sanctions available to discretionary principals such as the public. This principal is limited, in the main, to utilizing what one interviewee described as 'embarrassment sanctions'.[2]

One of the participants in this study questioned whether delivering accountability on a wider scale would undermine the role of those who are elected. This issue has not been specifically addressed in this research, but it does indicate the political dimension of accountability. The relationship between the Council Executive (the steward) and the Scrutiny Committee (representing the local Principal) is a complex arrangement. For example, the principal both has power over the steward but, at the same time, as this study has shown, is dependent upon the steward for continued participation in the process.

Joined-up e-government presents new challenges for public accountability [26]. It would appear that partner accountability silos are being erected, preventing members of joint arrangements from being fully held to account for all the e-government activity in which they participate. Some councils have the aspiration of being jointly and severally accountable for joined-up working. Few are actively scrutinizing all joined-up service delivery. As this is a model of service delivery which is increasingly being used, there is an urgent need for further research into this area.

8. Postscript - recent developments

Let us now return to the underlying question behind this study: to what extent might ICT lead to a paradigm change in the accountability relationship between government and its citizens? We can begin to answer this question by considering recent developments in policy, practice and technology that have occurred in the two years since this empirical study was undertaken.

Firstly, government terminology is changing. 'Modernization' was once the buzz-word at the policy level [27]. This is now being replaced by 'innovation'. The latter term is used repeatedly in recent Government strategies. It is also finding its way into the naming of organizational structures[3]. Innovation is used loosely in practice to encompass small-scale improvements through to paradigm shifts in service delivery. In order to evaluate practice, a more precise definition is required. A commonly-accepted definition of innovation is 'an idea, practice or object perceived as new by an individual or other unit of adoption' [28:11]. Osborne [29] further assists our analysis by categorizing different types of service improvement. He distinguishes organizational development, process changes that lead to an improved service to existing users, from actual innovation. Innovation may be evolutionary, new services provided to existing users; expansionary, existing services provided to new users; or, total, in which new services are introduced to meet the needs of new users. Using ICT to make service efficiency improvements does not significantly alter the relationship between government and the public. However, it is argued that using ICT in an expansionary manner to reach previously disaffected citizens or deploying it in an evolutionary manner to enhance the accountability services already received by active citizens may begin the process of re-definition of the accountability relationship.

Secondly, new technological channels are now becoming available to councils to supplement the Internet-based applications that form the mainstream e-government components. Recent government policy is encouraging councils to experiment with mobile technologies to engage with citizens [30]. The mobile phone, for example, offers the possibility to engage the young in particular and, through its ubiquitous take-up with this age-group, the prospect of reducing the digital divide.

Thirdly, the Government has recognized that, whilst electronic service delivery by councils has progressed in response to government targets, similar developments have not occurred to support democratic processes [30]. Democratic participation has been steadily diminishing and this is most noticeable amongst the young [31]. e-Democracy is an under-developed and emerging area of research. Scholars and practitioners are beginning to explore how digital technologies may be employed to improve consultation with the public and to engage them in novel ways to help raise their participation in democratic processes. Some of the pilot projects using SMS texting to consult young people, for example, are currently more likely to represent evolutionary innovation as they tend to involve those already actively engaged as youth citizens, such as youth club and youth parliamentarians [32]. However, they do offer the prospect of being developed into total innovations capable of connecting with non-active youth citizens as well.

It remains to be seen to what extent these recent developments will contribute to accountability to the public at the local level. Osborne's [29] framework identifies two significant contributors to the relationship between the government and citizens: the service and the user of the service. By adopting services from other sectors and using digital technologies to reach otherwise disaffected citizens, the relationship may start to be transformed. One area to watch, in this respect, is the developing area of e-democracy. Using new technologies to enable electronic forms of voting, consultation and participation, particularly with younger citizens, might re-invigorate local government accountability. Further research is needed into the scrutiny process and its actors, the elected members, council officers and members of the public, to explore approaches for delivering the paradigm shift in the accountability relationship.

Endnotes

1. What forms of ICT-enabled formative action do we have in mind. One example, from the private sector, might be disgruntled citizens deciding to undertake a denial of service attack on the council's web server. … Another possibility might be a citizen sabotaging the web page of the specific elected member. Either of these courses of formative action might have a significant effect on the reputation of the affected council.

2. In chapter 7 of this book, Meijer suggests that this type of sanction is likely to become the predominant one and will play a crucial role in holding government to account.

3. An example from central government is the Performance & Innovation Unit; an example from local government is the Yorkshire and Humber Improvement and Innovation Partnership;

References

[1] M. Bowerman, G. Francis, A. Ball and J. Fry, The evolution of benchmarking in UK local authorities, *Benchmarking: An International Journal*, **9**, 5 (2002), 429-449.

[2] ODPM, Creating sustainable communities: new constitutions, *Office of the Deputy Prime Minister*, www.odpm.gov.uk/stellent/groups/odpm_localgov/documents/page/odpm_localgov_605431.hasp (2004).

[3] J.Kelly, The Audit Commission: guiding, steering and regulating local government, *Public Administration*, **81**, 3 (2003), 459-476.

[4] G. Boyne, J. Gould-Williams, J. Law and R. Walker, Plans, performance information and accountability: the case of Best Value, *Public Administration*, **80**, 4 (2002), 691-710.

[5] A. Lawton, D. McKevitt and M. Millar, Coping with ambiguity: reconciling external legitimacy and organisational implementation in performance measurement, *Public Money and Management*, **20**, 2 (2000), 13-19.

[6] A.J. Fowles, Changing notions of accountability: a social policy view, *Accounting, Auditing and Accountability Journal*, **6**, 3 (1993), 97-108.

[7] A.J. Meijer, Transparent government: Parliamentary and legal accountability in an information age, *Information Polity*, **8**, 1/2 (2003), 67-78.

[8] M. Wisniewski and D. Stewart, Performance Measurement for Stakeholders: the Case of Scottish Local Authorities, *International Journal of Public Sector Management*, **17**, 3 (2004), 222-233.

[9] D. Griffin, A. Foster and E. Halpin, Joined-up e-Government: an exploratory study of UK local government progress, *Journal of Information Science and Technology*, **2** (2004).

[10] F. Finger and G. Pecaud, From e-Government to e-Governance, in *Proceedings of the 3rd European Conference on e-Government*, D. Remenyi and F. Bannister (Eds.), Dublin (2003).

[11] B. Stahl and C. Butler, E-Government and Transformation of Bureaucracies: Some Remarks About the Development of a Customer-Centred Information Society in Ireland, in *Proceedings of the 3rd European Conference on e-Government*, D. Remenyi and F. Bannister (Eds.), Dublin (2003).

[12] G. Mather, Beyond targets, towards choice, *The Political Quarterly*, **74**, 4 (2003), 481-492.

[13] A. Gray and B. Jenkins, Government and Administration: Checking, Not Enough Doing?, *Parliamentary Affairs*, **57**, 2 (2004), 269-287.

[14] I. Horrocks and . Bellamy, Telematics and community governance: issues for policy and practice, *International Journal of Public Sector Management*, **10**, 5 (1997), 377-387.

[15] T. Ling, Delivering joined-up government in the UK: dimensions, issues and problems, *Public Administration*, **80**, 4 (2002), 615-642.

[16] Cabinet Office, *Wiring it up. Management of cross cutting policies and services*, Performance and Innovation Unit, London, 2000.

[17] D. Griffin and E. Halpin, An exploratory evaluation of UK local e-government from an accountability perspective, *Electronic Journal of e-Government*, **3**, 1 (2005), 13-28

[18] D. Griffin and E. Halpin, Local Government: a digital intermediary for the Information Age?, *Information Polity*, **7**, 4 (2002), 217-231.

[19] I. Horrocks, The 'webbing' of British local government, *Public Money and Management*, **10**, 5 (1998), 39-44.

[20] M. Flinders, Governance in Whitehall, *Public Administration*, **80**, 1 (2002), 51-75.

[21] S. Richards, Four types of joined up government and the problem of accountability, in *Joining Up to improve Public Services*, National Audit Office, www.Nao.gov.uk/publications/nao_reports/01-02/0102383article.pdf, (2002).

[22] M. Barnes, J. Newman, A. Knops and H. Sullivan, Constituting 'the public' in public participation, *Public Administration*, **81**, 2 (2003), 379-399.

[23] M. Noordegraaf and T. Abma, Management By Measurement? Public Management Practices Amidst Ambiguity, *Public Administration*, **81**, 4 (2003), 853-871.

[24] G. Johnson and K. Scholes, *Exploring Corporate Strategy*, Prentice-Hall, New Jersey, 2002.

[25] ODPM, *National Local e-Government Strategy*, Office of the Deputy Prime Minister, The Stationery Office, London, 2002.

[26] S. Page, Measuring Accountability for Results in Interagency Collaboratives, *Public Administration Review*, **64**, 5, (2004), 591-606.

[27] Cabinet Office, *Modernising Government White Paper*, The Stationery Office, London, 1999.

[28] E.M. Rogers, *Diffusion of Innovations*, 4th Edn. Free Press, New York, 1995.

[29] S.P. Osborne, *Voluntary Organisations and Innovation in Public Services*, Routledge, London, 1998.
[30] Cabinet Office, *Transformational Government Enabled by Technology*, The Stationery Office, London, 2005.
[31] K. Parry, *e-Democracy Standard Note*, House of Commons Library, London, 2004.
[32] D. Griffin, P. Trevorrow and E. Halpin, Using SMS texting to encourage democratic participation by youth citizens: a case study of a project in an English local authority, *Electronic Journal of e-Government*, **4** (2006), forthcoming.

Developments in e-Government
D. Griffin et al. (Eds.)
IOS Press, 2007

e-Government and Active Participation by Young Citizens

Philippa TREVORROW
Innovation North: Faculty of Information and Technology,
Leeds Metropolitan University, UK

1. Introduction

Participation and political engagement by young citizens in UK local and national government processes is reportedly low. The UK government have tried to address this by a move towards Internet-based activity; this is a step in the right direction as young citizens tend to be users of the medium [1]. However, research has shown that more young people have a mobile phone than have access to the Internet on a regular basis. The mobile phone is a technology that has been adopted world wide with vigor especially by young people with SMS text messaging (referred to as 'text messaging' throughout this study) being the phenomenon of the 21st Century [2]. Can the mobile phone text messaging function be used to encourage and support participation and democracy amongst young citizens?

This chapter will commence with an outline of previous work conducted by Trevorrow and Orange [3] on modeling active youth citizenship. The use of the Internet and mobile phones by young people will then be considered. This will be followed by a discussion of new empirical research conducted by the author in two separate studies: (Study 1) a text messaging service piloted by a local council, based in North England, and (Study 2) research conducted with university students to assess the potential of text messaging, as a tool with which to engage and support young citizens.

The combination of this information suggests that text messaging is a viable tool to use in order to engage young people. However, there are major considerations that need to be made for it to be successful in the government arena. Text messaging has the potential to transform how young citizens engage with government issues – however, the overriding outcome that needs further investigation, is that they have to WANT to engage, regardless of the devices being used to entice them in.

2. Active young citizens

Coles has defined a 'young person' (or 'youth') as "an interstitial phase in the life course between childhood and adulthood" [4 p.4]. The precise age at which this period begins and ends has become more and more vague [5]. For the purpose of this chapter the age range 11-24 will be referred to when discussing young citizens/people.

The development of young people into 'good citizens' has been high on the political agenda in the UK over the last decade [6, 7]. School pupils are expected to become "informed and interested citizens" through the development of communication, enquiry, action and participation skills [8]. The UK National Curriculum includes citizenship as an important element to be covered in order to increase understanding of social and moral responsibility, community involvement and political literacy [8]. Now in a bid to develop citizenship at an EU level, a 'Citizens for Europe' programme has been developed for the period 2007-2013 which aims to "promote young people's active citizenship in general and their European citizenship in particular" [9]. Other non-governmental organizations such as the National Youth Agency are also actively trying to engage young people with their communities by establishing initiative drives [10].

What makes a young citizen an active member of society? There are a number of models of active youth citizenship available that identify required elements such as skills and knowledge that young people need in order to become an active citizen [11-15]. In a previous study these models were combined with research conducted with youth organizations spanning five countries and resulted in the development of a model by Trevorrow and Orange of the major dimensions that influence active youth citizenship [3]. The Trevorrow and Orange model (see Figure 1) highlights three dimensions of active youth citizenship: environment, personal traits and behavior that in combination influence an individual's contribution to active citizenship; this model will be referred to in this chapter.

The environment dimension defines the external elements that impact **on** the individual such as societal conditions, structures, experiences and resources; these will enable or constrain the individual in terms of participation [16, 17]. The personal traits dimension includes the qualities, competencies and attitudes needed for the young citizen to become an active participant in society, i.e. that which is resident **within** the individual and has been shaped to some extent by the environmental factors. These include skills, beliefs and knowledge that are significant to the individual if they are to have a meaningful contribution to the community [10, 18]. The behavior dimension highlights the **actions** taken by the individual and represents the degree to which an individual may engage as an active citizen. This includes a 'desire' to be involved regardless of whether they have the personal traits or environment in order to be able to do so competently [19, 20].

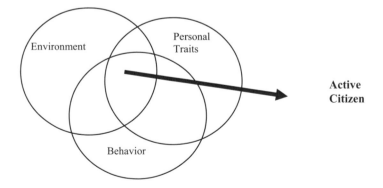

Figure 1. Trevorrow and Orange [3] model of active citizenship by young people

3. New digital media

The Internet has become a predominant service delivery channel and the UK government has adopted the technology with a specific target of encouraging democratic participation and general interest by young citizens [21, 22]. The Internet provides the means to display up-to-date information and the "opportunity to publish far more information than would normally be read by citizens, at a time and place that is convenient to them" [1]. However, despite the fact that young people are observed as more active online than other age groups and the move by government to an Internet-rich activity base, young people are still disengaged from government related issues and still choose not to get involved [22].

Whilst young people have been shown to use the Internet, the phenomenon that is taking over with more impact is that of the mobile phone and the text messaging facility [23]. UK statistics have shown that 80% of the under-25s have a mobile phone with the average age of first owning one being only 8 years of age [24]. The mobile tends to be an immediate communication line. In a survey with young people by Nestlé Social Research Programme, 78% of the sample never or hardly ever turned off their mobile phone [2].

Mobile phone adoption has been reported as surpassing both TV popularity and the number of fixed line subscribers on a worldwide basis [25, 26]. Young people have adopted the mobile phone with extreme enthusiasm [26] and the most popular, if unpredicted, feature for young people has been the text messaging function, which now takes precedence over phone calls and letter writing [27, 28].

"More than eight out of ten people under the age of 25 are more likely to send someone a text message than call." [27]

Currently the text messaging facility is predominantly used by young people for social networking, such as arranging to meet friends and informing parents of their whereabouts [2]. However text messaging is beginning to gain interest from companies and organizations as a means to contact and communicate with young people. A Primary Care Trust in North Tyneside is piloting a project that allows teenage girls to receive sexual health advice and counseling, by experts, via text messaging. The project was developed following discussions with young people, the service allows an individual to send a text message to a 24 hour number, the individual will immediately be invited to an appointment with a member from the sexual health service [29]. A Safety Text solution has also been set up for parents and children to register and set up pre-paid credits so that the young person has the ability to raise alarm should anything happen to them[30]. In Australia and Malta some schools are sending exam marks to pupils via text messaging [26].

Whilst outside of the scope of this chapter, it is interesting to note that the mobile phone is more recently being considered as a potential solution to the disparity that is the digital divide [25, 31]. The high diffusion rate world-wide, the affordability, and ease of use, are just some of the attributes that are highlighting the mobile phone as a means to access information, instead of or in addition to the Internet [31]. Obviously there are draw backs to using such a medium, screen size, phone capability, etc which would need consideration for such an investigation.

The ubiquity of the mobile phone and the universality of text messaging skills among the young imply that they can send and/or receive information at any given time.

Could this be utilized by the government to encourage democratic participation by young people?

4. Empirical research

New empirical research has been conducted in two separate studies of which both will be discussed in the following sections: (Study 1) a text messaging service piloted by a local council, based in North England, and (Study 2) research conducted with university students to assess the potential of text messaging, as a tool with which to engage and support young citizens.

4.1. Study 1: Local council using text messaging with young people

The Youth Services Department of a council in North England had initiated a 'Youth Participation Project' which involved using a two-way text messaging service with young people in the community. A case study was conducted with the council which began eight months into the Project and continued to the end of its pilot year (the final third of the pilot year). The case study approach provided the opportunity to gain in-depth information from a variety of sources about the use of the text messaging service [32, 33]. Both qualitative and quantitative methods were used, gathering data via observation, questionnaires and interviews.

Semi-structured interviews were conducted with staff in the council including: the project leader, who was also the person responsible for sending out messages and collating any responses returned; Head of Youth Services for Students and Communities; Youth Service Manager; and Deputy Chief Executive. In order to attain a different perspective of the Project a young person, a Member of the Youth Parliament (MYP), was also interviewed.

As part of the study personal mobile phones were registered with the text messaging service in order to view the messages that were being sent out, by content and frequency. In addition, with permission from the council and Youth Department, a survey was conducted via the text messaging service with the registered participants (100 young people at the time of study) by sending out a series of four questions about the service to which the participants could respond with a pre-coded answer.

4.2. Study 2: Young people using text messaging to contact local councils

In a separate research project a paper questionnaire was conducted with 1400+ students attending a North England university to gather views from young people on whether text messaging was a viable tool for receiving and giving information on local council/government issues.

The combination of data collected from both studies has provided a wide source of information from which to draw ideas about how a text messaging service could be used as a communication and participation tool between government and young people.

5. New digital media and young citizens' active participation in practice

5.1. Local council text messaging project

The Youth Participation Project was introduced in order to satisfy an element of a public service agreement target to improve democratic participation by young people. Text messaging was adopted as a service that young people were already adept and enthused about using. The service consisted of a computer package with the ability to send text messages to registered mobile phones and collate any responses in a database. Young people were encouraged to sign up to the service and were provided with a financial incentive of a £10 voucher for every 50 consultation messages that they replied to. They had the ability to withdraw from the service at any time by un-registering.

The four questions sent out via the text messaging service for Study 1 went to all 100 young participants who were registered at the time. The response rate was very low to each of the four questions posed with the highest response rate being 12% to the final question. This was not unique to the particular survey; response rates to consultation messages sent out by the council were reported as equally low.

An interview with the project leader who was running the computer-based system highlighted that they had no formal training of the system and were apprehensive about using it. In addition the leader was a temporary employee and located externally from the council offices. The interview with the MYP highlighted a lack of awareness by young people within the community of the system that he had evidenced through his own research.

Personal mobile phones had been registered with the service in order to view the messages that were being sent out to the registered participants. In four months only two messages were received indicating that the service was not being utilized to its highest potential.

5.2. Young peoples perceptions of using text messaging with local councils/government

The survey conducted with university students showed that 98% of respondents owned a mobile phone; 69% sent 5+ text messages and 71% received 5+ text messages daily. 53% of the sample stated that they would be willing for the council to seek their views via text messaging although only 13% believed that the council actually listened to young peoples' views. With regard to giving their views to local councils/government on amenities for young people, the preferred means was via e-mail (38%), followed by not giving any views (17%), and text messaging or a letter both receiving only 16%. Only 20% would ask the council to empty a forgotten bin via text messaging, with phoning being the most popular method (60%). Other government related issues, such as voting, received similar ratings with regard to the use of text messaging, although it is important to note that 'not giving any views/taking part' appeared as a popular option in all scenarios.

6. Is text messaging a viable means of connecting young people and the government?

Some conclusions can be drawn from the information gathered in this chapter; these will be discussed in relation to the Trevorrow and Orange active model of youth citizenship outlined in Section 2 [3].

6.1. Environment

With regard to this study, the main external elements that would impact on the individual are the structure of the service, awareness of the service being offered, and with regard to the resources available this would include actually having a mobile phone and the available credit to use it to engage with community issues.

The service was controlled by a member of staff who was not adept at using the software which could have acted as a constraint on the delivery of the service to young people. Awareness that the Project was being trialled proved to be low and the messages that were sent out to the registered users were far and few between, this would not have been encouraging for future or continued use of the service. Study 2 showed that the majority of young people have at least one mobile phone and hence resource in terms of the actual device was not considered a problem. With regard to credit, an incentive of phone vouchers was offered by the local council in Study 1 to cover costs of text messaging. However, with as few as two messages being sent per three month period, being able to accumulate 50 sent messages appears difficult. The survey question sent out via the text messaging service in Study 1 that gained the highest response was also in relation to receiving the £10 voucher with the response that they would prefer to receive it sooner.

6.2. Personal traits

Study 2 showed that the personal traits dimension of the model is not an issue with regard skills and knowledge of sending and receiving text messages. Young people are comfortable using the device for communication purposes as the number of daily text messages sent and received indicates. In addition, the students surveyed in Study 2 indicated that they would be prepared to communicate about council issues by text messaging.

6.3. Behavior

The low return rate to messages sent out in general in Study 1 from the participants who had willingly signed up to the service, and could withdraw their number at any time, is a significant result. The tool is clearly not being used by young people as was expected, they are still not engaging despite using a communication device that they are comfortable with using as shown in Study 2. Although the students in Study 2 had claimed that they would be willing to communicate with the council via text messaging, in later responses this appeared lower in the 'preferred contact method' than e-mailing or phoning, or in some cases than not giving a response at all. Clearly there are still some practical issues that need further consideration.

Technology and users form a two-way bond, people will use the technology for their own means and in turn, the technology will have unforeseen affects on the users [34]. Can provision of a new channel of communication by the government foster demand by young people? Clearly not.

Even though text messaging offers the potential by which to engage with young people, as Gilbert *et al* discuss in Chapter 12 of this volume, it is not the use of the technology that is in question here, as indicated in Section 6.2, but more so whether the medium will, or can, be used for communication and participation in government issues. This is essentially more of a concern about the desire of young citizens to engage with the government at all, rather than having the skills or access to the medium being used. The fact that the young people in Study 2 did not believe the council listened to young peoples' views is a major concern. Possibly the real issue is not e-government policy or implementation, but rather one associated to civic and political engagement. The research presented here indicates that young people do not have the desire to be involved and participate, or believe that any involvement will be effective, in which case technology is not the answer and other mechanism are required to ensure active participation of young citizens.

References

[1]   Becta,   *Becta   ICT   Advice: ICT   Advice   for   Teachers*.   2003,
      www.ictadvice.org.uk/index.php?section=tl&catcode=as_cu_pr_sub_02&rid=1800&rr=1.
[2]   H. Haste, Joined-up texting: mobile phones and young people, *Young Consumers*, 2005. **6**, 3 (2005), 56-
      67.
[3]   P. Trevorrow and G. Orange, *A Model of Active Youth Citizenship*, Joint Actions Socrates Leonardo Da
      Vinci and Youth Programmes, 2004, 1-33.
[4]   B. Coles, *Youth and Social Policy. Youth citizenship and young careers*, UCL Press Limited, London,
      1995.
[5]   C. Wallace and S. Kovatcheva, *YOUTH IN SOCIETY. The Construction and Deconstruction of Youth in
      East and West Europe*, Palgrave, New York, 1998.
[6]   M. Marinetto, Who Wants to be an Active Citizen? The Politics and Practice of Community Involvement,
      Sociology, **31**, 1 (2003), 103-120.
[7]   A. France, Youth and Citizenship in the 1990s, *Youth and Policy*, **53** (Summer 1996), 28-43.
[8]   DfES,   *Citizenship.   The   National   Curriculum   for   England*.   2004,
      http://www.dfes.gov.uk/citizenship/section.cfm?sectionId=3&hierachy=1.3.
[9]   Commission of the European Communities, *Porposal for a Decision of the European Parliament and of
      the Council*. 2005, http://www.epha.org/a/1843.
[10] R. Parsons,*The National Youth Agency experience. Making a Success of Youth Action*, The National
      Youth Agency, Leicester, 2002.
[11] J.M. Johnson, *Design for Learning: Values, Qualities and Processes of Enriching School Landscapes.*
      Landscape, Architecture Technical Information Series, 2000(www.asla.org/latis1/LATIS-Process.htm).
[12] Active   Citizenship   Today!,   *ACT!   Cycle   of   Change*.   2003,   Institute   for   Citizenship
      www.citizen.org.uk/active/act.html.
[13] A. Osler and H. Starkey, Rights, Identities and Inclusion: European action programmes as political
      education, *Oxford Review of Education*, **25**, 1&2 (1999), 199-215.
[14] P. Treseder, *Empowering Children and Young People: Training Manual*, Save the Children, London,
      1997.
[15] B.l. Boyd, Bringing Leadership Experiences to Inner-City Youth. *Journal of Extension*, **39**, 4(2001),
      August 2001.
[16] G. Jones and C. Wallace, *Youth, Family and Citizenship*. Open University Press, Buckingham, 1992.
[17] S. Morch, *Youth and activity theory*, In *Youth, Citizenship and Social Change in a European Context*, J.
      Bynner, L. Chisholm, and A. Furlong, Editors., Ashgate Publishing Ltd: Hants, 1997.
[18] L. Cairns, Investing in Children: Learning How to Promote the Rights of all Children, *Children and
      Society*, 2001. **15**, 5 (2001), 347-360.

[19] T. Hall, H. Willliamson, and A. Coffey, Young People, Citizenship and the Third Way: A Role for the Youth Service?, *Journal of Youth Studies*, 2000. **3**, 4 (2000), 461-472.
[20] R. Sinclair and A. Franklin, *Young People's Participation*. Quality Protects Research Briefing, 2000. **3**(www.rip.org.uk/publications/QPB/qbp3.html).
[21] S. Harwood, Government places online at centre of educating youngsters, *New Media Age*, 2005. **17/02/05**, 5.
[22] J. Ward., An opportunity for engagement in cyberspace: Political youth Web sites during the 2004 European Parliament election campaign, *Information Polity*, **10**, 3/4 (2005), 233-246.
[23] D. Madell and S. Muncer, Back from the Beach but Hanging on the Telephone? English Adolescents' Attitudes and Experiences of Mobile Phones and the Internet, *CyberPsychology & Behavior*, 2004. **7**, 3 (2004), 359-367.
[24] J. Dhaliwal, Youth market is central to developing mobile, *New Media Age*, 2005. **21/04/05**, 9.
[25] R.E. Rice and J.E. Katz, Comparing internet and mobile phone usage: digital divides of usage, adoption, and dropouts, *Telecommunications Policy*, (2003), 597-623.
[26] L. Srivastava, Mobile phones and the evolution of social behavior, *Behavior and Information Technology*, **24**, 2 (2005), 111-129.
[27] BBC News, *Young 'prefer texting to calls'*. 2003, http://news.bbc.co.uk/go/pr/fr/-/1/hi/business/2985072.stm.
[28] C. Farr, Sealed with a kiss, *Times Educational Supplement*, **4625** (2005), 23.
[29] BBC News, *Girls text for morning after pill*. 2003, http://news.bbc.co.uk/go/pr/fr/-/1/hi/england/tyne/3227149.stm.
[30] Safetytext Ltd, *Safety Text*. 2005, www.safetytext.com.
[31] R.J. Kauffman and A.A. Techatassanasoontorn, Is there a global digital divide for digital wireless phone technologies?, *Journal of the Association for Information Systems*, 2005. **6**, 12 (2005), 338-382.
[32] V. Keddie, *Case Study Research*, In *The Sage Dictionary of Social Research Methods*, V. Jupp, Editor. Sage, London, 2006.
[33] R.K. Yin., *Case Study Design: Research and Methods*. 3rd ed., Sage, Beverley Hills, 2003.
[34] J.M. García-Montes, D. Caballero-Muñoz, and M. Pérez-Arvarez, Changes in the self resulting from the use of mobile phones, *Media, Culture and Society*, 2006. **28**, 1, (2006), 67-82.

Part 4

Evaluation of e-Government

Developments in e-Government
D. Griffin et al. (Eds.)
IOS Press, 2007

Macro, Micro and Pica: A Three-Level Exploration of e-Government Economics

Frank BANNISTER
Trinity College, Dublin, Eire

1. An old question

As a field of interest in information systems, e-government is not exactly new except perhaps in the purely semantic sense. The term e-government, by which Europeans mostly mean e-public administration, was coined in the 1990s, probably in the United States [1] . However the topic of informatization of public administration, which is electronic government by another name, has been widely discussed in the European literature since the early 1980s (indeed earlier, e.g. [2]). Examples of early contributions can also be found in the US literature and include Kraemer and King [3] and Perry and Kraemer [4]. To date, little of this literature (there are exceptions, see for example [5, 6]) has been concerned with questions of economics *per se*, despite the frequent use of the word 'economics' in a looser sense (as in Parker and Benson [7] and Wiseman [8]). Likewise, while there have been many studies which have considered questions of cost and value in the public sector (examples include Margretts [9, 10] and Willcocks [11]), this body of research largely eschews economics, focusing instead on a variety of other metrics. Part of the reason for this may be that this is a topic that sits at the intersection of three disciplines (Figure 1) and that there are few scholars who feel comfortable working in all three fields.

When considering the economics of ICT use in the public sector, it is important to have a sense of history. e-Government did not start in the mid 1990s when the wider world discovered the Internet, any more than did e-business. By 1995, many states had over three decades of computer development, implementation and operations behind them and many major systems were in place, supporting the day to day operations of public administration. In economic terms, many of these systems are of much greater significance than current developments. The reason for this is simple: as in business the first phase of computerization is to tackle those areas which are easily automated and from which a high return on investment can be expected. Thus basic systems such as computerization of government payrolls, Pay-As-You-Earn taxation or social welfare systems were the obvious targets for early computerization. In practice, computerization of these was not always terribly effective [10], but where it was done well, the return and savings to the taxpayer were substantial. The relevance of this legacy base to the discussion that follows lies in the fact that economic impacts of current investment may depend heavily on such existing assets and previous investments.

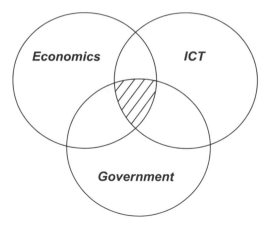

Figure 1. The locus of e-government economics as a field of study

2. Expenditure on e-government

In this chapter, the focus is on the impact of government spending on information technology rather than on the actual spend itself or its fiscal impact on national budgets or government borrowing. However it is worth commenting briefly on e-government expenditure.

Arriving at a reasonably accurate Figure for e-government spend is difficult for precisely the reasons set out in the Introduction, i.e. much of what is spent on ICT by governments is not necessarily recognized as such. There are also many problems in arriving at a true cost [12]. Figures therefore need to be treated with caution. Many of the estimates of e-government spend come, not from governments themselves, but from research companies. For example, Kelly [13] cites Gartner Group as estimating that Western European governments would spent US$67.8 billion in 2003 (one cannot but wonder at the precision of the decimal place). The UK research company Kable (cited by Rogers [14]) estimated that between 2001 and 2006, e-government projects would cost the UK government £7.4 billion (comprising £3.0 billion for central government and £4.4 billion for local government). More recently, Kable have claimed that total expenditure in the UK to date is about £13.5 billion and that the annual spend in the European Union would rise to $68 billion by 2007 [15].

These are large sums of money and it is important to know what the taxpayer is getting in return for his or her largesse. In what follows, this question will not be addressed directly in terms of, say, cost benefit analysis or return on investment. But it will look at how this spend impacts on the economy at a number of levels.

3. Definitions

A great deal of the discussion of e-government, even in academic circles, is imprecise as to what exactly 'government' is in this context. Most states have a core of central administrators and several layers radiating out from this. In Ireland, for example, the central civil service is quite small, being vested in 16 departments of state which between them employ under 40,000 people, about 1% of the population. However, as in other countries, much government is delegated to a series of executive agencies. In Ireland these vary from the National Roads Authority to the Health and Safety

Executive. Most of these are answerable to a central government department and are a *de facto* extension of that department's operations. In the next circle out, are the local authorities which have limited governmental powers over a particular county or city. Further out reside areas like health, education, policing and the army; all part of the public sector, but not quite government. Beyond them, on the fringes so to speak, is the state commercial sector. Even today in Europe many states still own electricity supply companies and airlines, to give but two examples. This concept is illustrated in Figure 2.

A pertinent question is: where in this model, does e-government stop? To illustrate the problem consider the following question: which of these are examples of e-government:

- Paying taxes on-line;
- On-line car registration;
- A citizen advice web-page;
- A system for processing planning applications on-line;
- Hiring a public football pitch for a game on-line;
- A new police system for processing penalty points;
- A new police crime control computer system;
- A laboratory control system in a public hospital;
- A new command and control system for the military;
- A new reservation system for the state airline?

Most people, whether scholar or citizen would agree that the first item on this list is definitely e-government and the last is certainly not. The answer is not so clear in the case of some of those in the middle. At one e-government conference held in 2005, there were papers on 'e-government' in or on:

- a regional ministry;
- educational services;
- a local authority;
- the courts system;
- the taxation of e-commerce;
- epidemiology;
- local mobile phone services in a city.

Under the banner of e-government, others have written about areas as wide apart as coastguard services and e-voting. In fact, much of what is described as e-government is in practice about e-governance or e-operations in public sector entities. The exchange of information on epidemics is clearly an important and potentially powerful application of communications technology, but it is not government as such.

Bearing all of the above in mind, for the purposes of this discussion, e-government will be defined as comprising:

- The central administrative core;
- Agencies which are a *de facto* extension of that core and
- Local authorities,

and the definition of 'economics' used will be:

> *"The study of methods of allocating scarce resources in production, the distribution of the resulting output and the effects of this allocation and distribution"* [16].

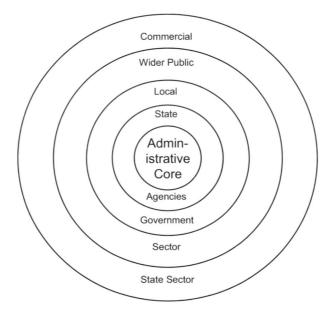

Figure 2. An onion model of a typical public sector

Taking information technology, in terms of people and material, as being one scarce resource, questions to be explored in e-government economics therefore include how much should be invested in such resources, how such resources should be allocated and what impact this allocation may have? This is a wide brief. In taking it on, it is possible to choose several different vantage points ranging from the impact of e-government on national or international economies as a whole down to its impact on the individual citizen or organization. Here, a simple three tier approach will be used.

4. Three Levels of Analysis

As a field, economics is traditionally divided into macro- and microeconomics. Macroeconomics is concerned with the aggregate effect of many localized decisions on the behavior of national or regional economies. Microeconomics is concerned with the decisions and behaviors of individuals or firms and their consequences. As such, much of microeconomics is about topics such as prices, markets, productivity, factors of production and so on. In terms of e-government, microeconomics might be thought of encompassing government departments or agencies or even the administrative public sector as a whole. However, when considering e-government, it is useful, with apologies to professional economists, to introduce a further distinction, which will be entitled 'picaeconomics'. Picaeconomics is concerned with the economic impact of e-government on individuals or small communities

When applied to e-government, each of these levels is problematic in its own way. At the microeconomic level for example, there is no market as such for many public sector products and no competition for most of them. The government is frequently a monopoly supplier and the consumer may have no choice but to buy from the government if he she or it wants to engage in certain activities or obtain certain services. This applies to a wide range of goods from a passport to a mobile telephone license. These problems are well known of course, but it is worth reiterating them here if only to be clear that the expression 'economics of e-government' needs to be approached with care at this level, as at the other two. For a technical discussion of these issues, see Soete and Weehuizen [5][1].

To illustrate some of the issues, the example of the Irish Department of Agriculture and Food (DAF) will be used throughout what follows. The DAF is one of the major Irish departments of state, employing over 4,000 administrative and professional staff. It manages approximately €2 billion in funds each year including €1.3 billion in EU payments of various sorts. In terms of operations and policy and their impact on e-government, the DAF is one of the most complicated of the 16 departments of state in Ireland which makes it a particularly useful source of informative examples.

5. e-Government and macroeconomics

Macroeconomics, in this context, can be defined as the impact of e-government on the economy of the nation as a whole[2]. The macroeconomic question is whether or not e-government is a significant factor in, or has a material impact (directly or indirectly) on, economic performance at a national level. A good starting point for this line of enquiry is national competitiveness.

States and nations have always competed with each other. Sometimes they raided each other's territory and fought wars either to establish ascendancy or simply to survive. Wars are still fought for such reasons, but between democracies in the first world at least, today's battles are economic, diplomatic and cultural. It the case of the first of these, the locus of conflict is the marketplace and the weapons of choice include monetary and fiscal policy as well as variety of other tools such as production subsidies, launch aid and import tariffs. Governments use a multiplicity of means, both overt and covert, to try to help their industries and citizens compete in a world market. States also compete for highly mobile investment capital and the employment and wealth creation that follow it. Tables of comparative international competitiveness and economic performance are published regularly. One example of this is the World Competitiveness Ranking [17] published by IMD[3] which uses 325 criteria to rank countries. Competitiveness tables attempt to measure the economic performance of countries across a range of metrics from wage rates and inflation to political stability and the quality of the educational system. The question asked of the impact of e-government might therefore be broken down into two: what impact does e-government have on national competitiveness and on national economic performance?

These are difficult questions even when dealing with less elusive concepts than e-government. To isolate, say, the comparative marginal impact of even a variable like average hourly industrial wage on economic growth, requires detailed, accurate and comparable data. Even where such data exist, comparisons can be clouded by a variety of other factors such as worker productivity, social security costs and benefits, the income tax regime, leave entitlements and exchange rates. It has almost become a cliché that workers in France work fewer hours than those in any other European country, but that French productivity approaches that of the United States [18]. In Ireland there has been much debate on the factors that led to the Celtic Tiger boom which started in the latter half of the 1990s. The boom has been variously attributed to:

- A low tax regime;
- A large English-speaking and young labour force;
- The education system;
- EU transfers;
- The dot.com boom;
- Far sighted industrial policy

and so on [19, 20, 21, 22]. If it continues to be hard to find a consensus, even amongst professional economists, on the causes of such a phenomenon, the challenge of distilling out the impact of e-government from amongst 300+ other criteria is likely to be formidable indeed. Nonetheless, given the huge investment in e-government world-wide, a question that needs to be asked and, if possible, answered is at least how, if not to what extent, can e-government contribute to competitiveness or better economic performance?

5.1. Ease of doing business?

One way in which e-government can improve national economic performance is by improving the ease of doing business. The phrase 'ease of doing businesses encompasses everything from the degree of political corruption to the amount of red tape in getting things done. An inefficient public sector acts not only like a drag anchor on local businesses; it can also be a major deterrent to inward investment. Aggressive multinationals operating in world markets will seek an edge wherever they find one and countries which are seen to have efficient and effective state machinery will, *ceteris paribus*, be more attractive to potential investors than states where it is necessary to deal with cumbersome bureaucracies for the most mundane of tasks - a fact recognized implicitly in the European Union's Lisbon Declaration. This is a topic of interest in the business literature. Baron [23] uses the term non-market strategies to describe how firms can gain advantage from exploiting the services of the state to their advantage.

In this battle, e-government is certainly a factor. The Irish government's flagship project in this arena is BASIS (*www.basis.ie*). Other states have similar sites. BASIS provides a wide range of information on everything from starting a business to employment legislation and, if (s)he drills down far enough, BASIS will eventually take a user to the requisite state agency, document or form. This is all very well, but a distinction must be made between the messenger and the message. Good systems can enable the business user to get to the information she wants, obtain forms, make returns and so on. But for business it is the number of forms, the complexity of the regulations and the financial and temporal costs of compliance that really matter. Some indication of this can be obtained by observing the depth of drilling required to reach base information. For example, using BASIS to find out about information requirements for company registration gives: Home, Legal and Regulatory, Company Set-Up and Registration, Information Obligations, Requirements following Incorporation of a Company

This suggests a simple piece of research looking at e-government business site maps as proxies for the complexity of national business legislation! More seriously, if a country's public administration tends toward the bureaucratic and operates a convoluted and heavy-handed regulatory regime for businesses, simply making it easier to interface with that regime is only going to have a marginal impact on business decision makers, especially external investors.

5.2. National efficiency?

A wider question is the impact of e-government on national efficiency. The cumulative impact of small savings, particularly time savings, can be significant on a national scale. To take a simple example, if taxing one's motor car requires a trip to a motor tax office and such offices are only open during office hours, then many car owners will have to take time off work to tax their cars. If doing this takes an hour and a half (say) and there are 10 million cars in the country, assuming an eight hour working day, this amounts to a little over 1,000 man-years of output lost each year while people tax their cars (assuming that the time would otherwise have been productively used of course). So if one takes a wide view of economics as encompassing citizens' personal time and that that time is worth money and that that time should be included in measures of economic output, then there are potential savings (or productivity gains) realizable using a range of e-tools from web-based personal income tax calculators to purchasing a dog license on-line. While the impact of such savings will be moderated by the fact that those who have most contact with the state are often the least economically active (see below) and are therefore less like to use them, nonetheless there could be a significant overall effect. Of course, such impacts might be negative. For example, if citizens have to invest in equipment (computers, communications devices etc.) in order to do business with the state or if the advent of e-government encourages states to make processes more complicated, there many be no net benefit to the economy.

5.3. Macro impact examples

To see the real impact of economically effective e-government, it is necessary to go beyond the web-sites and on-line services and look at the state's underlying computer systems and how well they service the consumer and the economy. The potential of this can be seen by looking at the impact of the DAF computer systems on Irish agriculture and, indeed, on the Irish exchequer. Because of the effectiveness of its monitoring systems and control systems, Ireland has the lowest level of disallowances (penalties imposed by EU Commission under the Common Agricultural Policy for breaches of rules) in the EU. Of course this is an avoided cost and such costs are notoriously hard to evaluate, but it is probable that without such systems the country would incur disallowances of several hundred million euro per annum. Effective use of computer systems, including a Cattle Movement and Monitoring System which tracks the location of every cow in the country, by the DAF also contributed to the containment of a foot and mouth outbreak in Ireland in 2001 (at a time when the UK industry was brought to its knees by the same outbreak) and may also have helped control BSE[4]. The national economic impact of these systems alone dwarfs the impact of even the best designed web pages for state agencies.

Consequently, if e-government is defined narrowly as the interface between the state and citizen, it is unlikely to be a major factor in national economic competitiveness. Factors such as corporate tax rates, ease of hiring and firing, availability of a skilled labour force or quality of infrastructure will loom much larger in the mind of a worker, businessman or potential investor than how easy it is to fill in a form on-line. The reality may be that, at this level, good e-government systems may be more of a must-have than a competitive edge, although, as noted above, the impact of small improvements on a large scale should not be underestimated. If e-government is taken as the application of ICT to all aspects of governance and administration, the picture may be quite different. As in the case of the DAF, the real economic value may lie beneath, below the radar of traditional economic measurements.

Finally there should be some mention of the halo effect [24]. The image of a country, as of individuals, is determined by many factors and its public image, which includes the public face of its government, is one. The EU is one of a number of bodies which publish 'beauty contest' data of this type [25, 26, 27]. Others are published by Accenture [28], the United Nations [29] and Brown University [30]. The conclusion is therefore that, at a macroeconomic level, e-government matters and does have an impact, but at the surface level that the impact may not be that large. At a level of depth, it may be significant. This is a field which is worth exploring further.

6. e-Government and microeconomics

e-Government offers a wide range of potential economic benefits for state agencies and for corporate entities dealing with those agencies. A corporate entity might be a business (from small to multinational). This is the largest single category. However there are many other such entities, for example charities, private schools, private hospitals, professional associations and so on.

Benefits to such entities can be divided into two broad categories:

- Generic benefits and
- Agency specific benefits.

Generic economic benefits are those that are available to any agency. In general, these are the traditional benefits of information technology such as automation of manual processes and the resultant labour savings, elimination of paper, business process simplification and so on. In particular, there are substantial potential cost savings which can be realized from converting hitherto face-to-face delivery to self-service. Even at the trivial level of eliminating paper circulars, putting paper based discussion or management of parliamentary questions on-line using groupware; it is not difficult to see how ongoing savings to the taxpayer can be made.

That said, there are several key differences between commercial/private organizations and public sector bodies which make this picture more complicated:

- First is the fact that public servants usually have job security; they cannot be hired and fired as workloads fluctuate. This means that the financial benefits of process re-engineering and simplification are not always easy to realize as new jobs must be found for displaced staff.
- Second, the public sector is large and mobility is not as high as in commercial enterprises.
- Third, many public sector organizations are heavily unionized. This can sometimes (though not always) mean that there is more resistance to change than would be the case in the private sector.
- Fourth, as already noted, many state agencies are monopoly suppliers. The citizen cannot shop around for a driving license.
- Fifth, the public sector is multi-ethical, i.e. its value system is a great deal more complex than that of a commercial firm. In the latter, the primary (sometimes even sole) ethic is profit or wealth creation. The public sector on the other hand is concerned with factors such as equity, access, fairness, universality and so on, not to mention the presence of multiple stakeholders, all of which means that the conventional rules of economics do not always apply. The civil service cannot simply close down a service because it is losing money, nor can it always engage in differential pricing to give but two examples.

In considering the economic impact of e-government on the state agency or department of state, it is, therefore, important to realize that the rules are different.

A key question at this middle level of economics is whether investment in e-government is the best or at least a justifiable, use of scarce resources. This leads to some subtle issues. For example, by shifting service delivery on-line, state agencies frequently transfer the work from the agency to the customer/citizen. A classic example of this which pre-dates e-government is self assessment tax. By requiring taxpayers to compute their own tax, governments shift workload from the collective taxpayer to the individual taxpayer. There is certain logic in this. Why should a citizen with simple tax affairs pay for computing the tax of somebody whose tax affairs are far more complicated?[5] As more and more services become self services thanks to e-government, an interesting dynamic emerges which is illustrated in Figure 3.

An interesting conjecture is that, if one takes a purely short term economic perspective, certain types of investments will often show a poor return to state agencies either because there is public resistance (or indifference) to them or because structural rigidities prevent the type of labour shedding or process change that should result. The latter is not, of course, just a problem with e-government. A number of recent government reforms in Ireland have run into precisely this problem[6]. On the other hand, if one takes a long view, it may be that the government can use this slack to create new services. The danger in this situation is that agencies fall victim to Parkinson's Law [31] and end up finding things to keep people busy. Where resultant slack is used to create new services, the problem then becomes putting an economic value on such services, especially if they are not yet clearly defined.

This is even more the case when it comes to *agency specific* aspects of e-government. Agency specific services are those targeted at an agency's primary customer. The latter is often some subgroup of citizens or stakeholders. For example, social welfare departments generally deal with the poorer or more vulnerable, foreign affairs departments largely deal with citizens who are temporarily or permanently outside the country and so on.

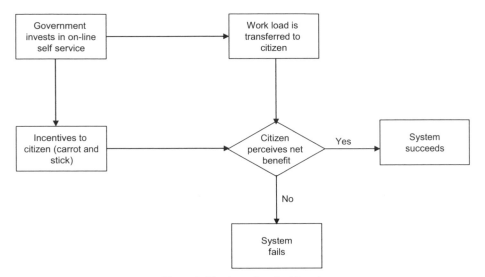

Figure 3. The dynamics of self service

In most countries there is a myriad of agencies dedicated to specific social or economic groups or collective needs in the community.   Other agencies, such as departments of defense may, in the normal run of things, have little or no direct economic dealings with the public at all.

To illustrate these points, consider the position in the DAF. The DAF has several constituencies including farmers and the European Commission. Farmers, the most politically important constituency, numbering about 200,000 (of whom about 130,000 are full time) in Ireland. The nature of the services provided by the DAF to farmers is highly specialized and of no relevance to the average office worker in Dublin. To meet these needs, the DAF runs a large number of highly technical IT applications. Several of these systems support a wide range of EU subsidies and farm-support schemes from export refunds to rural environment protection. As already noted, other systems are used for management of animal health, tracking herds and individual animals as well as controlling testing regimes and helping to cope with disease outbreaks (such as BSE and foot and mouth). If one looks at such systems through the lens of conventional investment analysis, some of these systems will show a high return on investment. Others may show a negative return for a variety of reasons including that they are mandatory or that they support wider national or EU goals such as protection of the environment or maintaining food quality. When e-government and the economics thereof are talked about in the context of the DAF, it is not only these systems, and not the department's public website, that matter, but a full understanding of the first, second and even third order effects of what are often highly complex systems.

This point needs to be stressed. A great deal of the debate about e-government takes place at a relatively superficial (in the literal sense of being near the surface) level, i.e. at the point at which the systems meet the public. However, without the engines underneath, much e-government is little other than gloss. The power of the e-government services delivered by the DAF lies in its ability to pay farmers the correct amount on time, to manage animal health and to provide accurate accounts to the EU. ICT priorities in the DAF are often driven by external events. An outbreak of foot-and-mouth disease, such as happened in 2001, is a national emergency and IT resources will inevitably be diverted into dealing with such a threat.

The position is therefore far from simple. The important lesson is that the work of government agencies is complex and multifaceted. Generalizations are dangerous and what may be important for one agency may be irrelevant for another.

7. e-Government and picaeconomics

The term 'picaeconomics' will not be found in economics textbooks, but is here used for those aspects of e-government which affect the economics of the family and the individual. Clearly individuals can benefit indirectly as members of corporate entities. However picaeconomics refers to the impact on citizens in their private lives, i.e. benefits which accrue to them personally, not to some larger group to which they happen to belong. Furthermore, while there is an overlap at each of the three levels discussed in this chapter with the thorny issue of IT value, this overlap is at its greatest here. It has already been noted that one aspect of the microeconomics of e-government is reducing cost to the general tax payer by transferring work to the consumer of the service. An e-government system that simply increased the burdens on the citizen would not be a saleable proposition. Although government can shift workload by stealth, if it is to be economically attractive for the citizen to accept this, it needs to do some or all of:

- Reducing the cost to the user of using the service;
- Simplifying the process for the user;
- Increasing the level of service to the user;
- Saving the user time;
- Eliminating the need for a process altogether.

Given the complexity of many government processes, none of these should be difficult to achieve. For example, a common phenomenon, typical of this type of problem, is the state seeking from citizens information which it already has or does not need. This can be eliminated. Eliminating the need to travel to a government office to transact business (as in the example of motor taxation cited above) saves the citizen time. Permitting automation of processes (such as direct debiting or money transfer) also saves the citizen time and is of direct economic benefit. There are many possibilities.

7.1. Citizen time and citizen money

The cost, in time and money, to the individual citizen of dealing with the government varies greatly. Many citizens may spend little time during the year dealing with the state. Others may spend many weeks over the course of a year transacting their personal business with the state. Examples of the latter might include those claiming extensive state benefits or people entangled in complex tax negotiations or planning wrangles. It is here that one of the significant problems of picaeconomics arises as the citizens that have most interaction with the state tend to be the poorest and (to a lesser extent) the most wealthy. All citizens deal with the state for so-called life events (e.g. birth, marriage, first employment, having a child, etc.). But groups like the unemployed, single mothers and other disadvantaged groups will have constant contact with state services, possibly weekly or, in some cases, daily. At the other extreme, the wealthy, because of their more complicated tax and business affairs will also have more contact with the government than a 'typical' middle class salaried employee. The paradox is that when it comes to the technology of e-government, those who have most contact with the state have least access (Figure 4). Consequently, at a citizen level, the picaeconomic impact of e-government may be limited by such structural factors.

7.2. Pica impact examples

Nonetheless, there are areas where impacts can be made. From the viewpoint of a farmer dealing with the DAF, the key service factors include immediate payment of monies due and an easy to use and efficient service when dealing with the department. DAF systems save time for farmers in a variety of ways. Reporting of cattle movements is now done automatically by marts. The farmer does not have to report to the department that he has sold the animal; the department systems will get this information from the mart's computer system. Likewise, if a farmer purchases an animal, the system will know that he now has that animal together with any payments attached to it. It will also know if the animal needs to be tested for any diseases. If these systems were not in place, the onus for this would rest with the farmer (as it has in the past). Even though Irish farmers still have to fill out what they would probably regard as too many forms, the aggregate impact of the DAF's systems on the productivity of farmers is considerable. By automating a variety of activities that were heretofore manual and by providing farmers with access to information on everything from marts to animal health, the DAF computer systems save the farmer time and help him (or less commonly her) increase his productivity. For the individual farmer, this is a significant contribution to his economic welfare.

Farmers, however, are a special case. The impact of computer systems on the personal lives of social welfare recipients is much less significant in economic terms. In the case of social welfare, the benefits are indirect, i.e. by automating systems and making them more flexible, resources can be released to concentrate on case work and on those social welfare customers/clients who need personal and detailed attention. In a similar way, the picaeconomic impact of each state agency will impact different groups in different ways. Detailed analysis of this is way beyond the scope of this chapter. What can be said, to paraphrase Abraham Lincoln, is that when it comes to picaeconomic effects, e-government will impact on the economics of some of the people all of the time and all of the people some of the time, but not on all of the people all of the time.

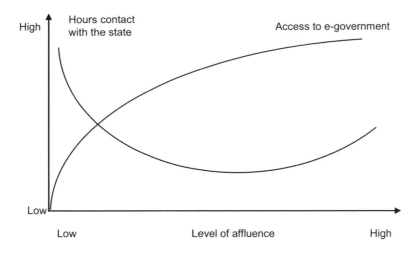

Figure 4. Relationship between potential usage and access for e-government

8. Conclusion

This chapter provides a preliminary look at some of the issues in the economics of e-government. There is much work to be done to develop this field.   The objective here has been to map out the field and to demonstrate that it offers many rich possibilities for research at a number of levels. While these levels have been treated separately, it is clear, even from the above discussion, that the lines between then are blurred and that an issue at any one level may have resonances at one or both of the others.

Research into the economics of e-government is important for (at least) three reasons.   First, it is important to gain an understanding of the contribution of government IT spend to the national economy. It has been claimed (and some assert that it has been proved) that almost all of the increase in productivity in the US over the past 20 years can be attributed to information technology [32].   Even if this is only partially correct, there must already have been significant and measurable economic improvements from the deployment of ICT in government.   After all, in many countries, including Ireland, it was the public sector which led the way in computing in the early years. The problem is that the real impacts are often hidden and that much of the value of e-government is to be found in nuts and bolts systems which support economic groups in a variety of ways, but which do not get recorded in the economic data. This needs to be corrected, in retrospect if necessary.

Secondly, research into the economics of e-government is useful if it can provide a guide to future investment. A great deal of money has been and is being wasted on e-government projects that have delivered little or will deliver little. Such money could be better spent. Governments and public servants, no less than anybody else, are often attracted to the glamorous rather than the grunt work of deep systems. It has been argued before now [33] that much so called e-government is little more than a fresh coat of paint over a crumbling structure. It is time to declare the days of adequate e-government being just an information website with a few on-line forms have passed. The focus must now move from optics to real added value including economic value.

Thirdly, following from both of the above and to use the definition of economics adopted in this chapter, it is about the allocation of scarce resources. While it may be politic to throw bread and circuses to the populace, the real work of e-government happens beneath the carapace. A good understanding of the economics of e-government can only lead to better allocation of resources and the potential, as shown by some of the examples cited in this chapter, is enormous. The best ICT professionals in the public sector have long known this. It is not clear that the economists or the politicians are as aware. It is up to the research community to provide this insight.

Endnotes

1. Soete and Weehuizen use a much wider definition of e-government, incorporating the wider public sector e.g. hospitals, schools, security forces etc. in their discussion.
2. This could also apply to a state or a region. For simplicity, this concept of a national economy will be used here.
3. The International Institute for Management Development business school. Current rankings can be found at http://www01.imd.ch/wcy/
4. Bovine Spongiform Encephalopathy
5. Probably because they are wealthier!
6. Notably a plan to decentralise the civil service and the re-structuring of the country's health administration.

References

[1]   J. Kaaya, Towards Implementation of E-government Services in East Africa: Content Analysis of Government Websites, *The Electronic Journal of e-Government*, **2**, 1 (2004), 39-54.
[2]   LAMSAC, *Costing the use of computers in local government: report of the Computer Panel of Local Authorities Management Services and Computer Committee Computer Panel*, Local Authorities Management Services and Computer Committee, London, 1978.
[3]   K. Kraemer and J. King, *Computers, Power, and Urban Management: What Every Local Executive Should Know*, Administrative and Policy Study Series, Sage Publications, California, 1976.
[4]   J. Perry and K. Kraemer, *Technological Innovation in American Local Government/ The Case of Computing*, Pergamon Press, New York, 1979.
[5]   L. Soete and R. Weehuizen, The Economics of e-Government: A Bird's Eye View, *International Journal of Communications, Law and Policy*, **8** (2003), Winter.
[6]   M. Freeman and S. Nelson, Economic Competitiveness is Vital in the 21st Century, *Public Management*, **85**, 1 (2003), 22-27.
[7]   M. Parker and R. Benson, *Information Economics: Linking Business Performance to Information Technology*, Prentice-Hall, Englewood Cliffs, New Jersey, 1988.
[8]   D. Wiseman, Information Economics: a practical approach to valuing information systems, in L. Willcocks, (Ed.), *Information Management, The Evaluation of Information Systems Investments*, Chapman Hall, London, 1994.
[9]   H. Margretts, The Computerization of Social Security: The Way Forward or a Step Backwards?, *Public Administration*, **69** (1991), 325-343.
[10]   H. Margretts, *Information Technology in Government: Britain and America*, Routledge, London, 1999.
[11]   L. Willcocks, Managing Information Systems in UK Public Administration: Issues and Prospects, *Public Administration*, **72** (1994), Spring, 13-32.
[12]   F. Bannister, P. McCabe and D. Remenyi, IS costing: the case for a reference model, *Southern African Business Review*, **7**, 1 (2003), 1-16.
[13]   P. Kelly, e-Government must offer value for money, ElectricNews.net, 2003, available at: http://www.enn.ie/news.html?code=9379230.
[14]   J. Rogers, *E-government savings will outweight costs as the UK government focuses on improving services*, ComputerWeekly.com, 13th June, 2003, available at: http://www.computerweekly.com/Article122624.htm

[15] Nomensa, *E-government Investments Drive IT Spending*, 2005, available at: http://www.nomensa.com/news/industry-news/2005/6/e-government-investments-drive-it-spending.html

[16] A. Bullock, O. Stallybrass and S. Trombley, *The Fontana Dictionary of Modern Thought*, Fontana Books, London, 1988.

[17] P. Purcell, New infrastructure board will need help of special High Court division, *The Irish Times*, 17/10/2003.

[18] O. Blanchard, The Economic Future of Europe, *Working Paper 10310*, National Bureau of Economic Research, Cambridge, MA., 2004, Available at http://papers.nber.org/papers/w10310.pdf

[19] J. Fitzgerald, Understanding Ireland's Economic Success, *ESRI Working Paper*, No. 111, 1999.

[20] C. O'Grada, Is the Celtic Tiger a Paper Tiger?, *ESRI Quarterly Economic Commentary*, Summer (2002).

[21] F. Barry, The Celtic Tiger Era: Delayed Convergence or Regional Boom?, *ESRI Quarterly Economic Commentary*, Summer (2002).

[22] P. Honohan and B. Walsh, Catching Up With the Leaders – The Irish Hare, *Brookings Papers in Economic Activity*, 2002.

[23] D. Baron, Integrated Strategy: Market and Non Market Components", *California Management Review*, **37**, 2 (2005), 47-65.

[24] S. Plous, *The Psychology of Decision Making*, McGraw-Hill, 1993.

[25] A. McLinden, *Ireland Tops EU e-Government Rankings*, Electric News, 2002, http://www.enn.ie/news.html?code=7890738

[26] Economist Intelligence Unit (with IBM), *The 2004 e-readiness rankings*, The Economist, London, 2004.

[27] Capgemini, *Online Availability of Public Services. How is Europe Progressing?* Web-based Survey on Electronic Public Services. Report of the Sixth Measurement, e-Europe, 2006, available at: http://ec.europa.eu/information_society/soccul/egov/egov_benchmarking_2005.pdf

[28] Accenture, *e-Government Leadership: Building the Trust*, Accenture, Dublin, 2006.

[29] UNPAN, *Global E-government Readiness Report 2005: From E-government to E-inclusion*, United Nations, 2006, available at: http://unpan1.un.org/intradoc/groups/public/documents/un/unpan021888.pdf

[30] D. West, *Global E-Government, 2005*, Center for Public Policy, Brown University, RI, USA, 2005. Available at: http://www.insidepolitics.org/egovt05int.html

[31] E. Brynjolfsson and L. Hitt, Paradox Lost? Firm Level Evidence on the Returns to Information Systems Spending.", in L. Willcocks, and S. Lester (Eds.), *Beyond the IT Productivity Paradox*, Wiley, 1999.

[31] C.N. Parkinson, *Parkinson's Law or the Pursuit of Progress*, Penguin Books, London, 1965.

[32] F. Bannister, Dismantling the silos: extracting new value from IT investment in public administration", *Information Systems Journal*, **11** (2000), 65-84.

Developments in e-Government
D. Griffin et al. (Eds.)
IOS Press, 2007

Information and Communication Technology Evaluation: Role, Methods and Practices in the Public Sector

Luca BUCCOLIERO and Stefano CALCIOLARI
*Centre for Research on Health and Social Care Management,
Bocconi University, Milan, Italy*

1. e-Government: challenges and opportunities

The recent and pervasive diffusion of ICT into commerce, industry and the public sector has led to a revolution whose consequences are potentially comparable to those produced by the industrial revolution. ICT has been assigned a key role in promoting the development of what is generally termed the "new economy", which is defined as [1]:

- *Informational*, as the productivity and competitiveness of its actors largely depend on the ability to efficiently generate process and transfer information.
- *Global*, as production, consumption and circulation are organised at the world level.
- *Networked*, as production, consumption and competition take place in a web of business networks.

The typical organisational form of production in this new economy is the *networked company*, which applies ICT to redesign processes and relations in a useful (effective) and cost-effective (efficient) way.

This substantial and far-reaching change also affects the public sector as it is directly involved in productive processes and it also governs social and economic activities. The effects and perspectives of this change on the public sector are generally termed *e-Government*, which is also defined as the renewal and innovation of public administration through the strategic application of ICT [2]. However, public action is subject to the principle of '*value for money*' because of scarcity of resources. Therefore, the ability to prioritise investments and the ability to identify the best alternative are two key issues.

In this context, ICT evaluation represents a key means of enhancing the decision-making process in the public sphere. Essential to determining the value of ICT investment is the relation between the costs incurred for the acquisition and introduction of ICT and the gain from better management. In addition, since e-government initiatives gain from the "network model", ICT evaluation can improve planning at a national level by coordinating ICT strategies adopted by individual public institutions.

2. ICT evaluation approaches

The scientific literature reports a significant variety of evaluative approaches for ICT. The heterogeneity of measures and principles formalized and adopted in actual practice leads to the conclusion that ICT evaluation has a multidimensional, complex nature. This is essentially due to the fact that each approach implies a particular role for evaluation and aims to meet particular information needs.

The scientific community has long been interested in understanding the relationship between ICT and aggregate productivity of companies. The need for measuring the value of ICT as a specific factor of production is therefore clear. Early studies [3, 4, 5] revealed the alarming "IT productivity paradox". Despite substantial, increased investment in Information Technology (IT), no significant increase in productivity was observed. The key evaluative criteria of these studies were based on financial indicators (e.g. return on investment, return on assets and similar measures). These studies addressed the US economy only. Starting in the mid-1990s, the results of these studies were increasingly criticised [6, 7]. Observations include:

- a long period is necessary for the benefits of IT investments to become discernible (*time lag*)
- The full range of benefits of IT investments is difficult to identify and/or measure, as performance can be evaluated only through methods capable of measuring intangible improvements (e.g. in quality, variety, etc.).
- A significant variability exists across organisations in regard to their ability to productively use information technologies. Therefore performance reflects processes and strategies as well as IT investments.

The contrasting outcomes of these studies led to the development of business-oriented approaches which viewed the organisation as something other than a mere "black box". For example, Shang and Seddon [8] propose a framework based on five categories of benefits:

- operational
- managerial
- strategic
- IT infrastructure
- organizational.

They list 25 sub-dimensions of these benefits and emphasized how different benefits can follow diverse development paths· For instance, operational and organizational benefits were found to be negative at the beginning of a technological investment. They tended to be positive after the organizational learning that followed the change. These are results one would expect to find. Consequently, net benefits are the sum of separate benefits flows each of which needs to be considered.

Rockart [9] proposes the *Critical Success Factors* evaluation model. It is based on the definition of critical success factors (CSFs) that managers need to include in their decision-making when considering ICT investments. Once CSFs have been identified, managers establish the priority of CSFs relative to the mission of the organisation. Specific functions or processes that allow the organisation to focus its efforts on CSFs are identified. The priority of a given ICT investment is measured by the benefits it offers for each function and/or process related to each CSF. This establishes the most rational investment strategy for the attainment of strategic goals. This method provides insight into the mediating role of processes in the relationship between ICT and performance.

Other methods refine the tools useful in investigating the relationship between ICT and CSFs, taking into consideration organisational factors which mediate the relationship between technologies and success factors. The *Strategic Value Analysis* method [10], for example, focuses on organisational issues. The *Cost-Benefit Analysis* method (CBA) evaluates the impact of public programmes on a community's well-being [11, 12]. In the public sphere, economic evaluation techniques can be used to:

- Analyse all costs and benefits having an impact on society;
- Determine methods for measuring costs and benefits that lack tangible market value.

The analytical instruments developed for CBA are particularly useful for our discussion. Governments are interested in understanding the social impact of innovative actions they undertake. The application of ICT produces important 'intangible benefits' whose evaluation requires ad-hoc methods. When the costs and/or benefits can be expressed in monetary terms, the method provides an indicator establishing the value of an investment, e.g., net present value (NPV), or internal rate of return (IRR). This requires a full understanding of processes, activities and their input/output factors.

Both subjective and objective values can legitimately contribute to valuing investments in technology. We elaborate on this in the next section.

3. A broad perspective on evaluating ICT

This variety of evaluative approaches suggests the complexity of appraising ICT investments. There are two distinct aspects of this. First, the range of impact of ICT investments requires different evaluative tools to identify which factors play a role in the introduction of ICT: strategic priorities, tangible costs and benefits, intangible benefits, risks, flexibility, interactions between different ICT projects (i.e. complementarities). Second, the diversity of interests and information needs of different stakeholders generates varying, but relevant viewpoints about the priority and impact of ICT investments. Therefore, both qualitative and quantitative aspects are normally part of the evaluation process. The fact that multiple interests are involved in ICT investment decisions reiterates the need to incorporate multiple viewpoints on objectives and measures into the assessment [13].

Serafeimidis and Smithson [14] define four possible ICT evaluation orientations:

- control
- social learning
- sense-making
- exploratory.

Each orientation emphasizes a particular role and, consequently, a different evaluation approach. The first two orientations are linked by a consensus about the expected objectives. The control orientation is based on a predictable relationship between outcomes (usually quantitative and easily measurable) and a defined strategy. The social learning orientation considers a broader range of strategies to fulfil the aims. The last two orientations are both characterized by lack of clarity in defining expected objectives. However, while the sense-making orientation is useful when the relationship between actions and impacts is predictable (tactical level), exploratory evaluation operates when uncertainty characterizes both objectives and the strategy to fulfil them (strategic level).

The last classification emphasizes how the choice of an approach depends on context-based issues. These are the business, organizational, and technological pressures faced by the stakeholders involved in the decision-making process [14]. Since the results achieved by each single method are partial, Hamilton and Chervany propose participatory evaluative approaches to incorporate multiple viewpoints and the use of standardized measures to make results comparable. In so doing, evaluation is no longer regarded as a mere support tool to decide whether ICT investments are feasible. Instead of being a simple external judgement of a technological solution, evaluation becomes an instrument to manage innovation and make users feel committed to the project.

The issue regarding user commitment is particularly interesting. Changchit, Joshi and Lederer [15] emphasize the persuasive function of evaluation to commit managers and their subordinates to a project. It is crucial to make users understand the value of the new system and to engage them in realizing benefits once the system is implemented [15]. For those benefits which depend primarily on processes and people (i.e. organizational and operational benefits), this part of implementation is particularly relevant and can justify time and resources earmarked for evaluation.

Below we describe the results of the evaluation approaches as applied to two Italian healthcare projects. We then draw conclusions from these results.

4. An example of control evaluation: The use of telematics in treating oncology patients

The first project we consider was launched by a non-profit organization with the goal of assisting oncology patients. The project was developed to modify the traditional perception of home care through the introduction of technological and telematic instruments at so-called "listening centres" all over the country. The listening centres provide home care services through skilled personnel who are specially trained to assist this type of patient. They allow constant monitoring of the health condition of assisted patients through data recording into a local database within each location (so that all caregivers have up-to-date information on diagnosis, medical reports, medicine prescriptions, etc.), and into a central database (for statistical purposes).

All the patients treated at the listening centres are registered in a database. Not all of them use the special telemedical devices however. The devices include:

- Videophone or video-camera enabling the patient to see his/her listening centre counterpart.

- BP Tel for blood pressure measurement, which allows data to be transferred to the local database through a telephone connection.
- Clinic Analyser for the most frequent exams.
- Cardio Vox for teleECG.

The project's main goal is to make the remaining life of terminally-ill patients as relaxed and peaceful as possible.

Below we estimate the costs and the economic effects of this service (i.e., tele-oncology) for patients who are undergoing palliative treatments during the final phase of cancer, analyse the costs associated with the "traditional" methods of assisting patients with similar clinical backgrounds and propose a reference framework for a successive evaluation of the benefits perceived (for instance for each single patient).

4.1. Standard tele-oncology costs

The cost analysis below for tele-oncology is useful for comparison – in the next subsection – to the other two treatment options available: day-hospital and hospitalization. The tele-oncology costs are summarized in Table 1.

Table 1. Tele-oncology costs

Cost category		Cost per patient (€)
Video assistance (see Table 2 for details)		6,011
Telemonitoring devices and services	*Blood pressure and heart rate measurement devices*	128
	Telespirometres	34
	Tele-ECGs	43
	Personnel costs	331
	Data transmission costs	10
Total cost/patient		**6,558**

Video assistance represents the most advanced communication channel between the patient and the institute. However video assistance requires several devices and services:

- *Maintenance and technical assistance fee for video-link equipment: €20,454 yearly for the management of at most 4 devices for 5 patients Cost per patient: €818 yearly.*
- *Rental fee for video-link devices: €13,274 for the rental of at most 4 video-link devices for 5 patients. Cost per patient: €531.*
- *ISDN line activation. Cost per patient: €155.*
- *ISDN line charges:* the two-month fee has been calculated proportionally to the average 65-day device use length. Cost per patient: €56.
- *Throw-away injection pumps:* the single cost is €47 and it has been calculated proportionally to the average number of pumps used by a

patient (6) and to the percentage of patients who need it (70%). Cost per patient: €195.

- *Video-link phone traffic:* this figure has been estimated by referring to the average consumption levels registered from 1997 to 2000. The total consumption, amounting to €388, was divided by the number of days the service was used (2.449). The phone traffic cost refers only to the video-link for the monitoring of the utility perceived by each single patient. Cost per patient: €10.

Personnel cost: the calculation of this cost refers to a study carried out by the National Institute of Tumours (in Milan) about the teleassistance actually provided by doctors, social workers, registered nurses and co-ordinators to 36 patients over the three-year period. According to the simplest assumption, the personnel cost should increase in a directly proportional way vis-à-vis the number of tele-assisted patients; the possible fixed costs are however structural costs, not differential ones. Cost per patient for three-year tele-assistance: €4,246. These costs are summarized in Table 2.

Table 2. Video assistance costs

Item	Cost per patient (€)
Maintenance and technical assistance fee for video-link equipment	818
Rental fee for video-link devices	531
ISDN line activation	155
ISDN line charges	56
Throw-away injection pumps	195
Video-link phone traffic	10
Personnel costs	4,246
Total costs	**6,011**

Tele-monitoring device and service costs (equipment, installation, and services) are shown in Tables 3, 4 and 5. In addition, the personnel costs related to the telemonitoring services are estimated at €331 per patient, while the phone charges for data transmission are assumed to equal the video-link cost (i.e. €10 per patient). Therefore the daily cost per patient is: €6,556/65 days ≈ €101 per day. The numerator is the total cost per patient (see Table 1). The denominator is the patient's assumed life expectancy. This is the cost of tele-oncology services only (i.e., excluding eventual pharmaceutical treatments, etc.). It is the basis for the comparative analysis in the following section.

4.2. A comparative analysis of the various options available

This section presents a comparison of the costs related to three methods of assisting terminally-ill patients: tele-oncology assistance, day-hospital assistance, and complete hospitalization. The costs of the options have been estimated based on data collected at primary oncology hospitalization treatment and research centres.

Table 3. Costs related to blood pressure and heart rate measurement devices

Item	Parameters	Per patient costs
Device at home	€542	
Depreciation (annual)	€108	
Patients/year	5	
Cost/patient		**€21**
Receiving station management software	€10,618	
Depreciation (annual)	€2,124	
Patients/year	20	
Cost/patient		**€106**
Total cost/patient		**€127**

Box 1. Technical service characteristics and evaluation assumptions

---

Technical service characteristics:

- Installation of a special videoconferencing device at the patient's house;
- Equipment management;
- Management of daily video-links (average length: 12 minutes) between central institute and patient's house, as well as constant updating of the electronic record database regarding the usefulness of the service as perceived by individual patients;
- Electronic patient record database;
- Injection of pain-relievers by means of throw-away pumps (one pump can be used for a maximum of 7 days);
- Routine medical and nursing home care;
- Possible telemonitoring of the patient's main cardiovascular and respiratory values.

Assumptions:

- The patient's life expectancy is 65 days (criterion for granting teleassistance to patients), same as the service delivery time length;
- Any device installed at the patient's house can be used by 5 patients a year. This assumes full employment of all equipment
- Costs are calculated based on the assumption of offering services to a maximum of 4 patients at the same time. That is to say, 4 devices are available on a total number of 20 patients per year;
- A depreciation rate of 20% is assumed for each device;
- All installation costs are charged to the institute providing the service, either directly or on a reimbursement basis.
- the patient also requires a constant telemonitoring of both blood pressure and heart rate. For this purpose, the equipment given to the patient includes special devices (e.g. telespirometers, teleECGs, etc.).

Table 4. Telespirometres costs

Item	Parameters	Per patient costs
Spirometre (purchase cost)	€858	
Depreciation (annual)	€172	
Patients/year	5	
Cost/patient		**€34**

Table 5. Detailed costs related to tele-electrocardiograph for ECG (about 50 ECGs per year for 20 patients)

Item	Parameters	Per patient costs
Electrocardiograph (purchase cost)	€1,550	
Depreciation (annual)	€310	
Patients/year	20	
Cost/patient		€16
Subscription to medical report service		€28
Cost/patient		**€43**

The first option considered is **hospitalization.** We estimate that the average daily hospitalization cost for the same patients is €465 (including the cost of clinical exams) - with an average of 40 in-hospital days - for the remaining 65 days of life (Sources: National Institute of Tumours and European Oncology Institute). This figure includes

- personnel cost directly imputable to the wards
- equipment depreciation rate
- administrative costs directly imputable to ward activities
- hotel costs
- healthcare service costs.

The average total cost for hospitalization therefore totals €18,592.

Aside from hospitalization costs, the cost for medication administered to the patient at his/her own house (€646) as well as the cost for transportation to the hospital (€33) are included.

The second option is **day-hospital assistance**. We estimate that in 1999 the *day-hospital single access* cost for a patient undergoing a palliative treatment at €214, with an average number of 5 oncology patients provided with the service. The total cost borne by the medical centre therefore is €1,072. Analysis of the clinical data shows that a day-hospital patient requires on average 2.35 hospitalization days for exams, visits and special treatments. Using the average daily hospitalization cost per patient (i.e. €465), the total hospitalization cost for this option is €1,092.

Another cost is medication administered at the patient's house at a daily cost of about €26 for a total of €1,618. Travel costs to and from the hospital (6.5 trips on average) are €84.

Telemedicine is the last option and it is mainly based on the tele-oncology cost analysis in the previous subsection. The total cost of tele-oncology assistance is the daily cost per patient (i.e., €101) times the number of days that the patient spends at home on average before death – for a total cost per patient of €6,200 . The clinical data show that the patient also requires on average of 3.55 days in the hospital. At the average daily hospitalization cost per patient (i.e. €465), the total hospitalization cost is to €1,650.

Added to this is medication administered at the patient's home at the same daily cost as the previous options (€26), plus travel costs to and from the hospital (1.5 trips on average) for a total of €19.50.

Table 6 shows the full estimated costs for the three options available to patients: telemedicine, day-hospital, and stay in hospital.

It is important to emphasize that the cost analyses of the telemedicine and day-hospital options do not take into account the opportunity cost of the time families dedicate to their sick relatives. As a consequence, with an average stay-at-home period of 62.65 days - with no external support - the day-hospital option turns out to be extremely costly. Relatives and patients face the burden of self-administered assistance both in monetary terms and terms of time. This likely imposes psychic costs - for example increased anxiety - on the people involved.

The next project we consider had a goal of paperless –that is, all-electronic - documentation, whilst at the same time meeting legal requirements for signatures. To do this, management opted for an electronic document management system which incorporates digital signature technology (as established by legislative decree DPR 28/12/2000 no. 445, art.1, paragraph 1, letter 'ee').

Four health care units participated in the project, one of which was the lead partner in the project. Its goal was to electronically transmit medical reports from/to a number of local health care departments and services, specifically: the diagnostic services department, various hospital departments, the social and health care districts and a selected number of general practitioners. After a successful trial period at the lead site the system was implemented at the other three health care units.

5. Blurring the line between control and social learning evaluation: Technology for paperless healthcare

The cost-benefit analysis for the project focuses on two key issues:

- The effects produced by the introduction of the ICT system, omitting the decision-making process which led to the launching of the project.
- The medical reports produced by the hospital's diagnostic services department and transmitted to internal departments (internal medical reports) or to the social and health care districts located in the area surrounding the leading health care unit (external medical reports).

We first looked at the resources needed to implement the project. Our study encompassed the medical reporting processes in the health care unit's diagnostic services departments (Microbiology Lab, Clinical Chemistry Lab, Anti-Diabetes Centre, Radiology and Neuroradiology department, Anatomy and Pathologic Histology department) and in various hospital departments. We identified the following processes to which we could attach costs

- personnel assigned to the reporting function,
- space allocated to filing of documents,
- technological tools used to support the reporting process,
- medical reporting production costs (paper, labels, etc.).

Table 6. The three clinical options

	Telemedicine		Day-hospital		Hospital	
	Parameters	**Cost**	**Parameters**	**Cost**	**Parameters**	**Cost**
Overall stay in hospital (number of days per patient)	3.55	€1,650	2.35	€1,092	40	€18,592
Day-hospital access (number of patients)			5	€1,072		
Medication treatment at patient's house (treatment days per patient)	61	€1,587	63	€1,618	25	€646
Patient transportation (trips)	1.5	€20	6.5	€84	2.5	€33
Tele-oncology assistance (number of days per patient)	61	€6,200				
Total cost/patient		**€9,457**		**€3,866**		**€19,270**

Table 7 shows the savings in personnel and filing space used for reporting after the introduction of the ICT system. The last column gives the yearly operating costs of the ICT system[1].

Investment in the ICT system includes system design, hardware, software, customised applications, advisory services and internal personnel permanently assigned to the project. These costs total €600,000. Table 8 summarizes savings and costs over a five-year time period. On the basis of these data, the project's net present value (using as a discount rate the rate on five-year Italian treasury certificates:- CCT) is a negative value: € (55,414).

The negative value indicates that it is difficult to justify infrastructure projects like this solely on the basis of measurable costs and savings. In regard to intangible benefits, it is worth noting that once the trial period was over the project arranged for transmission of the digital medical reports to patients at their homes. This new service was offered through an agreement with the national postal service. Once the health care unit transferred the electronic data, the postal service printed the reports and delivered them to the home address of the patients.

Table 7. Annual savings/(costs) from implementation of electronic document system (in €)

Organisational Unit	Personnel	Filing space	Operating costs
Microbiology Lab.	41,026	3,000	0
Clinical Chemistry Lab.	76,924	3,000	0
Anti-Diabetes Centre	0	3,000	0
Radiology and Neuroradiology	0	3,000	0
Anatomy and Pathologic Histology	25,641	3,000	0
Hospital departments	0	0	0
Social and Health Care Districts	92,309	0	0
Common-shared costs	51,283	0	(2,000)
TOTAL	102,565	15,000.00	(2,000)

N.B.: the figures in brackets represent additional expenditures, while the other figures indicate cost savings

Table 8. Savings/(costs) during the five-year investment horizon (in €)

	Year 1	Year 2	Year 3	Year 4	Year 5
Investment	(600,000)	0	0	0	0
Personnel	102,565	102,565	102,565	102,565	102,565
Filing space	15,000	15,000	15,000	15,000	15,000
Operating costs	(2,000)	(2,000)	(2,000)	(2,000)	(2,000)
Total	**(484,435)**	**115,565**	**115,565**	**115,565**	**115,565**

N.B.: the figures in brackets represent additional expenditures, while the other figures indicates cost savings

We factor in the cost of producing and mailing the reports to patients' homes in table 8. Operating costs include the costs for each medical report produced and mailed (we estimate an average of 272,000 reports per year).

The technical tools are the same as before, but there are additional costs related to the purchasing of a specific IT application, to the number of days used to integrate it to the system, then interface it with the ICT architecture. Thus, overall costs total €606,960. Table 9 shows the cash flow over the five-year investment horizon adopted for the analysis.

Table 9. Annual savings/(costs) (in €)

Organisational Unit	Personnel	Filing space	Operating costs	Reporting
Microbiology Lab.	41,026	3,000	0	0
Clinical Chemistry Lab.	76,924	3,000	0	0
Anti-Diabetes Centre	0	3,000	0	0
Radiology and Neuroradiology	0	3,000	0	0
Anatomy and Pathologic Histology	25,641	3,000	0	0
Hospital departments	0	0	0	0
Socio-Medical Districts	30,770	0	0	12,930
Common-shared costs	51,283	0	(99,196)	0
TOTAL	**225,643**	**15,000**	**(99,196)**	**12,930**

N.B.: the figures in brackets represent additional expenditures, while the other figures indicates cost savings

Table 10. Savings/(costs) (in €)

	Year 1	Year 2	Year 3	Year 4	Year 5
Technological platform	(606,960)	0	0	0	0
Personnel	225,643	225,643	225,643	225,643	225,643
Filing space	15,000	15,000	15,000	15,000	15,000
Operating costs	(99,196)	(99,196)	(99,196)	(99,196)	(99,196)
TOTAL	**(465,513)**	**115,565**	**141,447**	**141,447**	**141,447**

N.B.: the figures in brackets represent additional expenditures, while the other figures indicates cost savings

These cash flows equate to a positive project net present value of **€43,656**. This positive net present value compared to the negative value calculated earlier shows the value of extending the analysis from operations within the *front office* alone to activities further down the information chain, in this case to getting the reports into the hands of the patients.

In addition to these quantified benefits, there are intangible benefits:

- improved and more efficient services provided to users (such as the reduction in reporting times);

- improved quality of services, as fewer mistakes occur in sorting reports (according to the health care units' estimates, mistakes occurred 10% of the time);
- improved image of the health care unit;
- improved accessibility to and effectiveness of operative processes (for example services available on-line to patients and other parties).

These benefits represent value added to the investment. Unlike quantified benefits however, the choice and use of appropriate indicators is not always an easy task. For example we evaluated reporting turnaround times through direct surveys and questionnaires administered to health personnel. We limited the survey and questionnaires to the interaction between the Clinical Chemistry Lab (LAB) and the Anatomy and Pathological Histology department (APH) in a sample of 13 wards of the hospital. The results of the randomly chosen sample of patients participating in the study are reported in table 11.

Table 11. Characteristics of the sample of patients participating in the study before and after the technological innovation

Characteristics	before	after
No. of patients	159	155
No. of patients with urgent requests only	9	6
Average no. of patients involved for each ward	12.2	11.9
No of wards	13	13
Total no. of requests	369	369
No. of urgent requests	124	120
No of requests to the LAB	346	357
% urgent	*35.8%*	*33.6%*
% programmed	*64.2%*	*66.4%*
No. of requests to the APH	23	12
% urgent	*0.0%*	*0.0%*
% programmed	*100.0 %*	*100 .0%*
Average no. of hospitalisation days	10.5	9.9

From this analysis we can see two significant and comparable values:

- the average waiting time between the submission of a request for a diagnostic exam and receipt of the medical report (S/R waiting time index)
- the average waiting time between the availability of a medical report in a ward and its use for treatment purposes (W/U waiting time index).

In Table 12 the two indexes are calculated and compared before and after the introduction of the ICT system. A distinction is made both between the reports produced by the LAB and by the APH and, for each category, between those referring to urgent requests and those referring to non-urgent ones. Overall, a reduction in waiting time is reported.

The remarkable reduction in S/R waiting time is also confirmed by the answers to the questionnaires submitted to the staff working in the departments involved. These show a consistent perception of reduced waiting times. Reduced waiting time improves treatment. For APH, values are less significant. The diagnostic process is generally time-consuming (for technical reasons). The number of requests for the sample chosen is also very low. On the basis of these results management of the unit decided to keep a record of the reporting times. This can be done by extracting data from the *log files* produced by the new document management system.

Table 12. Reduction in waiting time before and after the technological innovation (values are in hours + minutes)

Phase	Indicator	LAB		APH	
		Urgent	*Non-urgent*	*Urgent*	*Non-urgent*
before	S/R waiting time	5.17	17.02	-	173.97
	W/U waiting time	1.03	6.44	-	4.73
after	S/R waiting time	2.0	10.8	-	98.0
	W/U waiting time	0.6	6.3	-	14.7

Finally, since the sponsor of the project is a public body, we decided to evaluate external benefits, that is, the social benefits produced by the new system, especially by home delivery of medical reports. We identify the benefits as reduced travel costs and increased time for patients who no longer need to physically pick up their reports at the health care unit. We estimated an average distance from patient home to the unit which we multiplied by the average cost per kilometre (obtained from Italian AAA) to calculated travel costs. We estimated time saved at one hour multiplied by the average hourly wage (from ISTAT statistics) to calculate the value of time saved (see Table 13). The resultant savings are about €4 million.

Table 13. External benefits for the local community (in €)

Type of benefit	Cost per report	Annual reports	Annual benefits
Reduced travel costs	3.46	272,000	941,120
Increased time	11.51	272,000	3,130,720
TOTAL			**4,071,840**

Conclusions

Our analysis of these two cases shows that ICT investments have a range of impacts. We need multiple measures to identify the full range of costs and benefits. There are two issues that require particular attention:

- intangible benefits which mainly fall into the effectiveness sphere, but often cannot be quantified in monetary terms;
- synergies among different investments which can be sources of long term benefits (e.g., use of the postal service)

In addition, since we are evaluating a public sector service, e-government should improve the quality of life of citizens, regardless of whether the improvement can be quantified. The first case is an example of *control orientation evaluation*, mainly focused on objective values. The evaluation is based on standard financial measures. However, it is worth remarking that the analysis did not take into account:

- costs of assistance to patients' families during an extremely difficult period
- longer-term improvement in the effectiveness of treatments
- measurable improvements in the efficiency of processes
- cost implicit in the time that patients' families devote to assisting patients.

This last item is difficult to measure. Benefits consist of improved quality of life for terminally-ill patients, reduced anxiety and increased well-being of both patients and family.

The second case evaluates the impact and the intangible benefits accruing from the introduction of a technological innovation. The cost-benefit analysis provides useful tools (e.g., survey, questionnaire) to evaluate social benefits and treatment quality for example. However, neither the first nor the second case takes into account perceptions of the beneficiaries of care.

It is important to emphasize that formal and informal approaches are equally legitimate means of assessment, depending on the evaluative role and shareholders' information needs. In particular, formal approaches are a common part of organizational culture. However, formal approaches need to be used together with informal approaches, especially for projects led by public or non-profit organizations, to overcome the limits of their restricted focus [14]. Further research is needed to quantify intangible benefits, thus gaining stakeholders' consensus on their value.

Despite the limits of our study, the resulting information seems useful for prioritising investments and identifying the best alternative consistent with ICT strategy. Evaluative study supports strategic alignment and forces ICT public investments to adhere to the principle of '*value for money*'. Not only does this help to determine whether ICT investments are feasible, it also helps to manage innovation by highlighting the organizational impact and identifying opportunities for improvement.

Finally, it is evident that any kind of evaluation requires resources (in terms of time and costs) and information. Information cost represents one of the crucial problems of the evaluation process. It is one of the most important reasons for promoting a participatory approach. The mediating role of complementary factors in the relationship between ICT and its positive impacts [16] makes it difficult to identify information needed for effective evaluation. Participatory evaluation can help in this regard. This leads decision-makers toward solutions whose implementation is more likely to find stakeholders' support.

Endnotes

1. The costs to produce medical reports remained the same: reporting previously done by Diagnostic Services was later done by the Social and Health Care Districts or by hospital departments, which are part of the same health care unit.

References

[1]   M. Castells, *The Rise of the Network Society*, Blackwell Publishers, Oxford, 2000.
[2]   E. Borgonovi, *Principi e sistemi aziendali per le amministrazioni pubbliche*, Egea, Milan, 2002.
[3]   S. Roach, *Macro-realities of the information economy*, National Academy of Science, New York, 1986
[4]   T. Landauer, *The trouble with computers: usefulness, usability and productivity*, MIT Press, Cambridge, 1995.
[5]   Q. Hu and R. Plant, *Does IT spending impact firm productivity and performance?,* University of Miami Paper, Florida, 1998.
[6]   K. Kraemer and J. Dedrick, IT and economic development: international competitiveness, in W. Dutton (ed.), *Information and Communication Technologies*, Oxford University Press, Oxford, 1996.
[7]   E. Brynjolfsson and L. Hitt, Paradox lost? Firm-level evidence on the returns to information systems spending, in L. P. Willcocks and S. Lester, (eds.) *Beyond the IT productivity paradox,* John Wiley and Sons, New York, 1999.
[8]   S. Shang and P.B. Seddon, Assessing and managing the benefits of enterprise systems: the business manager's perspective, *Information Systems Journal*, **12** (2002), 271-299.
[9]   J.F. Rockart, Chief executives define their own data needs, *Harvard Business Review*, **57** (1979), 81-93.
[10] R. Curtice, *Strategic value analysis*, Perentice Hall, Englewood Cliffs, 1985.
[11] F. Nuti, *La valutazione economica delle decisioni pubbliche,* Giappichelli Editore, Torino, 2001.
[12] M. F. Drummond, B. O'Brien, G.L. Stoddart and G.W. Torrance, *Methods for the economic evaluation of health care programmes,* Oxford University Press, New York, 1997.
[13] S. Hamilton, and L.N. Chervany, Evaluations Information Systems Effectiveness – Part I: Comparing Evaluation Approaches, *MIS Quarterly*, **5** (1981), 55-69.
[14] V. Serafeimidis and S. Smithson, Information systems evaluation as an organizational institution – experience from a case study, *Information Systems Journal*, **13** (2003), 251-274.
[15] C. Changchit, K.D. Joshi and A.L. Lederer, Process and Reality in Information Systems Benefit Analysis, *Information Systems Journal*, **8** (1998), 145-162.
[16] M. Ko and K.M. Osei-Bryson, Using regression splines to assess the impact of information technology investments on productivity in the health care industry, *Information Systems Journal*, **14** (2004), 43-63.

Developments in e-Government
D. Griffin et al. (Eds.)
IOS Press, 2007

Citizen Adoption of e-Government in the UK: Perceived Benefits and Barriers

David GILBERT, Pierre BALESTRINI, Ailsa KOLSAKER
and Darren LITTLEBOY
School of Management, University of Surrey, UK

1. Introduction

In response to the prevailing discourse of consumer-centricity many organizations have sought to realign their structures and processes to focus upon meeting customer needs. Customer Relationship Management (CRM) is employed widely by companies eager to develop and maintain fruitful, and profitable, relationships with their customers. CRM activities are increasingly Internet-based, as companies exploit the potential of the technology to communicate directly and interactively with consumers as well as handle and mine data, customize products and personalize offerings [1]. Whilst there exists a growing body of empirical evidence about consumers' perceptions and evaluations of electronic service delivery generally [2, 3, 4], hitherto there has been little evaluation of this specifically in relation to the delivery of e-government services. Official reports, such as the annual European Commission report (see [5]) concentrate upon the *provision* rather than *usage* of public services (for a critique of this approach see [6]). Yet understanding citizens' perceptions, attitudes and intentions is of particular importance if the government is to achieve widespread acceptance and usage of its electronic services. Without an understanding of why UK citizens would choose to use electronic service delivery channels rather than more traditional service delivery methods, government organizations are likely to fall further and further behind e-delivery targets. Against this background we investigate citizen usage intentions based upon perceptions of benefits and barriers and based upon these results assess whether e-government services are likely to be successful in terms of citizen usage.

2. Theoretical models of consumer acceptance

Existing empirical research into the use of the Web for service delivery tends to focus around models of technology acceptance and usage, applied in various contexts. Despite increasing acceptance, a recent study by O'Cass and Fenech [7] suggests that perceived risk in using the technology remains an important antecedent of stated intention to use. The Technology Acceptance Model (TAM), developed by Davis [8] suggests that beliefs influence attitudes about information technology and, in turn, attitudes lead to specific intentions to use and subsequently actual use of technology. According to the TAM there are two key antecedents of technology adoption; perceived usefulness and perceived ease of use. Whilst the model provides a useful starting point for exploring consumers' use of online services, its original purpose was to expose how employees make decisions about using technology in the workplace. Thus, a number of extensions have been proposed to help explain an individual's use of the Web. From these, two key elements emerge as extremely influential, both being composite parts of the Theory of Reasoned Action (from which the TAM was developed); subjective norms, and social norms (see [9, 10]). These are of interest both individually and in relation to each other, the latter specifically because the networked nature of the Internet encourages interaction with others, and as both the technology and consumers' acceptance of it continue to grow, so does the significance of its multi-nodal, integrative characteristics in relation to social norms.

Reflecting a growing recognition of the importance and complexity of attitudes in Internet adoption, Bobbitt and Dabholkar [11] integrate the various attitude-based theories (Theory of Reasoned Action, Theory of Planned Behavior, Theory of Trying) with external factors (such as the product/service category and perceived risks) to explain why individuals may choose technology-based self-service options. Bobbitt and Dabholkar's findings highlight the importance of attitudes in the growth of technology based self-service, thus where negative attitudes towards technology exist, these must be converted through an attitude change strategy before users will adopt technology-enabled services. The importance of consumer attitudes is also highlighted in Lee and Turban's [12] Internet trust model in which 'trustworthiness of the Internet shopping medium' is identified as a key antecedent of consumer trust (and usage) of Web-based retailing.

Whilst the bulk of empirical research is concerned with those attributes which increase an individual's propensity to use the Internet and disregard those that are not significant, O'Cass and Fenech's [7] study identifies those factors reducing that propensity, that is to say, factors which discourage individuals from using the technology. Although O'Cass and Fenech's data collection was by means of an online survey, possibly impinging upon validity, nevertheless the results are of interest, suggesting that not only technology acceptance but individual characteristics; such as opinion leadership, impulsiveness, Internet self-efficacy, and perceptions; such as perceived Web security, Web shopping compatibility, shopping orientation and satisfaction with Web sites can discourage consumers from shopping online. Thus, it must be recognized that even though the Web now may be commonplace, attitudes towards the medium are developing at a significantly slower pace than the technology itself. It is useful to consider the diffusion of innovation model in this context.

The Diffusion of Innovation (DOI) model [13] conceptualizes the decision to adopt technology as a process of information gathering and uncertainty reduction. The individual's decision on whether to use the technology is based upon perceptions of the technology such as relative advantage, compatibility, complexity, trialability and observability. Diffusion is the process by which people adopt new innovations, new products, and different ways of doing things. According to Siegel [1] the second Internet revolution is diffusing far faster than the first – within five years after its release, the World Wide Web had spread around the world, with people who were unaware of its release in 1991 – 1992 using it to shop, learn, play, communicate and work. Agarwal and Prasad [14] report three main influences upon diffusion that are most supported by empirical studies; relative advantage, compatibility and complexity. However, whilst commonly applied to explain consumers' decision to use the Internet, the model was originally developed as a conceptual framework for understanding the use of information systems for performing job roles, and as such may not be valid to current contexts. The identified antecedents of technology usage may be significantly different for a consumer adopting technology to receive a service and an employee using technology to perform his or her job. Molesworth and Suortfi's [15] study of consumers buying cars online indicates resistance to completing the purchase online, but a clear recognition of advantage at the information search stage. Innovation resistance appears to stem from the need to test the product prior to purchase and uncertainty over after-sales service. Thus, the level of complexity and risk associated with the online alternative appear to influence innovation diffusion. In a recent study of the launch of e-government in the State of Iowa's Treasury Department, Tat-Kei and Ya Ni [16] also identified resistance as a key determinant of the rate of innovation diffusion, suggesting that organizational features and peer influence play key roles.

Drawing upon a humanistic perspective, Chen and Tan's [17] study expands both the TAM and DOI models to propose an extended model which considers both the technology itself and the user's predispositions. They suggest that consumer acceptance of a virtual store is influenced by a number of factors, including product offerings, information richness, usability of storefront, perceived trust and perceived service quality. Chen and Tan's findings echoes a number of earlier exploratory studies, suggesting that although consumers are becoming more accustomed to the Web environment, their intention to engage in online transactions remain highly influenced by non-technological factors. Thus, as the online environment becomes increasingly mainstream and the medium increasingly accepted, we can anticipate that technology will become less of a barrier to usage, challenging firms to differentiate themselves through factors unrelated to the technology, such as product range, product quality, responsiveness, reliability of delivery and service quality. This may be difficult to achieve in practice – an interesting study by Douglas *et al* [18] of the quality of e-services in the provision of legal practices reaffirms the importance of high quality e-service delivery. Defining e-service operations as 'hard': right place, right time, right price, right condition, and 'soft': site design, information readiness, smooth transactions, they identify a number of barriers erected not by the technology, but by the inability of the profession to adapt to the new high-tech world. It may be anticipated that this reticence to embrace change is not restricted to the legal profession and may be uncovered in various guises even within large innovative organizations.

3. Importance of service quality

The TAM and DOI models focus specifically upon perceptions, attitudes and intentions to use technology. Recently, however, reflecting the growing acceptance of technology and the increasing importance of service quality as a differentiator, research studies have begun to consider the role of service quality in consumers' use of the Web. Parasuraman *et al*'s [19] SERVQUAL model is most commonly used to measure service quality, however as it largely ignores technical aspects it is of limited value in the current context. Cronin and Taylor's [20] perceptions-based model, SERVPERF, is potentially useful, however the removal of pre-consumption expectations on the basis that customer evaluation of performance already includes an internal mental comparison of perceptions against expectations, appears to be an important limitation in the current context.

Drawing upon Grönroos' [21], Higgins and Ferguson [22] suggest that functional quality (how the service is provided to the customer) dominates when the consumer has only limited ability to make technical evaluations. However, while the concepts of technical and functional quality are easily understandable, it is less simple to test them through empirical means since consumers find it difficult to separate the *what* from the *how* [23]. This is of particular importance in the current study as it is anticipated that individuals may find it difficult to evaluate the service quality of e-government services because of unfamiliarity with an electronic delivery method. In addition, Kuo's [24] study of service quality amongst members of a Web community is of interest in the current context. Kuo employs Kano's two-way quality model to reaffirm the importance of customer perceptions in service delivery and the influence of perceptions upon customer satisfaction. Thus, if citizens are to be encouraged to use e-government services, it is of key importance that such services offer overt and unambiguous added value over and above those provided by the offline alternative. Piccoli *et al* [25] propose that the design and functionality of Web sites are key to their usage, as they must both offer value and the opportunity to maximize individual utility and suggest that currently a number of sites fail to offer sufficient personalization, support and explanation to browsers, resulting in disappointments and sub-optimal usage. Dissatisfied browsers are unlikely to continue to utilize the Web - in their study of continued use of e-services, Meng-Hsiang and Chao-Min [26] propose that continuance intention is determined by Internet self-efficacy and satisfaction. They suggest that satisfaction may be a much more complex concept than its current definition. In relation to online services satisfaction appears to be influenced not only by Web site characteristics, functionality etc., but jointly influenced by technical and psychological factors, namely perceived usefulness, interpersonal influence and perceived playfulness.

In a study of consumer evaluation of self-service delivery through technology, Dabholkar [27] proposes two models to capture the influence of service quality on intention to use: one based upon quality attributes, the other upon affective predispositions towards technology. In common with studies of technology acceptance, Dabholkar found that a number of factors affect perceptions, namely ease of use, reliability, speed of delivery, enjoyment and control. Shaohan and Minjoon's [28] study of Internet users' perceptions identifies Web site design/content, trustworthiness and effective communication as key elements of online service quality for browsers and browsers/buyers alike. Those who bought online also included prompt, reliable service delivery in their evaluation. Studies by Meuter *et al* [29] and Szymanski and Hyse [30] suggest that consumers, quite naturally, compare the novel technology service delivery with the traditional alternatives. A study by Kolsaker, Lee-Kelley and Choy [31] of Web consumers in Hong Kong identified that some consumers consciously choose *not* to use the online alternative simply because they actually enjoy High Street shopping and being on the High Street anyway, and perceive few 'time saving' or 'convenient place' advantages. Thus, as well as removing barriers, online providers may also need to take positive action to encourage people to move online where offline alternatives exist. This has important implications for e-government services where, unlike some private companies (such as Easyjet, or Amazon) the provider can not simply offer only one, online, channel.

A recent development which may impact upon the delivery of high quality e-government services is the overt refocusing by government from citizen-centricity to efficiency gains. Acknowledging the impact of the 2004 *Efficiency Review,* a statement by the Institute for Public Policy Research (IPPR) in the 2004 report Society of Information Technology Management (SOCITM) *Local e-Government Now* notes a recent shift of emphasis:

"It seems clear that e-government policy is now at a turning point. On the one hand, more pressure is being placed on local authorities to link e-government activity to the Treasury's Public Service Agreements'… on the other hand, the Efficiency Review is taking centre stage and the potential savings facilitated by e-government are coming centre stage with it.... Central government is now signaling that it wants some serious return on its e-government investment".

It is not difficult to imagine that shifting to a 'bottom line' focus may affect citizen-centricity and the quality of e-government services.

4. Discussion

The literature review has focused specifically upon technology adoption, highlighting areas where either the approach or the previous applications have limitations that may be reduced by combining all three approaches. Attitude-based methods are of interest because they are supported by accepted behavioral theory linking perceptions to usage intentions. By combining the attitude-based and service quality based approaches, the strong theory linking attitudes to behaviors can be exploited (DOI, TAM), with the service quality literature being used to help identify the antecedents that affect these attitudes (see Tables 1 and 2 for an abridged account of the literature sources that generated the study variables). This enables a grounded approach to measuring the variables associated with technology adoption, placing the onus on both the factors affecting consumer intentions to adopt an online service channel (considered in a comparative manner, that is to say relative benefits) and the factors representing a barrier to adoption.

A further dimension to the problem of the prediction of self-service technology adoption is the importance of including the variable of age. Age difference has an impact on the ability to use and subsequently the intention to adopt new technological advances [32, 33]. However, there is not a representative distribution of age in the technology adoption studies. For example, the respondents for Liao and Cheung's study [34] are all between 20 and 35, Dabholkar (1996) reports an average age of 25, and Shim *et al.* [35] have the large majority of respondents in the 35-44 range.

The objective of the current study is based upon two stages of enquiry: firstly, to identify factors that may predict consumer take-up of the Web-based option of service delivery, and secondly; employing the results of the initial stage to identify factors which do not predict intention to use the electronic delivery option.

5. Methodology

The factors impacting on the individual's intention to use the technology self-service option, both the relative benefits and the barriers, have been drawn from Diffusion and Innovation studies, TAM studies and approaches to service quality and theory (see Tables 1 and 2). While many of the principles from the reviewed studies can be used, the following reasons justify a modified approach taken in this research:

- The context here is a publicly available service, not one within the workplace.

- While people are aware of the Internet they are unlikely to have received training on how to use it or received direct marketing encouraging them to use it. This is in contrast with potential users in a work environment.
- The delivery of government services via the Internet is relatively new so there are few people who have actually used it.

Table 1. Relative benefit factors sources

Factor	Definition	Source references
Avoid personal interaction	The ability to be able to receive public services without having to interact with members of the service provider's staff	[36][37][29][38]
Control	The ability to exert more control over the delivery of the service than through another method	[39][27][34][40][25]
Convenience	The ability to receive the service how and when the individual wants to	[39][29][30][40]
Cost	The electronic delivery of public services saving money	[34]
Personalization	The ability to tailor the delivery of the service more towards the individual	[41][25]
Time	The time saved by obtaining the service electronically	[42][27][37][34][29][17]

Table 2. Barrier factors

Factor	Definition	Reference
Confidentiality	Personal data must be kept private and not used for other purposes	[39][41][40]
Easy to use	The delivery mechanism must be straightforward to use with minimum effort required	[14][27][43][29]
Enjoyable	Using the system must be an enjoyable experience	[27][44][34]
Reliable	The website must have services that are required, and individuals must trust that a requested service will be delivered	[42][45][37][40]
Safe	The website must be secure with respect to entering financial details	[39][42][45][30][34]
Visual appeal	The website should look good	[43][7][28]

Thus, rather than questioning individuals on their perceptions developed from actual system usage and relating this to whether they are actually intending to use it further, the study investigates the importance of the candidate benefit-barrier factors relating to potential *willingness to use*. That is, the study does not measure actual perceptions, but investigates the factors that individuals consider important in evaluating whether or not to use the service and whether this willingness varies with age. These factors are important to the service providers (government departments) because they contribute towards the development of attitudes in making the delivery of public services on-line more acceptable. This structure of the research is illustrated below.

5.1. Instrument development

A self-administered postal questionnaire incorporating five-point Likert scales was developed. The questionnaire contained three parts:

- Part A: factual questions (demographics and previous Internet experience).
- Part B: attitude questions relating to the candidate benefit and barrier factors.
- Part C: question for 'willingness to use' on-line public service delivery.

5.2 Sample selection and pilot testing

The survey was conducted in the city of Guildford, Surrey employing a stratified random sampling technique to select 50 streets and subsequent street addresses at random from the list of all streets, using the SPSS random selection facility. A pilot study was carried out whereby an identification of the related factors and content of the research instrument (based upon the literature) was first discussed with identified industry experts. The resultant questionnaire was then discussed in a focus group involving representative members of the general public of Guildford. Finally the improved questionnaires were distributed through postal services within ten streets selected randomly from the sampling frame.

The reliability of the scales was calculated using Cronbach's alpha, which indicates the consistency with which each item represents the construct of interest. This is achieved by averaging the coefficients that result from split-half reliability testing, producing a coefficient from 0 – 1, where values below .60 generally indicate unsatisfactory internal consistency reliability. The scale items in the pilot for benefits and barriers were .75 and .72 respectively and for the final survey were .83 and .80 respectively. However, the reliability may indicate that together the questions measure benefits and barriers, but that they may not group under the 12 factors proposed. Therefore, factor analysis was used to identify the underlying constructs that do characterize the data response and to investigate the convergent and discriminant validity of the emerging factors.

Based upon the response rate of 18% from the pilot study, 555 questionnaires were distributed. Following up non-respondents produced a data set of 111 completed questionnaires, equivalent to a 20% response rate.

6. Analysis and Results

Compared to the total population of the UK (1991 census data), the age ranges 25-34 and 55+ and people not working full time were respectively over-represented and under-represented in the sample (Table 3).

6.1. Summary of responses to questions

Table 4 contains the means and standard deviations (SD) for each benefit and barrier construct. The constructs with the largest means (5 = "Strongly Agree" to 1 = "Strongly Disagree") are those that the respondents have deemed to be the most

Figure 1. Research Model

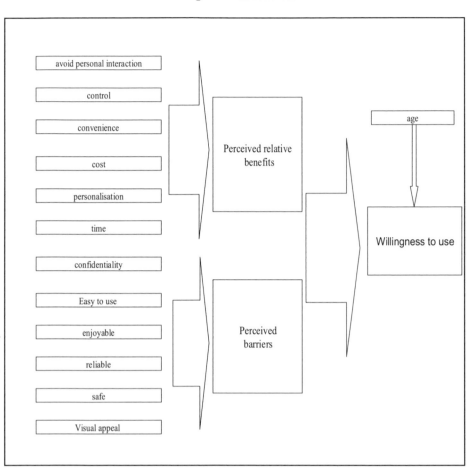

Table 3. Comparison of demographic data

Category	Response	Study response (%)	1991 census (%)
Age	18-24	14	13
	25-34	42	20
	35-54	35	33
	55+	9	34
Work status	Full-time	89	46
	Not full-time	11	54

Source: Fieldwork and [46]

important. Of those constructs with means of 4 and above, two relate to 'relative benefits', namely 'time' and 'control'. Whilst the 'time' factor reflects the findings of numerous extant studies, 'control' is of particular interest as it *may* suggest a shift in perceptions of empowerment within the context of public service consumption and a tentative shift in government/citizen relations. That four of the 'relative barriers' constructs have means of 4 and above suggests that currently citizens are more concerned about perceived risks than potential benefits. This may be due to the current immaturity of the offering and the lack of exposure of the general public to online government services. The largest means are those relating to safety, confidentiality and reliability. This is a potentially important observation given that the only potential barrier included within the attitude based models is the 'ease of use' of the technology option. It is interesting to note that one of the questions ("prepared to pay for the online service", 2.05) within the cost construct has the lowest mean for all questions across constructs, suggesting that people certainly would not expect to pay for electronic service delivery even if the level of service exceeded other methods.

Table 4. Descriptive Statistics attributed to Construct

Construct	Mean	SD
Perceived Benefits		
Avoid Personal Interaction	3.60	0.94
Control	4.20	0.76
Convenience	3.96	0.96
Cost	3.17	1.10
Personalization	3.55	1.00
Time	4.15	0.80
Perceived Barriers		
Confidential	4.80	0.54
Easy to use	4.34	0.64
Enjoyable	3.46	1.00
Reliable	4.55	0.62
Safe	4.57	0.61
Visual Appeal	3.81	0.89

6.2. Factor analysis

Exploratory factor analysis was used to identify the constructs that characterize the attitudes towards the on-line delivery of public services. To identify the number of key (also called principal) factors that explain the majority of the variance within the data and satisfying the assumptions of the test [47], the principal component method was used. Nine factors were identified (high factor loadings (>0.5) have been highlighted in bold, while moderate loadings (>0.3) have been highlighted in light grey). Four of these are factors identified in empirical research whilst five are new factors. Interestingly, contradicting earlier studies the factors of convenience, control and personalization no longer appeared important to attitude formation. We suggest tentatively that this may be due to the particular context of this study, that is to say the online delivery of government rather than commercial services.

Turning to barriers, ease of use, security, confidentiality, reliability and enjoyable to use have all been replaced with factors that are a combination of the items within the original factors. This is potentially important since the attitude-based models (such as the Technology Acceptance Model) all have 'easy to use' as the single barrier to adoption. Here, easy to use was not found to be a factor used in evaluating such technology options but there were five other barrier factors, namely, experience, financial security, information quality, low stress and trust.

An important observation is that the reduction in factors has come from the relative benefits side rather than the barriers, indicating again that the barriers to use are especially important in determining whether people will adopt public sector on-line service delivery.

6.3. Hypotheses Testing

While the nature of the data is ordinal (use of Likert scale for each statement considered on their own) the use of parametric tests is warranted in line with previous research as the underlying scale is continuous for each construct [48]. The assumptions of the tests used, namely linearity, homoscedasticity (the latter two assumptions were checked after generating scatterplots), random sample, normality and independence of observations are here all satisfied. Pearson's linear correlation was used to identify whether any relationships exist between variables, followed by multiple linear regression testing to measure whether each identified factor does/does not predict the intention to use the technology service delivery option. Actual dependency between the nine factors and willingness to use was investigated as to whether there is any potential relationship by considering the correlation between each of the factors and that of 'willingness to use'.

All results were statistically significant at the 95% confidence level except for the 'avoid interaction' factor, indicating a relationship between willingness to use and each of the factors identified except for the 'avoid interaction'· factor. More specifically there are strong correlations ($r \geq 0.5$) between time, financial security, trust, information quality and willingness to use e-government services; and medium correlations between cost, experience, visual appeal, low stress and willingness to use e-government services. This is reflected in the variance shared by the variables (r^2), with time accounting for 58% of the variance in respondents' scores on the willingness to use scale, financial security at 42%, trust at 38%, information quality at 28% and cost at 23%. The other factors have an explained variance of 15% or lower.

Since the correlation analysis demonstrates a relationship between some of the constructs, multiple linear regression analysis was performed to investigate whether any of the factors actually predict willingness to use e-government services and ascertain which variables have the greatest effect.

The result of the reression indicate that the linear combination of the factors is related to willingness to use the online option, accounting for approximately 32% of the variance. It may be seen that the strongest significant predictors of willingness to use the technology at the 95% confidence level, are time, financial security, trust, information quality and cost. However, it was found by means of an ANOVA test that the over 55s are less likely to adopt online services than younger respondents.

7. Discussion and conclusion

The present research identifies nine factors that determine citizens' attitudes towards the use of the Web as a delivery platform for public services. Three relate to relative benefits, specifically time savings, cost savings and avoiding interaction, and six to perceived barriers, specifically experience, information quality, financial security, stress, trust and visual appeal. In identifying emergent determinants the current results offer a more detailed understanding of consumer behavior than earlier studies. In addition, existing empirical evidence previous focus on the positive benefits are insufficiently cogniscent of negative aspects that may actually prevent usage. In addition, it may be that government sector employees who deal directly with the public are perceived as particularly inefficient compared to private sector employees.

The results indicate that all factors except 'avoid interaction' correlated with a willingness to use electronic government services; where time, cost, financial security, trust and information quality were the significant predictors of usage. This result suggests that previous models are restricted in that they ignore barriers to adoption and fail to acknowledge that the benefits of usage will never be realized if users' concerns are not addressed. This supports the results obtained for the attitude models in earlier research that capture only 50% of usage intention [49], and that successive modifications have only increased this percentage incrementally [50]. It is proposed here that existing models capture the majority of the usage intention from the benefits perspective, but that significant advances will not be achieved unless the barriers to adoption are fully understood. Furthermore, the current results differ from some of the published literature in that ease of use and some aspects of perceived usefulness did not emerge as important. This may be because previous applications [37, 14] were predominantly applied in the work environment to technologies introduced for employees, rather than to online services.

The results have some implications for management. Strategically, a public organization could initially focus upon the barriers to adoption in order to encourage individuals to use Web-based services. Two-thirds of the important factors identified were barriers to usage, suggesting that there are major areas of concern for this relatively new mode of delivering public services. The strategic aim could be to develop a trust relationship with the public, providing assurances that data (both personal and financial) will be secure and that the information contained on the website is both current and accurate. Operationally, each department within a government organization that provides services through an electronic channel will need to ensure that the information displayed is relevant, accurate and up-to-date - in other words of high quality. This may well require a realignment of organizational processes to ensure that information quality is maintained at a high level and that there is consistency across the whole organization. In addition, departments will need to concentrate on how the online delivery of services could save citizens time and money. For some services that traditionally take a long time it should be ensured that requests are straightforward to make and that processing is expeditious. Delivery on-line could involve providing responses to a set of questions that are asked individually rather than as part of a complicated form. Providing the ability to track the progress of online applications could also save time in terms of removing the need to telephone the appropriate office. In terms of savings citizens' money, discounts could be offered for obtaining services on-line, for example, discounts could be offered for council tax or leisure centre tickets paid on-line. In these circumstances care would have to be taken not to exclude citizens who cannot access the Internet, since this would contradict the government's social inclusion mandate, that is to say that all citizens must have access to the same level of services.

The results suggest a significant age-related difference in the willingness to use online services. Earlier studies, with the exception of Dabholkar [27], have paid scant attention to demographics in technology adoption. Overall, by considering the factors identified in this research government departments may identify greater potential for technology adoption amongst citizens, thereby reducing the risk of spending resources unnecessarily on online services which remain underutilized, rather than directing resource allocation towards citizen need. By optimizing resource utilization in this way government agencies may not only be able to better meet the electronic service delivery targets, but will also be making better use of their overall resources by targeting them at those areas where needs are greatest. This is a key aspect of delivering value for money, a fundamental objective under constant scrutiny by the National Audit Office.

Finally, we must acknowledge aspects of the research that may limit the usefulness of the results. Firstly, the data was collected in Guildford which may or may not be representative of the UK population. Secondly, the small number of respondents aged over 55 may affect the validity of the 'willingness to use' results. In addition, further research is also recommended both to validate the current scales identified in this research and to see whether other factors emerge. Overall, we offer the current results as an exploratory study of factors which *do* and which *do not* affect citizens' willingness to use online government services.

References

[1]   C. Siegel, *Internet Marketing: Foundations and Applications,* Houghton Mifflin, Boston, MA, 2004.
[2]   D. Gefen and D. Straub, Consumer Trust in B2C and the importance of social presence: experiments in eProducts and eServices, *Omega (Oxford), 32,* 6 (2004), 407 – 425.
[3]   B. Corbitt and T. Thanasankit and H. Yi, Trust and e-commerce: a study of consumer perceptions, *Electronic Commerce Research and Applications,* 2, 3 (2003), 203 – 216.
[4]   J. Sweeney and W. Lapp, Critical service quality encounters on the Web: an exploratory study, *Journal of Services Marketing,* 18, 4 (2004), 276-280.
[5]   European Commission DG Information Society report, *Online Availability of Public Services: How is Europe progressing?,* Cap Gemini Ernst and Young, 2004.
[6]   E. Lee-Kelley, and A. Kolsaker, e-Government: the 'fit' between supply assumptions and usage drivers, *Electronic Government,* 1, 2 (2004), 130– 140.
[7]   A. O'Cass and T. Fenech, Web retailing adoption: exploring the nature of Internet users web retailing behaviour, *Journal of Retailing and Consumer Services,* 10, 2 (2003), 81-94.
[8]   F.D. Davis, Perceived usefulness, perceived ease of use and user acceptance of information technology, *MIS Quarterly,* 13 (1989), 318-339.
[9]   E. Karahanna, D.W. Straub and N.L. Chervany, Information technology adoption across time: a cross-sectional comparison of pre-adoption and post-adoption beliefs, *MIS Quarterly,* 23, 2 (1999), 83-213.
[10] H. C. Lucas and V. K. Spitler, Technology use and performance: a field study of broker workstations, *Decision Sciences,* 30, 2 (1999), 291-311.

[11] L.M. Bobbitt and P.A. Dabholkar, Integrating attitudinal theories to understand and predict use of technology-based self-service, *International Journal of Service Industry Management,* **12**, 5 (2001), 423-451.

[12] M. Lee, and E. Turban, A Trust Model for Consumer Internet Shopping, *International Journal of Electronic Commerce,* **61**, 1 (2001), 75 – 92.

[13] E.M. Rogers, *Diffusions of Innovations,* 4th ed. Free Press, New York, 1995.

[14] R. Agarwal and J. Prasad, The antecedents and consequents of user perceptions in information technology adoption, *Decision Support Systems,* **22** (1998), 5-29.

[15] M. Molesworth and J-P. Sourtfi, Buying cars online: The adoption of the Web for high involvement, high cost purchases, *Journal of Consumer Behaviour,* **2**, 2 (2002), 155–169.

[16] A. Tat-Kei and A. Ya Ni, Explaining the Adoption of e-Government Features: A Case Study of Iowa County Treasurers' Offices, *American Review of Public Administration,* **34**, 2 (2004), 164–181.

[17] L-D. Chen and J. Tan, Technology Adaptation in e-Commerce: Key Determinants of Virtual Stores Acceptance, *European Management Journal,* **22**, 1 (2004), 74 – 87.

[18] A. Douglas, L. Muir and K. Meehan, E-quality in the e-service provision of legal practices, *Managing Service Quality,* **13**, 6 (2003), 483 – 492.

[19] A. Parasuraman, V.A. Zeithaml and L.B. Berry, A conceptual model of service quality and its implications for future research, *Journal of Marketing,* **49** (1985), 41-50.

[20] J.J. Cronin and S.A. Taylor, Measuring service quality: a re-examination and extension, *Journal of Marketing,* **56** (1992), 55-68.

[21] C. Grönroos, A service quality model and its marketing implications, *European Journal of Marketing,* **18**, 4 (1984), 36-44.

[22] L.F. Higgins and J.M. Ferguson, Practical approaches for evaluating the quality dimensions of professional accounting services, *Journal of Professional Services,* **7**, 1 (1991), 3-17.

[23] W. M. Lassar, C. Manolis and R.D. Winsor, Service quality perspectives and satisfaction in private banking, *Journal of Services Marketing,* **14**, 3 (2000), 244-271.

[24] Y. Kuo, Integrating Kano's model into Web-community Service Quality, *Total Quality Management and Business Excellence,* **15**, 7 (2004), 925 – 940.

[25] G. Piccoli, K. Brohman, R. Watson and R. Parasuraman, Net-Based Customer Service Systems: Evolution and Revolution in Web Site Functionalities, *Decision Sciences,* **35**, 3 (2004), 423– 455.

[26] H. Meng-Hsiang, and C. Chao-Min, Predicting electronic service continuance with a decomposed theory of planned behaviour, *Behaviour and Information Technology,* **23**, 5 (2004), 359-374.

[27] P.A. Dabholkar, Consumer evaluations of new technology-based self-service options: an investigation of alternative models of service quality, *International Journal of Research in Marketing,* **13** (1996), 29-51.

[28] C. Shaohan and J. Minjoon, Internet users' perceptions of online service quality: a comparison of online buyers and information searchers, *Managing Service Quality,* **13**, 6 (2003), 504-520.

[29] M.L. Meuter, A.L. Ostrom, R.I. Roundtree and M.J. Bitner, Self-service technologies: understanding customer satisfaction with technology-based service encounters, *Journal of Marketing,* **64**, 3 (2000), 50-64.

[30] D.M. Szymanski and R.T. Hyse, E-satisfaction: an initial examination, *Journal of Retailing,* **76**, 3 (2000), 309-322.

[31] A. Kolsaker, E. Lee-Kelly, and P.C. Choy, The reluctant Hong Kong consumer: purchasing travel online, *International Journal of Consumer Studies,* **28**, 3 (2004), 295 – 305.

[32] J. Sharit and S.J. Szaja, Aging, computer-based task performance, and stress: issues and challenges, *Ergonimics,* **37** (1994), 559-577.

[33] J.W. Milligan, What do customers want from you: everything!, *US Bank,* **107**, 12 (1997), 38-45.

[34] Z. Liao and M.T. Cheung, T., Internet-based e-shopping and consumer attitudes: an empirical study, *Information and Management,* **38** (2001), 299-306.

[35] S. Shim, M.A. Eastlick, S.L. Lotz and P. Warrington, An online prepurchase intentions model: the role of intention to search, *Journal of Retailing,* **77** (2001), 397-416.

[36] A.M. Forman and S. Ven, The depersonalization of retailing: its impact on the lonely consumer, *Journal of Retailing,* **67**, 2 (1991), 226-243.

[44] F.D. Davis, R.P. Bagozzi and P.R. Warshaw, User acceptance of computer technology: a comparison of two theoretical models, *Management Science,* **35**, 8 (1989), 982-1003.

[37] H.R. Hansen, A case study of a mass information system, *Information and Management,* **28** (1995), 215-225.

[38] G.P. Prendergast, and N.E. Marr, Disenchantment discontinuance in the diffusion of technologies in the service industry: a case study in retail banking, *Journal of International Consumer Marketing,* **7**, 2 (1994), 25-40.

[39] Cabinet Office, *Electronic Government: The View from the Queue,* HMSO, London, 1998.

[40] F.X. Zhu, W. Wymer and I. Chen, IT-based services and service quality in consumer banking, *International Journal of Service Industry Management,* **13**, 1 (2002), 69-90.

[41] A.C.R. Van Riel, V. Liljander, V. and P. Jurriens, Exploring consumer evaluations of e-services: a portal site, *International Journal of Service Industry Management,* **12**, 4 (2001), 359-377.

[42] B. Berkley and A. Gupta, Improving service quality with information Technology, *International Journal of Information Management,* **14** (1994), 109-121.

[43] A.L.Lederer, D.J. Maupin, M.P. Sena and Y. Zhuang, The technology acceptance model and the World Wide Web, *Decision Support Systems,* **29** (2000), 269-282.

[45] K. Evans, and S.W. Brown, Strategic options for service delivery systems, in C.A Ingene and G.L. Frazier (eds.) *Proceedings of the AMA Summer Educational Conference* American Marketing Association, Chicago, IL, (1988) 202-212.

[46] Local Government Association (LGA), *User satisfaction performance indicators: a pilot survey of the public,* LGA Publications, London, 2000.

[47] P. Kline, *An easy guide to factor analysis,* Routledge, London, 1999.

[48] B.G. Tabachnick and L.S. Fidell, *Using Multivariate Statistics*, 4th ed. Allyn and Bacon, Needham Heights, MA, 2001.

[49] V. Venkatesh and F.D. Davis, A theoretical extension to the technology acceptance model: four longitudinal field studies, *Management Science,* **46**, 2 (2000), 186-204.

[50] P. Legris, J. Ingham and P. Collerette, Why do people use information technology: a critical review of the technology acceptance model, *Information and Management,* **39** (2002), 1-14.

Developments in e-Government
D. Griffin et al. (Eds.)
IOS Press, 2007

A Study of UK Policy
Regarding Public Access to ICT

Robert BROOKES
Conwy County Borough Council, Wales

1. Introduction

The United Kingdom Government has set a target of making the UK the 'best' environment in the world for e-commerce. The Government has recognized that to achieve this aim it will be necessary to ensure that its citizens have access to ICT and the 'trust, skills and motivation to use them' [1].

The importance of this objective should not be underestimated. Whilst ICT can enable the transformation of economies and societies by generating wealth and helping to address social problems, it can also present major challenges. For example, citizens who fail to acquire ICT skills and knowledge will become incapable of participating in a society that is increasingly technology-dependent. Ironically, instead of helping to address social inequality, ICT may actually exacerbate it since citizens without the relevant skills and access to technology will be excluded from the knowledge opportunities presented through ICT to increase personal wealth and obtain better services [2]. This will lead to a polarization where the educated information-rich become richer and the less educated information-poor become poorer.

Exclusion in any form has both economic and social consequences. Ultimately, individuals who are less able to contribute to the wealth of the economy must be subsidized by the rest of the population whilst their reduced capacity to participate in social, cultural and political activities has implications for the quality of democracy. The exclusion of such individuals also hinders e-government initiatives to promote increased use of technology to improve the efficiency and availability of public services. This is particularly significant since many of those most likely to be excluded have the greatest dependency on public services.

The Government's policy goal for encouraging citizen engagement was to ensure that 'everyone who wants it has access to the Internet by 2005' [1]. A key element of the Government's strategy is the People's Network project which has seen the implementation of ICT facilities in more than 4000 libraries to provide free public access to the Internet. In Wales, which has historically contained some of the least-connected districts in the UK [3], the Welsh Assembly Government has financed the provision of public access personal computers linked to a national broadband network. This investment in broadband is an acknowledgement of particular challenges faced within the Principality including rural isolation and poverty.

The UK Government's strategy is based largely on the assumption that the main barrier preventing citizens from embracing the Internet is lack of access. However, there is increasing evidence that there are significant other factors that may prevent the Government from achieving its policy goal. National statistics for October 2002 revealed that 62 per cent of adults in the UK had accessed the Internet. By October 2003 this figure had increased slightly to 64 per cent but by July 2005, over a 21 month period, the figure had increased only a further 2 per cent to 66 per cent [4]. Analysis of non-users in July 2005 showed that 49 per cent did not want to use, had no need for nor interest in the Internet, while 39 per cent felt they lacked the confidence or knowledge to use it. Whilst 37 per cent stated that they had no Internet connection, only 10 per cent were not accessing the Internet because they thought the cost was too high.

In direct contrast to the statistics for new Internet users, there has been significant growth in the availability of Internet access in recent years. In the third quarter of 1998 just nine per cent of adults in Great Britain could access the Internet from home. However, by July 2005 this figure had grown to 55 per cent. The marked difference between the significant growth of access availability and the relatively slow growth in Internet usage seems to strongly suggest that availability of access does not necessarily guarantee usage.

In Spring 2003, an empirical study was undertaken of a semi-rural area with the aim of evaluating the effectiveness of Government policy. The main focus of this study was to establish public perceptions of ICT and identify barriers to uptake. This paper provides a summary of the 2003 study, and two years on reviews what significant developments have occurred to increase public engagement with ICT and considers the implications for e-government and e-democracy.

2. The digital exclusion literature

Prior to the 2003 study, a review of the existing digital divide literature was undertaken. The main purpose of the review was to examine the links between social exclusion and the use of ICT and to consider research undertaken regarding the digital divide. The review sought to show that the UK Government's emphasis on providing access to ICT to address the divide was inappropriate and based on an oversimplification of a range of complex social issues. A case was made that more research was required to provide a better understanding of the significant body of non-users and help determine how this group should be engaged. The following summary of the literature review focuses on three key areas: the emergence and impact of the Internet and the evolution of the information society; an outline of the main types of digital exclusion; and a brief history of UK policy.

2.1. The evolution of the information society

It is now evident that the world is experiencing a third industrial revolution, an information technology revolution that is reshaping the material basis of society and introducing a new form of relationship between economy, state and society [5]. The availability of new technology such as computers and telecommunications has provided a catalyst for processes of social and economic transformation including the phenomenon known as globalization [6].

ICT now enables vast amounts of information to be stored and accessed from potentially anywhere on the planet, and individuals and organizations use this information to generate knowledge, the main currency of the 'new economy'. The ability of the Internet to facilitate both access to, and communication of, information has enabled the formation of on-line or 'virtual' communities. The implications of such virtual communities are considerable, as Rheingold states:

> *"The technology that makes virtual communities possible has the potential to bring enormous leverage to ordinary citizens at relatively little cost – intellectual leverage, social leverage, commercial leverage, and most important, political leverage"* [7:4].

Politicians have been quick to recognize the potential of the Internet to 'empower' individuals by increasing civic involvement and facilitating easy and widespread access to education and other public and government services. Consequently, governments in industrialized countries are investing heavily in ICT programmes to ensure that their citizens do not get 'left behind' [8:3]. This rush to promote ICT is not without its critics. May [9] questions why there is such widespread acceptance of the 'new ICTs' and their consequences whilst other technological advances such as genetically modified organisms continue to arouse much suspicion. Others suggest that the ambitious claims made by governments are little more than political rhetoric and that the promise of ICT to provide a fix for social and economic problems is simply a useful distraction from the failure of previous initiatives to solve these problems [10, 11].

2.2. Exclusion and ICT

Whilst much of the digital divide literature focuses on wealth as a major cause of exclusion, several other factors such as geography, age, physical disability, gender, ethnicity and culture are recognized as being influential. Whilst on one hand ICT has the potential to help address the forms of exclusion traditionally associated with these themes, inappropriate implementation can lead to greater exclusion by inhibiting equality of access.

Geographic exclusion can occur at a variety of levels. Analysis of the telecommunications infrastructure in Europe reveals significant differences between countries in the rich industrialized north and the periphery, with ICT services being far more expensive in countries where ICT is less developed [12]. Meanwhile, within individual countries rural communities are more likely to suffer from exclusion as dispersed patterns of population and economic activity increase the costs of implementing ICT infrastructure.

In the UK, research by the Countryside Agency revealed major differences in the progress of local authority website development. For example in 2002, 47 per cent of rural authorities still had only basic promotional facilities compared to 34 per cent of urban districts [13]. This is ironic because rural communities potentially have the most to gain from the provision of electronic services, for example reducing excessive travel costs and countering rural depopulation.

This point is echoed in a paper by Kenyon, Lyons and Rafferty [14] that explores the concept that the Internet can help provide accessibility without recourse to physical travel, thereby helping to address existing problems of transport exclusion experienced in rural communities. However, there is a paradox in that in order to gain the 'virtual mobility' benefits of ICT, rural inhabitants must travel to training courses provided at educational establishments, libraries or community centers. Nevertheless, whilst this may be an issue for traditional rural inhabitants, it will be of little concern to the affluent knowledge workers for whom teleworking has provided the opportunity to relocate from the suburbs to the countryside.

Age is widely accepted to be a key factor for ICT exclusion. While Katz and Aspen's findings [15] revealed Internet dropouts in the US to be younger than Internet users, there is generally more concern about the slow uptake amongst older people. This concern is understandable given that Europe has an ageing population with over 65's estimated to form around 20 per cent of the UK population by 2025 [16]. A UK survey undertaken in 2000 [17] revealed that over 55's made up the bulk of non-users and that a significant proportion of these considered themselves to be 'too old for the Internet'. This is unfortunate given that the virtual mobility offered by the Internet could offer major benefits to this age group, which is significantly more likely to suffer from transport or disability issues.

ICT has the potential to help disabled people overcome social exclusion in a number of ways. Whilst sophisticated developments such as voice recognition and the ability to create text through the use of tuned keyboards are available, more simplistic facilities such as the ability to change font size and color and the use of abbreviations to reduce typing effort are provided as standard utilities. However, lack of awareness and training to make effective use of these facilities has been identified as a possible barrier to usage [18].

Gender has traditionally been a factor in ICT access and usage and UK statistics for 2000 showed that only 39 per cent of Internet users were women [17]. Although the number of females studying ICT courses has increased, the numbers involved still indicate lack of interest as a major factor. A UK Department of Trade and Industry (DTI) literature review of women and ICT concluded that women are less likely than men to have access to a PC and less likely to feel that ICT would be useful to them in their daily lives [19]. The DTI review also mirrored findings from the US regarding representation on ICT-related higher courses and employment in the ICT industry. Although lack of confidence in ICT skills is cited as a factor, the report also notes evidence from the US that suggests women are more likely to adopt the Internet and new technologies for business growth than men.

In many western countries, including the US [20] and the UK, [21] the correlation between ethnicity and wealth is a further source of digital exclusion, and there is evidence that related issues such as cultural attitudes and language also have an impact. Cullen [22] observes that the predominantly western culture of Internet content is of little relevance to some societies, and that within some groups computers are regarded as being the preserve of 'brainy' people or a middle-class 'white' culture. Research undertaken in the UK supports these findings, for example, a study of low-income neighborhoods raised concerns about the use of colleges and schools to facilitate community access to ICT:

> *"Many parents are disadvantaged by their own negative experiences of education and perceive colleges and schools as predominantly "middle-class" institutions and "not for the likes of us"* [23:30].

The dominance of English as the prime language for Internet content is predictably another source of exclusion. An obvious example is that in China the 95 per cent of the population who do not read English failed to show any interest in the Internet until Chinese content was developed [22]. In Europe, Greeks who want to communicate electronically with the European Commission have to use a degraded version of their language because of technological difficulties with Greek fonts [12].

2.3. The origins of UK policy

Current UK Government policy regarding public access to ICT began in 1998 with research undertaken to address concerns about growing levels of social exclusion [24]. From this, 18 policy action teams (PATs) were created to tackle perceived policy problems and gaps. Policy Action Team 15 (PAT 15) was tasked with developing a strategy to increase the availability and take-up of ICT among people living in poor neighborhoods. The team undertook research into existing projects, and facilitated workshops in deprived areas to measure attitudes to ICT [25]. An important part of their work involved holding seminars and commissioning papers to address specific target groups [18, 19, 26, 23].

PAT 15 published its report in 2000 entitled 'Closing the Digital Divide: Information and Communication Technologies in Deprived Areas' [25]. It concluded that there was enough evidence to show that the take-up of ICT among people living in deprived neighborhoods was lower than the national average. A number of barriers to take-up were identified including the lack of a joined-up approach, poor promotion, unattractive or unsuitable content, access problems, fragmented funding and costs. The report also highlighted particular problems associated with black and minority ethnic groups.

The PAT 15 report detailed 37 recommendations, the most significant of which were the policy goal, strategy and actions regarding public access summarized in the Office of the e-Envoy's UK online annual reports.

The first of these reports [1] outlined the Government's policy goal which was to ensure that 'everyone who wants it will have access to the Internet by 2005'. The initial strategy involved implementing measures to ensure that 'access is accompanied by significant levels of use, by addressing the key barriers: motivation; trust; and skills'. Actions in this report included implementing measures to improve access, embedding ICT skills in the education system; promoting trust in the Internet and increasing the amount and quality of social content.

The second report [27] retained the policy goal and expanded the strategy to include ensuring that 'everyone is aware of both the benefits of the Internet and the support available to help them access it, if they want to do so'. New actions included exploring hardware leasing schemes, driving the uptake of digital television (DTV) and undertaking 'aggressive marketing' in partnership with the private sector of the benefits of Internet connectivity.

The third report retained the original policy goal and activities, but this time the strategy focused on encouraging take-up amongst digitally divided groups. Significantly, the report cites research findings regarding the large number of non-users:

> "Although long-term growth remains positive, research shows that some people have entrenched negative views about the Internet. About half of all adults who have yet to access the Internet express a general lack of interest in doing so. Similarly, a third of the total adult population consider it very unlikely that they will access the Internet in the next year" [28:71].

Although the UK Online strategy applies to the whole of the United Kingdom, some activities are the responsibility of the various devolved administrations, namely, the Scottish Executive, the Welsh Assembly Government and the Northern Ireland Executive. For example, the Welsh Assembly Government has its own strategic framework, 'Cymru Ar-lein'.

3. The 2003 North Wales study

The review of the digital divide literature identified several areas where more research was required. However, to enable an assessment of the effectiveness of UK policy, two key objectives were identified: firstly, to obtain more data regarding public perceptions of ICT; and secondly, to identify and analyze barriers to uptake amongst non-users of ICT. The method chosen to collect this data involved a face-to-face public survey, which was undertaken at a number of locations. The face-to-face approach was preferred because it offers better control over respondents, is more successful for longer lists of questions and is more likely to elicit responses to complex questions. The main disadvantages of this approach are that it involves increased risk of interviewer bias and of respondents giving answers that they believe to be socially desirable.

The area selected for the survey was a North Wales unitary authority with a population of just under 100,000 of which 29 per cent were Welsh speakers and 26 per cent were over the age of 65 at the time of the 2001 census. The authority is largely rural with just over a third of its 1130 square kilometers being situated within the Snowdonia National Park. At the time of the survey the area had the lowest level of GDP in Wales and the lowest wage levels in the UK. Many of these elements, in particular geography, age, culture and low relative wealth are likely to increase the potential for ICT exclusion.

The sampling strategy was largely dictated by the need to generate the optimum number of statistically significant results for the proportion of the population that were non-users of ICT. Since Government statistics for 2002 indicated that 38 per cent of adults had not accessed the Internet [4], a sample size of 100 was considered sufficient. Most of the survey work was undertaken outside supermarkets due to their ability to attract sufficient concentrations of potential respondents. Selection criteria for each supermarket included its geographical location and the market sector served. This would ensure representative samples of urban and rural respondents from a wide range of socio-economic classes. Some limited stratification was applied to address any gender bias associated with the supermarket venues and a small snowball sample of ten non-users included to ensure sufficient data was collected about this group.

Question topics were primarily drawn from the literature review and previous surveys, and to reduce the risk of aborted interviews the questionnaire was designed to take no more than eight minutes to complete. To maximize the amount of data generated the questions were mainly closed and fixed-response in nature with single value, multiple-value or likert-scale responses as appropriate. All data was initially entered onto a single database before being exported to a series of spreadsheets for detailed statistical analysis. Separate data subsets were generated for ICT users and non-users with the latter being defined as those who answered 'never' or 'not in the last three years' to a question regarding frequency of Internet access.

The first section of the questionnaire concerned potential barriers to computer usage. Comparison of Internet users and non-Internet users showed the former group to have been far more likely to use a computer in the last three years with 84 per cent of Internet users being regular computer users. The home and the workplace appeared to be the most popular venues for gaining regular access to a computer with just three Internet users considering public access facilities as a regular venue. None of the non-Internet users suggested they would consider public access facilities for regular access to a computer.

Analysis of reasons for not wanting to use a computer revealed significant differences between Internet users and non-users. Confidence levels in using computers were much higher in Internet users (77 per cent) compared to non-users (23 per cent) while 76 per cent of non-Internet users showed a lack of interest in using a computer compared to 24 per cent of Internet users. Both groups indicated a need for more knowledge or training but Internet users were more likely to disagree that home computers are too expensive (84 per cent) compared to non-Internet users (16 per cent).

Age was revealed as a potential barrier to computer usage with significantly more non-Internet users (79 per cent) considering themselves too old to use a computer when compared against Internet users (21 per cent). There was also a significant difference between the two groups in terms of discomfort with using technology. Only 39 per cent of Internet users suggested that they were uncomfortable using technology compared with 61 per cent of non-Internet users.

The second section of the questionnaire concerned potential barriers to Internet usage with some of the questions applying only to the 39 per cent identified as non-Internet users. Analysis of potential barriers to existing non-Internet users suggested that the cost of connecting was an issue with 54 per cent indicating that this was a factor. Lack of knowledge or training was again identified as a concern with 73 per cent agreeing that this was an issue. Marginally more non-Internet users (54 per cent) agreed that they had a lack of interest in using the Internet but lack of confidence was certainly an issue, with 76 per cent indicating that this was a concern.

Despite their apparent lack of interest, non-Internet users tended to disagree with the proposal that the Internet provides nothing they cannot find elsewhere with only 38 per cent believing this to be the case. Only 28 per cent of non-Internet users suggested that non-representation of their language or culture was a barrier. Non-Internet users tended not to consider the ease of availability of inappropriate material via the Internet as a barrier to usage with only 34 per cent stating this as a concern.

In terms of access, 64 per cent of non-Internet users agreed that they would use the Internet if available in their own home. However, although 31 per cent of non-users suggested that they would access the Internet on a regular basis at some point in the future, some 61 per cent stated that they would never access the Internet on a regular basis. Analysis of potential venues for Internet access gave broadly similar results to the corresponding question about computer access in the first section, with home and work again proving to be the most popular venues. Just six Internet users and three non-Internet users indicated public access facilities as a venue for regular access to the Internet.

The third section of the questionnaire focused on awareness and attitudes regarding public access facilities. One question, concerning barriers to public access facility usage, was directed only to those who stated that they would not use such facilities. Attitudes towards public access facilities were broadly similar between Internet users and non-Internet users. A majority of both groups stated that they were aware that the local authority had installed computers in public buildings with free Internet access and although more Internet users stated that they would consider making use of the facilities than non-Internet users, the difference was not statistically significant.

For those who would not consider using public access facilities, both Internet users and non-Internet users tended to disagree that getting to the nearest facility was a problem. However, more non-Internet users (60 per cent) than Internet users (40 per cent) tended to disagree that the opening hours of public access facilities are an issue. When asked if they would be uncomfortable using a computer in public, a significant 73 per cent of non-Internet users agreed this to be the case compared with just 27 per cent of Internet users. Nevertheless both groups tended to agree that public access facilities were a good thing whilst disagreeing that the nature of the environments in which public access facilities were located was a barrier.

The final question in the third section asked respondents to select up to three ways in which free public access to the Internet should be provided. A subsidized home computer was the most popular option, especially amongst existing Internet users. Public access facilities and set-top boxes for televisions were the next most popular with Internet kiosks in pubs or other entertainment venues being the least popular.

Section four of the questionnaire examined general attitudes towards the Internet. Both Internet users and non-users agreed that 'the Internet is now part of everyday life' with only ten per cent of the sample disagreeing with this statement. When questioned about what the Internet was mainly used for, both groups again gave broadly similar answers. Information gathering was by far the most popular choice, followed by e-mail, shopping and business. Non-Internet users ranked shopping slightly higher than e-mail and business.

Perhaps in contradiction to earlier answers, both Internet users and non-users tended to agree that public access facilities are the most suitable way to provide 'free access to the Internet for all those that want it'. This highlights the significance of the Government's policy wording and would seem to indicate that whilst the public consider this to be the best approach in theory, in practice they would not necessarily wish to use such facilities themselves. The final question in this section asked whether it is more important to make public services available via the Internet than to improve existing methods such as the telephone. Both Internet users and non-users tended to agree that improving existing methods was more important, with no significant difference between the two groups.

The final section of the questionnaire concerned demographic information. Age was shown to be an important factor with the percentage of respondents under the age of 55 using the Internet (77 per cent) being significantly higher than the percentage of Internet users in the older group (37 per cent). A significant difference was also found when analyzing the data either side of age 55. In this case the percentage of respondents under age 35 using the Internet (78 per cent) was higher than the percentage of Internet users in the older group (56 per cent).

Whilst there was insufficient data to support detailed analysis of ethnic minorities, analysis of first language revealed a significant difference between the two groups with the 19 per cent who stated a first language other than English being less likely to use the Internet. Of those who stated English as their first language, 67 per cent were Internet users compared to the rest of the sample of mainly Welsh-speakers of whom just 37 per cent were Internet users. Geographical analysis suggested that Internet use tended to be higher amongst urban dwellers although the difference was not statistically significant.

Analysis by occupational groupings revealed that the percentage within higher occupations that were Internet users (72 per cent) was significantly greater than the percentage within semi-routine and routine occupations and unemployed (40 per cent). Analysis of highest qualification obtained also revealed a significant difference with 72 per cent of Internet users having obtained level two qualifications or higher. In contrast, 65 per cent of those with no qualifications or of level one only were non-Internet users.

4. Recent developments

Some two years after the 2003 study, a review was undertaken to ascertain what significant developments have occurred in terms of public engagement with ICT. The review focused on recent published research and statistics, new Government initiatives and papers concerning digital exclusion. The main objectives of the review were to seek further confirmation that providing access alone does not guarantee public use of ICT and to consider if there had been any significant change in Government policy.

Statistics from various sources indicate continued growth in public use of ICT in the UK. For example, a market review published by the Government's Office of Communications, revealed that time spent online in households with dial-up connections had increased from an average of two hours a week in 1999 to an average of eight hours in mid-2004. Broadband customers spent even more time on-line, averaging 16 hours a week. The number of broadband connections grew by almost 50,000 a week, bringing penetration per 100 population to levels similar to those found in France and Germany [29]. Private sector research also suggests significant growth in UK Internet usage with a 13 per cent increase in the number of people actively surfing the Internet during the 12 months to October 2004. During the same period, the number of people surfing using high-speed connections increased by 93 per cent in the UK compared to an overall 60 per cent increase across Europe [30].

A Government-sponsored international benchmarking study suggests that UK businesses are now amongst the most sophisticated users of ICT in the world [31]. The study placed the UK third in an index of sophisticated use of ICT, which is an improvement of four places from the previous year. Whilst Internet access levels amongst businesses in those countries included in the study have generally stabilized, the UK is leading with the adoption of a variety of technologies including broadband and wireless networks. The study also revealed that 19 per cent of the total sales of UK businesses that sell on-line are now made over the Internet, representing a five per cent improvement since 2003.

In contrast however, a number of sources indicate a lack of awareness of e-government facilities by the UK public. Private sector market research undertaken by a web technology company concluded that 73 per cent of the public have yet to notice the impact of e-government [32]. Similar research by a communication services supplier indicated that whilst the public sector believes 40 per cent of Internet users to be aware of e-government initiatives, their own findings suggested that only 12 per cent were aware and just eight per cent were currently using on-line services on a regular basis [33].

Awareness of e-government initiatives is also low amongst those who can potentially gain the most benefits from its use. Research by the Joseph Rowntree Foundation concluded that ICT and the Internet in particular could significantly increase the quality of life of disabled people by enabling them to communicate with others and to access a variety of information resources. Whilst guidance and training was suggested as being a significant problem, only one in ten of the respondents knew the location of their local UK online centre or of the training facilities provided by these or other organizations. Around 40 per cent of disabled Internet users had been unsuccessful in their attempts to find suitable training locally [34].

Research undertaken by the Oxford Internet Institute in 2003 (2,029 respondents) and 2005 (2,185 respondents) provides further evidence that availability of access to ICT is now much less of a barrier. The 2003 survey established that only four per cent of the UK public lacked ready access to the Internet and both surveys supported previous findings that age is a key barrier. In 2003 whilst 98 per cent of school pupils and 67 per cent of people of working age were Internet users, the proportion dropped to just 22 per cent for retired people. Whilst the 2005 survey gave similar results for school pupils and people of working age the percentage of retired users had increased to 30 per cent [35, 36].

Analysis of data regarding non-users from the 2003 survey suggested that fear or dislike of using technology was not a major issue and that a far greater problem was people's failure to see how the Internet could help with their everyday lives. The research also suggested that around half of the non-users were informed but indifferent. For example, whilst they knew somebody who could send e-mails or access information on their behalf they had no interest in making use of such access. The 2003 research concluded that the Government may have to wait a generation or more before 90 per cent of the UK public regularly uses the Internet and accurately predicted that the percentage of non-users would reduce slightly to 34 per cent in 2004. The 2005 survey included an additional analysis of those people who had stopped using the Internet. Significantly, whilst 32 per cent indicated the lack of a computer as a reason for stopping accessing the Internet, the most popular reason cited was a lack of interest, being indicated by 35 per cent of this group.

Data from a major 2004 national survey commissioned by the Welsh Assembly Government supported findings from the 2003 North Wales study. Although 47 per cent indicated they now had a computer in the home, 78 per cent of the remainder considered themselves unlikely to obtain one in the next six months. Significantly, 70 per cent of this group suggested they had no interest or did not need a computer while only 20 per cent suggested cost was the main barrier. In contrast, 80 per cent of the population thought it essential that children learn how to use a computer. Training was again identified as a potential barrier with 41 per cent of the population considering themselves to be beginners or having no knowledge of using computers. This is significant given that 97 per cent of those who accessed the Internet did so using a computer. Knowledge was also an issue for those already accessing the Internet with 27 per cent considering themselves beginners and 28 per cent having some knowledge but occasionally needing help. Of those not planning to adopt Internet access just 20 per cent identified cost issues as a barrier whilst 32 per cent considered that they did not want it and 25 per cent suggested they did not need Internet access at home [37].

There has been increasing evidence that the availability of affordable broadband services is leading to a new form of geographic divide and this concern was a main driver for the Welsh Assembly Government's research project. Whilst broadband adoption amongst Internet users for the UK overall is around 20 per cent, the figure in Wales is nearly half this rate at just 11 per cent. The unavailability and relatively high cost of broadband in rural areas may well be a factor, with research by the Countryside

Agency suggesting that while 99 per cent of the urban population and 78 per cent of the UK population have access to affordable broadband, penetration was only 16 per cent for rural villages and just four per cent for remote rural areas [38].

Recent research by Selwyn raises concerns about attempts to engage socially excluded groups. In a survey of 1001 individuals in the West of England and South Wales, the findings suggested there was little evidence that public access facilities are attracting those social groups who may be excluded from the opportunities presented by ICT. Evidence from this research also supported findings from the 2003 North Wales study that public access facilities have a minimal profile compared to household access [39]. Selwyn has also recently raised concerns that politicians are taking an over-simplified approach to ICT exclusion and that access and education alone are not sufficient to address complex inequality issues. He repeats earlier assertions that ICT must be relevant and useful for excluded groups if they are to be successfully engaged [40].

Current UK Government activities suggest that there is now recognition that providing access alone will not address ICT exclusion. The main objective of the e-Citizen national project, which began in April 2004, is to encourage the take-up of services via electronic channels through the use of targeted marketing. Part of this project includes a major research programme to collect and review information about priority services, market segments and e-government take-up in an attempt to understand what tools and methods are effective for different groups. A budget of one million pounds has been reserved for the next stage, which will involve the implementation of proof of concept marketing campaigns in a number of local authorities.

Whilst the e-citizen project is intended to address visibility issues, the UK Government has also taken steps to gain a greater understanding of those groups who have yet to embrace ICT. The Digital Inclusion Panel, whose membership includes senior representatives of both the private and public sectors have produced a framework to tackle ICT exclusion [41]. Its three main objectives are to identify those groups most at risk from exclusion, identify ways of encouraging their engagement and to make recommendations regarding how industry, government and the private sector can collaborate to improve ICT take-up. An early outcome of this work has been the launch of the Alliance for Digital Inclusion, an industry body which aims to act as a think-tank and strategy advisor and promote corporate collaboration to help address ICT exclusion.

5. Conclusions

The findings of the 2003 North Wales study suggested that factors other than lack of access are responsible for ICT exclusion. Potential barriers identified by the research included demographic and socio-economic factors, lack of knowledge and training, lack of confidence and a general lack of interest. The findings supported previous assertions by Selwyn [8] that the UK Government's focus on providing access to ICT does not guarantee that the people it is aimed at will make use of it. To address ICT exclusion, it is necessary to provide meaningful access that takes into account the abilities and concerns of the uninterested. Most important of all, the non-users need to have some incentive to get on-line in the form of relevant and tangible benefits.

The review of recent developments shows that there has been significant growth in the availability of public access to ICT and that adoption of new technologies such as broadband is accelerating. However, the remaining number of non-users is decreasing only very slowly, averaging a two per cent annual fall over the last three years and it has been suggested that it may take a generation or more before 90 per cent of the UK public regularly access the Internet. One possible factor highlighted by a number of organizations is a lack of public awareness of e-government initiatives. Meanwhile there is also evidence that the uneven way in which broadband is being made available may lead to additional forms of exclusion, particularly in rural areas.

The UK Government has responded to concerns regarding the visibility of e-government initiatives by launching the e-citizen marketing project, which will attempt to understand what engagement methods are most effective for various target groups. Additionally, in developing a framework for digital inclusion, the Government has also shown that it now recognizes the importance of gaining a greater understanding of the significant number of people who are still not using ICT. The Government's approach to this problem involves close collaboration with the ICT industry as illustrated by the launch of the Alliance for Digital Inclusion.

It remains to be seen if the private sector will be prepared to make the necessary investments to guarantee the engagement of excluded groups. It could be argued that the uneven way in which broadband is being currently adopted does not set a good precedent. Given that still over a third of all UK adults have yet to access the Internet, the ICT industry may consider that this group offers significant potential commercial opportunities. However, there is a danger that those groups who offer the least profit are ignored and the Government must therefore ensure it demonstrates appropriate social responsibility to prevent such exclusion.

UK Government policy is still fundamentally about providing access to ICT for all those that want it. Consequently there will always be those who do notwant to engage with ICT or who are unable to due to their particular circumstances. As public sector organizations come under increasing pressure to focus on electronic channels of delivery there is a danger that funding for traditional channels is reduced and their scope subsequently limited. The Government therefore has a responsibility to ensure that traditional channels are maintained to prevent the exclusion of those who choose not to, or who are unable to engage with ICT.

The failure of a significant proportion of the population to engage with ICT does not prevent the Government from exploiting the advantages to be gained from electronic service delivery providing there is sufficient uptake by the public. However, the need to continue to maintain traditional delivery channels will inevitably limit potential efficiency gains. The implications for e-democracy are far more serious. Whilst the Government can introduce new technologies that might increase participation in government, such as e-voting and e-consultation, e-democracy cannot truly exist if large numbers of the population continue to be excluded. For e-democracy to succeed it must be fully inclusive and provide equal opportunity for participation. Without full participation any tools that are introduced to facilitate democratic processes will merely be another facet of e-government.

References

[1]   Office of the e-Envoy, *UK online annual report 2000*, Cabinet Office, London, 2000.

[2]   S.McNair, *The Emerging Policy Agenda, Learning to Bridge the Digital Divide*, Organisation for Economic Co-Operation and Development, Paris, 2000.

[3]   P.Foley and X.Alfonso, *The Digital Divide: The largest barrier to effective implementation of e-Government?*, Proceedings of the 2nd European Conference on e-Government, MCIL, Oxford (2002), 125-139.

[4]   National Statistics, Internet Access: 12.9 million households on-line, 2005. Retrieved: December 12, 2005, from: http://www.statistics.gov.uk.

[5]   M.Castells, The Rise of the Network Society, 2nd ed. Blackwell, Oxford, 2000.

[6]   A.Giddens, Globalisation, BBC Reith Lectures, 1999. Retrieved: January 25, 2005, from: http://www.bbc.co.uk/radio4/reith1999/lecture1.shtml

[7]   H.Rheingold, The Virtual Community: Finding Connection in a Computerized World, Secker and Warburg, London, 1994.

[8]   N.Selwyn, Defining the 'Digital Divide': Developing a Theoretical Understanding of Inequalities in the Information Age, Cardiff University School of Social Sciences, Cardiff, 2002.

[9]   C.May, *The Information Society: A Sceptical View*, Polity Press, London, 2002.

[10]   J.Servaes and F.Heinderyckx, The 'new' ICTs environment in Europe: closing or widening the gaps?, *Telematics and Informatics*, **19** (2002), 91-115.

[11]   N. Garnham, Europe and the Global Information Society: The History of a Troubled Relationship, *Telematics and Informatics*, **14**, 4 (1997), 323-327.

[12]   K.Sarikakis and G.Terzis, Pleonastic exclusion in the European Information Society, *Telematics and Informatics*, **17** (2000), 105-128.

[13]   Countryside Agency, The State of the Countryside 2002, Countryside Agency Publications, Wetherby, 2002.

[14]   S.Kenyon, G.Lyons, and J.Rafferty, Transport and Social exclusion: investigating the possibility of promoting social inclusion through virtual mobility, *Journal of Transport Geography*, **10** (2002), 207-219.

[15]   J.E.Katz and P.Aspden, Internet dropouts in the USA: The invisible group, *Telecommunications Policy*, **22**, 4/5 (1998), 327-339.

[16]   J.Gilbert, *Citizen-centric services and older people*, Proceedings of the 2nd European Conference on e-Government, MCIL, Oxford (2002), 155-165.

[17]   Which?Online, Can't surf won't surf – 15 million say 'no' to Internet, 2000. Retrieved: January 25, 2005, from: http://www.which.net/media/pr/jul00/general/survey.html.

[18]   Abilitynet, *People with Disabilities and ICTs: A paper for the Policy Action Team 15 work on ICTs and social exclusion*, Abilitynet, Warwick, 1999.

[19]   Department of Trade and Industry, Women and Information and Communication Technologies: A Literature Review, DTI, London, 1999.

[20]   J.E.Katz and P.Aspden, Motivations for and barriers to Internet usage: results from a national public opinion survey, *Internet Research*, **7**, 3 (1997), 170-188.

[21]   Social Exclusion Unit, Preventing Social Exclusion, Cabinet Office, London, 2001.

[22]   R.Cullen, Addressing the digital divide, Online Information Review, **25**, 5 (2001), 311-320.

[23]   K.Harris, *Everyone gets hooked: exploring ICTs in low-income neighbourhoods*, Community Development Foundation, 2000.

[24]   Social Exclusion Unit, Bringing Britain Together: A National Strategy for Neighbourhood Renewal, Cabinet Office, London, 1998.

[25]   Policy Action Team 15, Closing the Digital Divide: Information and Communication Technologies in Deprived Areas, Department of Trade and Industry, London, 2000.

[26]   J.Shaddock, Information and Communication Technologies for potentially excluded groups: PAT 15 Target Group – White males from manual backgrounds, Barnsley Information Society Development Group, Barnsley, 1999.

[27]   Office of the e-Envoy, *UK online annual report 2001*, London: Cabinet Office, London, 2001.

[28]   Office of the e-Envoy, *UK online annual report 2002*, London: Cabinet Office, London, 2002.

[29]   Ofcom (Office of Communications), The Communications Market 2004 – Telecommunications, Ofcom, London, 2004.

[30]   Neilson//NetRatings, Europe is at home online: 100 million and counting, November 2004. Retrieved: January   25,   2005,   from: http://www.nielsen-netratings.com/news.jsp?section=new_prandthetype=dateandtheyear =2004andthemonth=10.

[31]   Department of Trade and Industry, Business in the Information Age: The International Benchmarking Study 2004, DTI, London, 2004.

[32]   Transversal Corporation, The role of eService within the Public Sector: A Study of the Public's attitude to e-Government, Transversal Corporation, Cambridge, 2004.

[33] NTL, e-Government – if we build it, will they come?, 2004. Retrieved: January 25, 2005, from: http://www.ntl.com/mediacentre/press/display.asp?id=747.

[34] D.Pilling, P.Barrett and M.Floyd, Disabled people and the Internet: Experiences, barriers and opportunities, Joseph Rowntree Foundation, York, 2004.

[35] Oxford Internet Institute, *How much is enough for the Internet?*, 2003. Retrieved: December 12, 2005, from: http://www.oii.ox.ac.uk/research/oxis/oxis2003_results.pdf.

[36] Oxford Internet Institute, The Internet in Britain: The Oxford Internet Survey (OxIS), May 2005, 2005. Retrieved: December 12, 2005, from: http://www.oii.ox.ac.uk/research/oxis/oxis2005_report.pdf.

[37] L.Davies, C.Durrant and E.Winter, Report of the 2003 Broadband Wales Consumer Survey, NOP Social and Political, London, 2004.

[38] Countryside Agency, The State of the Countryside 2004, Countryside Agency Publications, Wetherby, 2004.

[39] N.Selwyn, ICT for all? Access and use of Public ICT Sites in the UK, *Information, Communication and Society,* **6**, 3 (2003), 350.

[40] N.Selwyn, *Increased use of electronic learning resources will not overcome the key issues of social exclusion and the digital divide*, Cardiff University School of Social Sciences, Cardiff, 2003.

[41] Cabinet Office, Enabling a Digitally United Kingdom: A Framework For Action, Cabinet Office, London, 2004.

Developments in e-Government
D. Griffin et al. (Eds.)
IOS Press, 2007
© *2007 The authors and IOS Press. All rights reserved.*

Subject Index

Developments in e-Government
D. Griffin et al. (Eds.)
IOS Press, 2007

Author Index